Nigel Costley

West Country Rebels

BREVIARY STUFF PUBLICATIONS

2012

About the author

Nigel Costley started work as an apprentice compositor – one of the last to be trained in 'hot metal'. While learning the trade it was changing rapidly and he was made redundant twice. It was his union, the National Graphical Association that helped him find new work and get re-trained as techology marched on.

Nigel was elected Father of the Chapel and then, at 24-years-old, the youngest full-time officer in the union. He spent fifteen years in the role through the most turbulent times for printing and trade unionism.

He particularly championed support for those out of work, including establishing a unique training co-operative. Having escaped school as soon as he could, Nigel returned to education on a part-time basis, eventually achieving a MSc with Leicester University.

He became South West TUC Regional Secretary in 1996. Nigel is responsible for the way the TUC remembers the Tolpuddle Martyrs and he has overseen the transformation of the annual rally into a hugely poular celebration of trade unionism.

Nigel Costley, senior steward at the head of the huge TUC march in 2011

First published by Breviary Stuff Publications 2012
© Nigel Costley 2012
All rights reserved

Breviary Stuff Publications
BCM Breviary Stuff
London WC1N 3XX
www.breviarystuff.org.uk

The centipede device copyright © Breviary Stuff Publications

ISBN: 978-0-9570005-4-4

A CIP record for this book is available from
The British Library

Contents

Foreword by Tony Benn

This is a scholarly, readable and relevant book, written by Nigel Costley, who has gone to the trouble to collect records of all the popular resistance that there has been over the centuries to injustice in the region. It tells you a great deal abut the people of the South West who are very independent and very principled.

Early resistance
The earliest account goes back thousands of years to the people resisting the Vikings and it reminds us that we were invaded by so many people and I suppose the resistance to foreign occupation is one of the absolutely clear examples all over the world of people getting together to protect the way they live.

The first section describes the actions of local people to deal with problems for example tax campaigns, the riots over Bristol Bridge tolls, mechanisation of agriculture and campaigns against poverty. Riots in the Forest of Dean, that has been a great centre of resistance over the years.

Tolpuddle
The book features the Tolpuddle Martyrs, where Nigel plays a leading role for thousands of people every year and has turned it into a festival. It is one of the great events of the socialist calendar.

I remember that Nigel was the first to invite me to Tolpuddle. I went from being the most dangerous man in Britain to a national treasure.

Unions and the vote
Nigel deals with the Chartists and the strikes associated with the formation of trade unions. Every one of these stories is riveting to read about and Nigel has done an excellent job of explaining it simply.

The later part of the book deals with the development of trade unions in the West Country. Ernie Bevan, was born into poverty, and defended the dockers so strongly he became known as the 'Dockers' QC'. At that time not only did people have their trade union membership but they now had the vote and they realised that influence could be achieved.

Pessimism, the enemy of progress
It may seem strange that after riots the book talks about the work of local

Tony Benn with Nigel Costley at Tolpuddle

authorities, socialists and trade unions who came together to achieve things. This is important because it gave people hope. Pessimism is the greatest enemy of progress. If anyone tries to change anything the media says it won't work or you're being unrealistic and that politicians are all corrupt. These ideas discourage anyone from trying to change things.

Two flames burn in the human heart: the flame of anger against injustice and the flame of hope to build a better world. And any sensible person will go around fanning both flames as much as they can. That's exactly what this book does. It gives people the confidence that something can be done.

Nobody can extend their own life by more than a minute, on the other hand if you study history you extend your experience by thousands of years.

Every generation has the same battles again and again, no issue is finally won and no issue is finally lost.

For West Country people it will relate to their own experience. It establishes a link between them and earlier generations and encourages the inheritance we get for future struggles.

It is a great achievement, a great deal of work, a great

deal of effort. I strongly recommend this book.

Progress is made by strange combinations and sometimes by chance people who are your enemy turn out to make a contribution that assists your cause. I daresay that would be true of Nancy Astor; I'm not sure. She is the only one whose appearance in the book really surprised me but I can understand why she is there.

Labour Party
The Labour Party is a coalition – it is not a socialist party although it's got socialists in it and that coalition is quite a difficult one to work within. You are living with the mistakes made by colleagues that have damaged the Party, on the other hand you know that within the hearts of everybody in the Labour Movement is the desire to improve and so you hope to build on the good and try to ignore or push aside the disappointing.

The Blair experience was similar to Ramsay McDonald in a way. He set up a completely new Party – I never joined it.

The answer is not to form a new socialist group but to work within the Labour Party and campaign for the things you believe in. The little socialist sects don't achieve anything and they accidentally damage the cause they are trying to support.

Riots and religion
The riots in 2011 tapped the frustration of many people who felt dissatisfied and excluded. They were frightening, in the sense they put people off, but they did represent a frustration with the system that has to be seen as a positive force.

The question is: is it right or wrong? And what they saw was injustice, this is wrong and we will campaign against it. This is where a religious element, Quakers and others, came in and added a moral dimension which strengthened the campaign and kept them on the right lines.

My mother once said to me: if you read the Bible it is the story of conflict between the kings who have power and the prophets who preach righteousness. Religion can go the wrong way – the Tea Party in America for instance, fundamentalists who are hostile to public services.

Every MP has to swear an oath of allegiance to the Queen. My allegiance wasn't to the Queen but the people I represented. In order to sit in Parliament I had to tell seventeen lies under oath. It is the role of the Crown that's the problem. The Chaplain comes to the House every day and looks at the Parliament and then says let's pray for the country!

Coming to Bristol
When I first came to Bristol, Cripps had just resigned. I was picked because they didn't want another minister. There was a man I beat who had been a cabinet minister but lost his seat a few months before and he was from Bristol, from my constituency, but they thought if we pick him he will be made another minister and you're locked into the policies of the government.

So they were looking for somebody young and a bit more independent. I was very lucky. I was only 25. They sent a national agent down from Transport House in the hope of getting this guy selected and not me.

I learned everything from listening to people at my surgeries. Listen to people's stories. Injustice upsets you. I made a big thing of learning how Parliament works so I could influence things for them.

Bristol Bus Boycott
Paul Stephenson came to me and I supported him. I went to Harold Wilson and he took a very courageous stand for a Party Leader to come out in support of this person. The T&G were very hostile to Paul. I saw the Bishop who called him a trouble-maker, which is the fate of everyone who comes along to try to make progress.

One thing I learnt in Bristol was that although so much was built on the wealth of the slave trade you never discussed slavery. There was a sort of collective guilt about it and now Paul has brought it into the open.

Giving people hope
The NHS and welfare state were formidable achievements. Giving people hope is the most important thing and that's what this book does. That's the great contribution of the book. It is a very remarkable book.

For Nigel
in unity
Tony Benn

Introduction

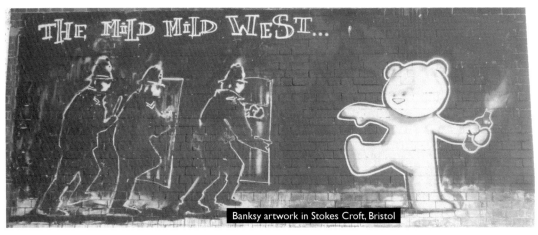

Banksy artwork in Stokes Croft, Bristol

The image of the West Country is of a beautiful coast and countryside, of charming cottages and lush meadows. It is full of history with plenty of places to visit to explore the past. The South West has more ancient monuments, national parks and heritage sites than other regions.

Few people connect the region with rebellion, riot and revolt. Surely the West Country has always been the sleepy, peaceful and rather conservative corner of Britain it appears to be today? Well, no!

For much of its past, the West Country has been in turmoil. It has provided the backdrop to rebellions that have shaped our society. The story of the South West includes many characters that have taken great risks and made huge sacrifices to defend their families and communities or to pursue a cause in which they passionately believed.

Rebels can be mavericks, lone crusaders standing up to overwhelming opposition. They can also be leaders, people who emerge or take hold of a situation. This book is about such people and about solidarity: ordinary people coming together to challenge authority and the status quo. Sometimes history has left us names and records of those involved but often the champions of social justice and democracy have been forgotten.

The book offers no clever definition of a rebel. It isn't a scholarly, academic record of social history across the region. It doesn't claim to be a comprehensive catalogue of events that have impacted on West Country life down the ages. It is hopefully a readable, enjoyable, digest of some of the less well-known people and stories that have pushed progressive ideas.

The book isn't a list of heroes, although many are. Some trouble-makers are unsavoury characters in whatever situation.

Radical campaigners who win power sometimes contradict their earlier promises. Some are sucked into the establishment they sought to challenge or overthrow. History is full of the twists and turns of politics, of betrayal, courage and human frailty.

The order of the book is roughly chronological but some themes span centuries and some individuals played key roles over many decades. The sequence is designed to be easily read. It tries to link the different influences upon radical thought. The development of democracy, non-conformist religion and trade unionism are often inter-woven.

The battle for women's liberation and equal rights runs through all progressive history but too many stories remain hidden.

It is a guide to the radical history of the West Country offering an alternative version of our past.

Thanks and apologies

Thank you to everyone who has contributed to this book and encouraged me to produce it. Thanks to those who share an interest in the history of working people in the West Country and who have helped me gather the material including, Keith Hatch, Dick Muskett, Steve Poole, Dave Chapple, the Bristol Radical History Group, Michael Walker and my wife, Gilda.

I suspect that errors will be discovered and I'm sure that I have missed out lots of stories that deserve to be included. Please forgive me. I have tried to track down the origins and ownership of all the photographs and given credits where appropriate. Please accept my apologies if I've missed any or got the credit wrong.

The battle for Wessex

The ninth century witnessed battles across the West Country that helped shape the region. It is not really possible to apply judgements on the political merits of the characters involved but the story of the South West would not be complete without including the struggle to defend what was known as Wessex.

In the mid-ninth century most of what we now call England had fallen to powerful Viking forces. The Danes sought to extend their control into the West Country and in 871 they defeated King Ethelred of Wessex at the battle of Merton. No-one is sure where Merton was but the King died as a result of the fight and was buried at Wimborne Minster in Dorset.

By 875 the Danes had taken Wareham and Exeter chasing out the new **King, Alfred** and his West Saxon supporters. Alfred made off to Gloucester and then Chippenham. After the 'twelfth-night' in mid-winter of 878 the Danes attacked and took Chippenham. Alfred escaped into Somerset where he established a base in the marshes at Athelney (burning some cakes along the way). He rallied support for the decisive battle that took place that Spring at Edington in Wiltshire.

King Alfred's Tower, a folly at Stourhead, Wiltshire, stands near where it is believed that Alfred rallied the Saxons before the Battle of Edington.

Alfred's troops drove the Danes back to Chippenham where, after a two-week siege, terms were agreed. The Treaty of Wedmore forced the Danes to retreat and their leaders to be baptised into the Christian faith at Athelney.

Around the same time, some 1,200 Viking raiders, led by Ubbe Ragnarsson, landed at Combwich in Sedgemoor. They were met and beaten at Cannington, near Bridgwater, by a force of Saxons led by **Ealdorman Odda** of Devon.

After Alfred's success he re-organised government and the military. A system of forts was built across the

Alfred's monument near Athelney

West Country so that no-one was more than one day's ride from safety. He reformed the administration of justice and supported education. He encouraged the translation of books from Latin into English.

King Alfred died on 26 October 899 and the Kingdom of Wessex became absorbed into England under King Athelstan in 927. The Norman conquest of England in 1066 broke up the area into new ownership and control.

Alfred's connection with Athelney and Somerset is marked by a stained glass window in East Lyng church, dating to about 1900, along with the King Alfred Inn at Burrowbridge.

The King Alfred pub

Alfred statue in Pewsey

Burrowbridge Mump, Alfred's troops are said to have used for a look-out

East Lyng church window to King Alfred

King Alfred's Tower at Stourhead, near the site of the Battle of Edington

The sculpture of Alfred on the Stourhead Tower

Exeter resistance

After William the Conqueror's victory at Hastings in 1066 he moved to assert his control on the country. A few stood out against his rule including those in Exeter loyal to the former King.

The new King William established his control and rewarded those who had supported his invasion. Land was seized and ownership distributed to his key French barons.

This wasn't just a change of king; it marked a wider culture change. 1066 proved a turning point for Britain with a change in government systems and structures, land owners, language and customs.

There was resistance to the new regime, however, especially in the West Country. Exeter refused to accept the new King, partly because it was home to Gytha, the former King Harold's mother.

When William demanded a tribute of £18 per year and that the city swear allegiance to him, the citizens of Exeter declared:

> " *We will not swear fealty to the King, nor admit him within our wall; but will pay him tribute, according to ancient custom.* "

In 1068, to secure his rule, William rode with 500 knights into the West Country. They laid waste to towns in Dorset on their way.

William's army approached Exeter from the north east by fording the Long Brook. At the East Gate, after the citizens refused to open the gates, he had a hostage blinded.

After 18 days of assault the city surrendered. Gytha escaped down the river and into exile. Properties were divided amongst the victorious French knights.

William's troops marched further west to deal with Cornish resistance.

The next year rebels loyal to the former King Harold, including his two brothers, landed at Exeter with 66 ships hoping that the West

THE LONG BROOKE CROSSED THIS ROAD SOME SEVENTY FEET SOVTH-WEST.→ THE WOODEN FOOTBRIDGE WHICH SPANNED IT, WAS REMOVED WHEN THE RIVER WAS ARCHED OVER A.D.1832. WILLIAM THE CONQVEROR AND HIS TROOPS,WADED ITS WATERS INTENT VPON BESIEGING OVR CITY. A.D.1069. *Harry Hems.*

A plaque in Longbrook Street, marks the Exeter siege.

Country could be a launch-pad for a fresh attack on William. But the rebellion was swiftly defeated.

The *Doomsday Book* census, begun at Gloucester Cathedral, was part of William's campaign to control land and suppress opposition.

Rougemount Castle, built by William to hold Exeter

The Cornish Rebellion

In 1497, Parliament levied a tax, to finance a war against Scotland. Cornwall was remote and poor and the tax hit the population hard.

Michael Joseph An Gof (Mychal Josef, an Gof in Cornish) was a smithy from the village of St Keverne. He organised a campaign against the tax and in May 1497 led a march to London with **Thomas Flamank**, a Bodmin lawyer.

In Wells, they were joined by **Lord Audley**, a disaffected nobleman. Many others joined from across the West Country. This was more than just a Cornish fight.

They drew up a declaration of grievances and on 13th June the march reached Guildford. Fearful of the rebellion, King Henry VII moved the Queen and Prince Henry to the Tower. The army confronted the rebels. The first skirmish led by Lord Daubeney, the Lord Chancellor and Chief General, was fought off and the Cornish camped at Blackheath.

The King's forces attacked early on the morning of 17th June. The Cornish, with home-made weapons, bill hooks, and scythes were no match for the trained troops. In the Battle of Deptford Bridge some 200 Cornish men died. Michael Joseph, Thomas Flamank and Lord Audley were captured and on the 27th June, they were taken to Tyburn, where they were hung, drawn and quartered. Lord Audley, because of his noble rank, was beheaded on Tower Hill the following day.

The Cornish remain proud of their history, including this early rebellion against the English tax. Each year in June, Michael Joseph An Gof is remembered by the people of St Keverne village.

In 1997, the 500th anniversary of the uprising, a special bronze statue of Michael Joseph An Gof and Thomas Flamank was made by Terence Coventry, a local sculptor.

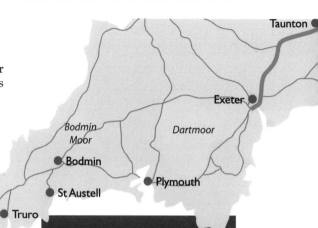

The sculpture of An Gof and Thomas Flamank in St. Keverne

photo: Helen Raynor

The Perkin Warbeck pub in Taunton

Second uprising

Soon after the rebellion, Perkin Warbeck, a pretender to the throne, tried to exploit the resentment felt in Cornwall to challenge King Henry VII.

On 7th September 1497, Warbeck landed at Whitesand Bay, near Land's End. Warbeck claimed that he would stop the hated taxes. He was declared 'Richard IV' on Bodmin Moor and his 3,000 strong Cornish army besieged Exeter unsuccessfully before advancing on Taunton. When Warbeck heard that the King's trrops were at Glastonbury he panicked and deserted his army.

Henry VII reached Taunton on 4th October 1497, where the remaining Cornish army surrendered. The ringleaders were executed and others fined.

Warbeck was captured in Hampshire and taken to Taunton, paraded at Exeter, then held in the Tower of London. On 23rd November 1499, Warbeck was taken to Tyburn and hanged.

The Prayer Book Rebellion

In 1549 the imposition of the new English Prayer Book was seen as an attack on old Catholic traditions and language, especially in Cornwall. It sparked a disastrous rebellion that led to the death of around ten per cent of the Cornish population, land seizures and suppression of Cornwall's culture and political aspirations.

Many worshippers wanted to retain their Catholic ways particularly in parts of the West Country. The use of English in church services was very unpopular in Cornwall where Cornish was widely spoken.

Resistance in Cornwall resulted in the murder of Sir William Body, the King's Commissioner and Archdeacon of Cornwall. He was a hated figure in the county and on 5th April 1548 a large crowd in

Helston set upon him after he tried to destroy church paraphernalia.

In January 1549 Parliament passed the Act of Uniformity to enforce the use of the *Book of Common Prayer* and eradicate the use of Latin Mass and other Catholic symbols.

In Sampford Courteney, Devon, local people resisted attempts to adopt the new service. On Easter holiday, people were out in force and drinking the local cider. William Hellyons, a yeoman farmer climbed up the steps outside Church House and tried to calm the crowd. Jeers

On Whit Monday 1549 SAMPFORD COURTENAY people killed a local farmer WILLIAM HELLYONS and then joined the Cornish in the Prayer Book Rebellion which ended in defeat by the King's army outside this village

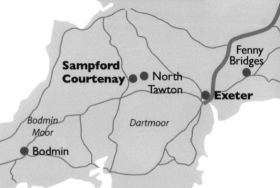

Sampford Courtney, the steps where William Hellyons was killed

Sampford Courtney church

The Arch-Prelate of St Andrewes in Scotland reading the new Service-booke in his pontificalibus assaulted by men & Women, with Crickets stooles Stickes and Stones.

Rioting against the reading of the new Prayer Book

turned to violence and he was run through with a pitchfork and killed.

The event sparked a rebellion that quickly spread into Cornwall. The imposition of the *Book of Common Prayer* followed a period of oppression and rampant inflation, in which wheat prices had quadrupled. After the rapid enclosure of common lands, the attack on the Church was the final straw.

Bodmin became the centre of the resistance until sufficient support was gathered to march on Exeter. Their statement declared "and so we Cornishmen, whereof certain of us understand no English, utterly refute this new English."

The rebellion besieged Exeter for five weeks. Cornish tin miners tried to tunnel under the walls but townsfolk poured water down a counter tunnel to drown out the rebel mine.

Lord Russell led the force sent to put down the uprising. He mustered his army at Honiton and battle commenced in the marshy meadows near Fenny Bridges. Russell's troops were strengthened by German and Italian mercenaries. They crossed the River Exe at Clyst St Mary and between North Tawton and Stone Cross.

The rebels were beaten and retreated back to Sampford Courtney where they were ruthlessly slaughtered. Lord Russell ordered his troops to slit the throats of 900 rebel prisoners.

Rebels executed

Memorial stones at Penryn in Cornwall and Fenny Bridges in Devon

The leaders were hanged from gallows across the West Country with some being taken to be executed at Tyburn in London. Some 5,000 people were killed in the uprising.

Although begun over the language and style of church services, the fight was as much about a changing way of life in rural communities, land and property. The final sharing of spoils saw the victorious gentry seize manors and swathes of countryside across Devon and Cornwall.

The defeat dealt a severe blow to the use of the Cornish language which never recovered.

Exeter Westgate plaque to mark the City's defence against the rebels

Revenge and retribution

Sir William Kingston, the English Provost Marshall led the retribution for the rebellion. He went to St Ives and invited John Payne, the Portreeve (port warden), to join him at the Old George and Dragon inn.

Kingston asked Payne to have gallows erected during the course of the lunch. Afterwards the Provost Marshall ordered the Portreeve to mount the gallows where he was hanged for being a "busy rebel".

Other well-known figures to be executed included Nicholas Boyer, the mayor of Bodmin and Richard Bennet, vicar of St Veep. Mayor Mayow of Gluvian was hanged outside a tavern in St Columb.

The stone in St Ives to remember John Payne

St Thomas Church Tower, Cowick Street, Exeter

Robert Welshe, vicar of St Thomas Church, in Exeter, joined the Prayer Book Rebellion. After the uprising failed he was tried and condemned to death. His tarred body hung from the church tower for four years until the Catholic Queen Mary succeeded her brother Edward VI in 1553 and ordered his body to be cut down.

In 1645, the tower crashed to the ground when the church was destroyed by the Royalist defenders of the city during the Civil War, to prevent Parliamentary troops occupying the structure.

The Western Rising

Between 1626 and 1632 there were a series of riots and rebellions against enclosures and de-forestation. Large numbers of people were involved in Gillingham Forest in Dorset, Braydon Forest in Wiltshire and the Forest of Dean in Gloucestershire.

The enclosure of open or common pasture occurred throughout the period after 1450 and forced many West Country tenants and commoners from their land.

It was in West Country forests where new fences caused most hardship and resentment. Locals, especially those with little if any land, who lived off the wood, were denied the means to survive.

Much of Wiltshire, Dorset and Somerset was covered by trees such as the large Selwood Forest. It meant work for carpenters, sawyers, coopers, tanners, charcoal burners and others. The fences threatened these trades and the independent life of rural artisans.

In the 1620s protests grew into a major uprising and the authorities, under the direction of the Star Chamber, struggled to quell the rebellion. In 1628 the Sheriff of Dorset bid a hasty retreat from Gillingham Forest in Dorset when he found the rebels to be numerous, well armed and resolute. The rioters declared:

> " Here were we born and here we will die. "

Skimmington Rebellion

Dressing up in women's clothes seems to have been a part of resistance to authority or a method of disguise at this time. Leaders of the uprisings used the alias: 'Lady Skimmington'.

A 'Skimmington' was a public shaming of individuals for a variety of offences or sexual behaviours. People would dress in smocks and parade an effigy to the victim's house. The term was used for other actions that caused the community's displeasure including enclosures.

In 1628 rebels established themselves on Cley Hill, near Warminster to protest at the enclosure of the forest at Selwood. The authorities could not find enough men to quell the uprising.

In 1631 the commoners rose in revolt at Braydon, north Wiltshire. Other incidents took place in the forests near

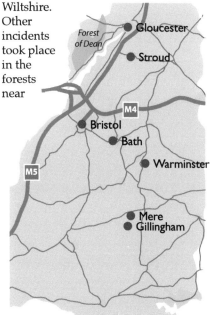

Frome, Maiden Bradley, Yarnfield, Melksham and Chippenham.

Riots were reported against the "new-gained grounds of Lord Berkeley" at Frampton and Slimbridge in Gloucestershire.

It is hard to be sure who led these uprisings. **Henry Hoskins**, yeoman and **John Phillips**, tanner from Gillingham faced arrest as "cheefe actors in theise disorders". Phillips was caught and held in Fleet Prison in London but Hoskins was never apprehended.

At Mailescott Woods, near Coleford in the Forest of Dean some 3,000 peope assembled with drums and ensigns. The filled in ditches, burnt down houses and attacked miners that had been brought it from outside the Forest.

Such were the problems in tracking down the leaders of the Dean riots, the Privy Council questioned landowners who employed suspects and even Peter Simons, curate of Newland Parish.

I'm John Williams

John Williams was a free miner from English Bicknor in the Forest of Dean. The importance given to his capture points to his role as leader of the riots in the spring of 1631. He escaped an attempt to catch him in his bed by the Sheriff of Gloucestershire with 120 men. In January 1632 he led another uprising at Cannop Chase.

He was finally caught in March that year by William Cowse, one of the King's Officers. Williams was taken to Newgate Prison in London where

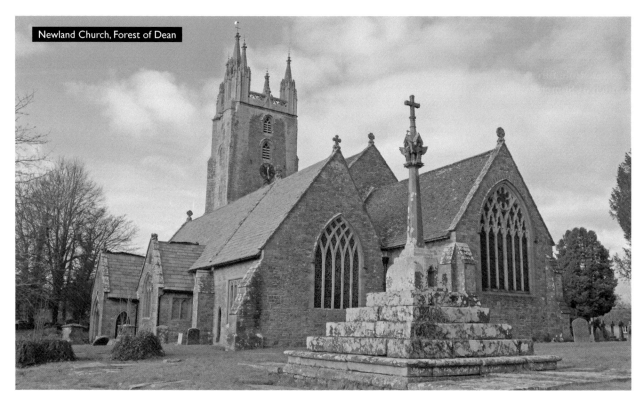

Newland Church, Forest of Dean

he was kept for five years before his release.

The reaction of the Foresters to his arrest was demonstrated when Cowse turned up at Newland Church. He was attacked and pistols were discharged. From then on Cowse required guards to enter the Forest.

The name John Williams and 'Skimmington' turn up in the uprisings in Braydon Forest and in Gillingham. News was spreading around the region and communities were sharing ideas or copying tactics. But it seems likely that the use of these names were a ploy to confuse the authorities and hide the true identities.

The law locks up the man or woman Who steals the goose from off the common But leaves the greater villain loose Who steals the common from off the goose.

17th Century poem

Land privatisation

In England between 1750 and 1850, over six million acres of common and waste land was turned into private fields. This created the hedge-lined fields, so much a character of the today's countryside. But it changed the rural society and class structures.

Enclosures led to a three-way division of rural life with landlords, tenant-farmers and hired labour that has since dominated the structure of farming and village life.

This process ran in parallel to the industrial revolution and the dramatic growth of towns and cities. The rural poor became a landless proletarian, relying on poverty level wages and Poor Law handouts.

No Mere Riot

At one time forests spread across much of Somerset, Wiltshire, Dorset and Devon.

The impact of the clearing of forests met with resistance from local people whose lives depended upon them. One example was the village of Mere on the edge of Selwood Forest in Wiltshire.

After opposition to the enclosures the early 1600s compensation was recommended of a one acre allotment for each cottage in Mere village. But it was only after more riots in the 1640s that concessions were given.

In April 1643 there was a proclamation issued by the men of Mere to summon the people of the forest to march with drums and muskets on 25th April to tear down the enclosures. This was Rogation Day on which there was a local market and a ceremony to ask for good growing and harvest.

A common feature of Rogation days was the 'beating the bounds', in which a procession of parishioners would proceed around the boundary of their parish and pray for its protection. It seems a fitting occasion on which to demolish the enclosures.

In 1643 orders from Parliament were read in the Mere and Gillingham churches warning that rioters would be arrested and brought before the House. The local reaction was shown by a quote from **Stephen Frye** of Mere: "that he cared not for their orders and that Parliament might have kept them and wiped their arses with them."

Groups of up to 300 joined in the destruction until no fences were left standing.

Much of the Forest around Mere and Gillingham was owned by Baron Bruce of Whorlton, the First Earl of Elgin. His agent was Thomas Brunker who was left to manage the woods

The centre of Mere

and try to keep out troublesome locals.

Riots occurred throughout the 1640s. The foresters took advantage of the chaos caused by the unfolding Civil War. It can hardly be coincidence that the 1643 uprising took place at the same time as the battle over Wardour Castle, just a few miles away.

The Royalist castle was seized by Parliamentary troops led by Sir Edward Hungerford. He sent a party of soldiers to intervene in the Mere riots but most were locals and were

Mere village

reluctant to act. They came upon a large group of rioters but let them escape. Only after Elgin's agents intervened did the troops capture seven rioters. They were taken to Blandford and spent two nights in irons.

On 7th May seven rioters were arrested but the justices were uncertain what to do with them and they were released on bail. Two days later the Earl's agent, Brunker, found some reluctant constables to arrest two more suspects. The party was met by some 200 people who freed the prisoners.

Only one of those arrested, **Richard Butler** a poor linen weaver and the leader of the riots, was re-taken and brought before the Lords. He was committed to Newgate Gaol but escaped in June 1644.

By March 1644, the Parliamentary position in the area worsened and Waldour Castle was recaptured for the King.

Elgin supported Parliament but his agent was accused of hiring Royalist troops to quell the riots. In 1645 a rioter was shot dead and one of Brunker's servants was beaten and left for dead.

It was around this time that bands of clubmen were formed in the area to defend their villages from troops of either side during the war.

An old tanner from Gillingham, **John Phillips,** seems to have taken over a leading role. Aged 66 he urged the men of Mere to beat down the fences. In 1646 he was jailed but when freed he continued his opposition to the enclosures. Aged 70 in 1648 he was back in prison.

Despite the end of the war, further riots broke out in 1648 and 1651

After yet more riots in 1652 John Kirke, who owned a third of the forest, conveyed 80 acres to trustees to provide an income for the poor of the town. But people didn't want charity, they

wanted access to common land and the fences were broken down again.

74 people were convicted in the Star Chamber for their part in the Gillingham riots – 45 of whom were artisans.

The forests were eventually felled and cleared for agriculture.

Fish-weir wars

In 1527 the monks of Tavistock Abbey, in Devon, built fish traps or weirs near Gulworthy so large that they prevented almost all fish passing upstream, including spawning salmon. This stopped local people from fishing the river and were hated by sailors trying to navigate the waters.

On Whit Sunday a crowd of about 200 gathered at Hingston Down. **William Harris** and **John Kelly** led the angry crowd and they smashed the weir. The Abbott mustered a posse of 160 men and the rioters dispersed.

In 1532, Henry VIII ordered all estuary weirs to be taken down. This efficient fishing method survived the orders and remained a cause of disputes.

Lydford Gorge, Devon

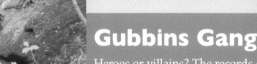

Gubbins Gang

Heroes or villains? The records of the Gubbins clan of Lydford show them as cut-throat outlaws. They lived in caves in the Lydford Gorge and stole sheep from Dartmoor.

Legend has it that the original family fled into 'exile' after one of the women was 'seduced' by a Royalist officer. The community existed for several generations and in the 1600s were led by Roger Rowle who some have described as the Robin Hood of Devon. They robbed travellers and lived off their wits during the years of the Civil War.

Fighting for Parliament

Re-enactment of the battle to lift the siege of Gloucester by Sealed Knot

The English Civil War was more than a battle between Parliament and an arrogant king who believed in his divine right to rule. It heralded the stirrings of a new order and unleashed radical ideas of democracy and freedom.

The West Country provided recruits for both sides in the war that divided communities and even families. The conflict swept back and forth across the region. Towns were taken, lost and taken again as the strength of each side ebbed and flowed.

Parts of the South West were particularly important for strategic control. Bristol was a key city and port; Gloucester was critical as it was the crossing over the River Severn and the route into South Wales; the Forest of Dean held substantial iron ore deposits and the south coast ports provided access for supplies and re-enforcements.

Kicking-off in Shepton Mallet

The first skirmishes of the civil war took place in the summer of 1642. King Charles issued a Commission of Array: an order to raise troops. Parliament responded with warrants to ignore the call to arms and called for a rally on 1st August 1642 in Shepton Mallet. Royalists claimed that the Parliamentarians were coming to 'fire' houses and a troop led by Wells MP, Ralph Hopton, rode into Shepton to face their leader, **Colonel William Strode.**

An argument ensued with Strode demanding to know why the Royalists came with such a show of force. When Hopton read the King's order, Strode said: "I come not to hear petitions but to suppress insurrections." Hopton tried to arrest Strode, tipping him off his horse.

Swords were drawn and pistols pointed. Hopton read the

Shepton Mallet market square: where hostilities began

Commission but only one man stepped forward. Angry at the lack of support, Hopton tried to take Strode prisoner. He learnt of a large crowd marching in support of Parliament. Realising that he was outnumbered, Hopton released Strode and retreated. On hearing of Hopton's behaviour Parliament removed him from office.

The Royalists mustered troops at Wells in Somerset while the Parliamentarians gathered at Shepton Mallet.

Marshall's Elm, where the Civil War saw its first battle

On 4th August the Royalist forces won the first round at the battle of Marshall's Elm. Some 10,000 Roundhead troops – as the Parliament forces became known – re-grouped at Chewton Mendip and the King's men withdrew towards Glastonbury.

Siege of Plymouth

Plymouth stood firm for Parliament against the forces of King Charles I throughout the period of the war. The Royalist army tried to take the city in December 1642 but was driven back. To blockade the town, Colonel Digby made his headquarters at Plymstock, with batteries at Oreston and Mount Batten whilst the army under Prince Maurice made its headquarters at Widey House.

Plymouth vowed not to surrender 'without the authority and consent of both houses of Parliament'. On 3rd December 1643 the 'Sabbath-day Fight' was waged on Freedom Fields. The King's forces were routed and driven into the marshes.

In April 1644 the Royalist forces again attacked Plymouth but were defeated in a battle at St Budeaux. Several

other attempts to take the town also failed. In September 1644 the King himself came to Plymouth but was no more successful.

The city was finally freed on Christmas Day 1644, bringing to an end one the longest and fiercest sieges of the war.

On 25th March 1646 Oliver Cromwell and Thomas Fairfax led a triumphal procession through the city.

Exeter

In Exeter loyalties were divided. Exeter defended itself in 1642-3 for Parliament against the Royalist forces of the west. Prince Maurice, for the King, captured the city in 1643. There were initial reports of Cavalier cruelty to townsfolk.

The city was held until April 1646 when a triumphant Parliamentary force led by Oliver Cromwell entered the city.

Lansdown

On 5th July 1643 the Royalists beat off an assault at Lansdown Hill near Bath although their leader, Sir Bevil Grenville was killed in the action.

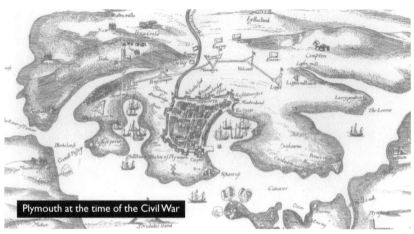

Plymouth at the time of the Civil War

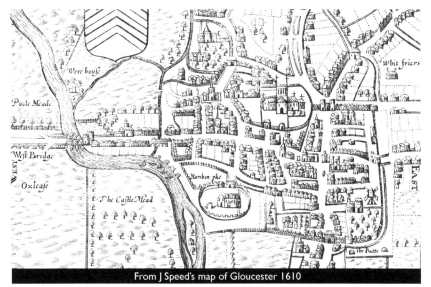

From J Speed's map of Gloucester 1610

the Royalists were determined to take the city.

The siege took place between the 3rd August and 5th September, 1643. The city's position guarded the lowest crossing point over the river to Wales and as such was strategically vital.

Colonel Massey, on behalf of the people of Gloucester, refused to surrender. Royalist forces dug in and set up artillery batteries around the south and east gates of the city. They severed or diverted water pipes and bombarded the city. The defenders burned houses and other obstacles outside the city walls.

The largest field army in the English Civil War sat outside Gloucester, trying to bring the city to its knees. The siege was lifted by a relief force of 'train-bands' from London just in time. 30-40 inhabitants had been killed but several thousand of the besiegers had died. It proved a turning point in the war.

Some believe that Humpty Dumpty comes from the siege engines used unsuccessfully in Gloucester.

Forest of Dean
Welsh Royalists raised an army to invade the Parliamentarian stronghold of the Forest of Dean. 500 residents took on the King's 1,500 troops.

Legend has it that Sir Richard Lawdley, Royalist commander was killed by a silver bullet fired from a window in the King's Head in Coleford.

Roundway Down battle
On 10th July 1643 the Parliamentary force led by **William Waller** laid siege to Devizes. Prince Maurice escaped the town to gather reinforcements from Oxford.

Waller's troops were attacked on Roundway Down and in the panic of battle many of the Parliamentary cavalry fled over the ridge to their deaths into what is now called Bloody Ditch.

Siege of Gloucester
In July 1643 Prince Rupert, supported by Cornish troops, broke through the walls of Bristol and took the town for the King. It was a serious blow for Parliament. Gloucester was the only Parliamentary stronghold left and

Gloucester's St Nicholas Church lost the top of its spire during the siege

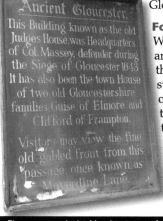

Plaque to mark the Headquarters of Colonel Massey in Gloucester

The Sealed Knot mark the skirmish in Coleford

Siege of Lyme Regis

Royalists under the command of Prince Maurice besieged Lyme Regis in June 1644. The town, led by **Thomas Sealey** and **Robert Blake** from Bridgwater, defeated the Royalist army which suffered between two and three thousand casualties.

Western Women

The women of Lyme Regis helped to dig trenches, guard earthworks and load muskets. After a five-week siege Prince Maurice withdrew, defeated by "this little vile fishing town".

Lostwithiel

The Earl of Essex marched into Lostwithiel for Parliament on 2nd August 1644. A skirmish took place at St Bartholomew's Church. Essex's soldiers held a blasphemous mock service christening a horse 'Charles'.

The Royalist army, led by King Charles himself surrounded the Roundheads and with the battle lost, Essex fled in a boat to Plymouth.

Crabchurch Conspiracy

In February 1645, the Parliamentary force holding Weymouth and Melcombe fought off a Royalist plot to take the twin towns.

Taunton is relieved

In 1645 Taunton was attacked by Royalist troops. When the three-month siege was lifted the local pubs were filled with songs of relief:

> The Cavaliers dispers'd with fear, and forced were to run,
>
> On th'eleventh of May, by break of day, ere rising of the sun.
>
> Let Taunton men be mindful then, in keeping of this day,
>
> We'll give God praise, with joy always, upon th'eleventh of May.

Battle of Langport

A key battle of the Civil War took place at Langport in July 1645. Cromwell's New Model Army routed Royalist troops having first marched through Dorset to Crewkerne and Yeovil and on to Langport.

Roundway Down and Bloody Ditch

The pub that overlooks Roundway Down now bears Oliver Cromwell's name

St James Church in Devizes still showing the holes from cannon fire during the seige of the town

The Blue Bowl Inn, Hanham, near Bristol was one of Cromwell's headquarters

Barnstaple

The north Devon town was taken twice by Royalist forces. After the first seizure, the townsfolk rebelled and evicted the troops.

Bristol Battle

Fresh from the victory at Langport,

Lyme Regis sea front

the Roundheads took control of Bridgwater, Bath and advanced on Bristol. Prince Rupert now returned to defend the city he had taken two years before.

The battle over Bristol was a bloody one but the Royalist army could not withstand the battering from the Parliamentarian forces. Prince Rupert withdrew into Bristol Castle but realising that his position was hopeless he sought a treaty. Sir Thomas Fairfax, for the Roundheads, granted him terms and the Royalist army was allowed to march out of Bristol with their colours flying but without their stores and ammunition. King Charles, furious over the defeat at Bristol, forced Prince Rupert into exile.

Clubmen

By 1644 some, weary of the war, organised local associations of Clubmen to keep plundering troops out of their areas. They claimed no allegiance with either side.

In 1645 Somerset Clubmen hunted down Royalist soldiers fleeing from the battle of Langport in revenge for earlier abuses. The victorious Roundheads, on the other hand, struck a deal with the Clubmen at Middlezoy with offers of supplies and promises that they would commit no offences against the local population providing they did not assist the Royalists.

In Dorset some 2,000-4,000 Clubmen made a stand against Cromwell's troops. Even though

The Lostwithiel font used to Christen a horse 'Charles'

Shroton Church and Hambledon Hill, near Blandford Forum where the beaten Clubmen were held, told off and sent home.

their leaders had been arrested in Shaftesbury, they gathered on Hambledon Hill. But they were no match for the professional and war-hardened New Model Army.

Most Clubmen fled but some were locked up overnight in the church of St Mary's in Shroton. The following day Oliver Cromwell gave them a lecture and let them go free, calling them "poor silly creatures".

Troops on strike?

On 6th October 1645 the Parliamentary western advance was brought to a halt at Chard, Somerset when the troops protested over arrears of pay. Five days later a treasury convoy reached the town to pay the men and the march into Devon resumed.

Parliament gains upper-hand

Through 1645 and 1646 the forces for Parliament were in the ascendancy. Cromwell had won the key battle of

Tiverton Castle

Naseby and his Roundhead troops led by Sir Thomas Fairfax swept through Amesbury, Blandford, Beaminster, Crewkerne, Bridgwater, Sherbourne and Devizes.

Berkeley Castle in Gloucestershire was captured by Colonel Thomas Rainsborough, for Parliament.

The Royalists were cornered in Devon and Cornwall and mutiny became rife. Tiverton Castle tried to hold out for the King but on 19th October 1645 a lucky shot broke the chains holding the drawbridge and surrender quickly followed.

After Tiverton, Fairfax and Cromwell met at Crediton and marched north to Great Torrington. On 16 February 1646 there was a fierce battle through the streets of the north Devon town. Lord Hopton commanded the Royalists using the church as a powder store. The Roundheads captured the church and used it to hold some 200 prisoners. There was a huge explosion killing all those inside and destroying the church.

To remember the events of the key battle, a torch-lit procession is organised each year and a re-enactment takes place of the proclamation of victory by Parliament.

Cornwall falls to Parliament

By 1646 Fairfax was in west Cornwall on his mission to root out remaining Royalists.

On 25th February 1646 he took Launceston, on 2nd March Bodmin fell and on 10th March at Tresillion Bridge, Sir Ralph Hopton met Fairfax to discuss terms. Four days later Truro was taken and Hopton fled into exile.

Charles, Prince of Wales escaped Falmouth for the Isles of Scilly and on 12th April twenty warships surrounded the island of St Mary's. Storms scattered the fleet and the Prince made his escape to Jersey and then to France.

Some 900 men still held Pendennis Castle in Falmouth under the command of Sir John Arundell.

Fairfax demanded the surrender of the castle but they held out for over two months. The garrison was reduced to "eating horses for beef". News of more Parliamentary victories led to some of the troops deserting.

Sir John Arundell surrendered on 17th August. The garrison marched out with their "colours flying, trumpets sounding, drums beating holding matches lighted at both ends, and bullets in their mouths". This was the end of the Civil War in Cornwall.

The last battle

With the King's forces in

Memorial stone in Stow-on-the-Wold Church

desperate retreat, the last battle took place at Stow-on-the-Wold, Gloucestershire.

Lord Astley was planning to join up with the King at Oxford. On 21st March 1646 troops from Gloucester intercepted the force. After street fighting in the Cotswold town, Astley surrendered.

Aftermath

King Charles was captured in June 1646 but tried again to outwit Parliament. He was executed on 30th January 1649.

Oliver Cromwell ruled until his death in 1658. Two years later Charles II returned from exile to take the throne.

West Country towns that had stood firm for Parliament were forced to take down their defences to prevent further resistance. King Charles II ordered that the walls of Gloucester be breached to prevent the city holding out again. Colonel Massey was elected as MP for the city. Taunton was ordered to dismantle its defences including the castle.

But it was the new ideas that the war unleashed that would prove harder to contain.

Pendennis Castle held out despite the Royalist surrender by Cromwell

South West War map

Few parts of the West Country escaped the horrors of war during the years 1642-46. But there were significant battles and sieges that helped shape the eventual outcome.

Devastation of war
The stone at the site of the battle of Lansdown Hill near Bath

Tewkesbury
Stow-on-the-Wold
Cheltenham
Gloucester
Forest of Dean
Stroud
Cirencester
Malmesbury
Swindon
Marlborough
Chippenham
M4
Bristol
Lansdown Hill
Bath
Roundway
Devizes
Chewton Mendip
Trowbridge
Shepton Mallet
Frome
Dunster Castle
Bridgwater
Marshalls End
Ilfracombe
Exmoor
Barnstaple
Bideford
Taunton
Langport
Salisbury
Yeovil
Babylon Hill
Sherborne
Tiverton
Hambeldon Hill
Blandford Forum
Chard
Stratton
Great Torrington
Crediton
Exeter
Dorchester
Poole **Bournemouth**
Lyme Regis
Launceston
Sourton Down
Exmouth
Weymouth
Bodmin Moor
Dartmoor
Newton Abbot
Bodmin
Torquay
Newquay
Lostwithiel
Braddock Down
St Austell
Modbury
Plymouth
Camborne
Truro
Penzance
Falmouth

✗ Battle
◯ Siege

Robert Blake

Born in Bridgwater in 1596, Robert Blake was the first of thirteen children. In 1640 Blake was elected as the town's MP until beaten by Royalist Colonel Wyndham, governor of Bridgwater Castle. When the Civil War broke out the two men faced each other in battle.

Blake became a hero of the Parliamentary cause by leading the defence of Lyme Regis. He helped lift the siege of Taunton and won Bridgwater Castle then Barnstaple and on 20th April 1646 took Dunster Castle.

Blake returned to Bridgwater as MP but his life turned to the sea. He helped lead the capture of the Royalist fleet. He re-built the Navy including introducing welfare reforms for sailors. Blake was killed in a battle at Tenerife. He left £100 to the poor of Bridgwater and is remembered in the town by a museum and statue.

ROBERT BLAKE
BORN IN THIS TOWN
1598
DIED AT SEA 1657

Civil war on the Isles of Scilly

Nowhere escaped the Civil War. But the Isles of Scilly held a key position in the approaches to the Cornish coast.

Like Cornwall, the Isles of Scilly held out for the King during the Civil War. Prince Charles took refuge in Star Castle on St Mary's before his escape to exile on the continent.

At the end of the war a garrison of Parliamentary troops were billeted in the homes of the islanders. No payments for board or pay arrived and the troops mutinied and declared for the Royalists.

Prince Charles sent 20-year-old Sir John Grenville to take advantage of this turn of events.

The last foothold for the King became a base to harass passing ships.

The islanders didn't like being occupied by a Royalist force either and in 1650 there was an abortive attempt to raise a rebellion against Grenville.

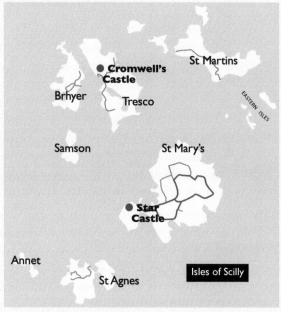

Isolated from supplies, the Royalists were forced into pirating, including taking a Dutch ship.

Fearful of this being used by the Dutch as an excuse to invade, Cromwell sent Admiral Blake to deal with the Royalists on the isles and the threat from the Dutch.

In April 1651 Blake took Tresco after three times being beaten off. Other islands soon fell but St Mary's was not taken. Blake built Cromwell's Castle on the island of Tresco in order to command the entrance to St Mary's harbour. Blockaded, Grenville had little choice but to surrender.

Star Castle, St Mary's, Isles of Scilly: refuge for Prince Charles and base for Royalist foothold after the war

Cromwell's Castle, Tresco

Twists and turns of the civil war in the West Country

1642
31 July **Confrontation in Shepton Mallet Market Place**
4 August **First skirmish at Marshall's Elm**
7 September **Battle of Babylon Hill hampers Royalist advance**
December **Royalists siege Plymouth**
5 December **Marlborough is taken for the King**
6 December **fighting in Modbury**

1643
19 January **Battle of Braddock Down**
21 January **Royalists storm Saltash**
2 February **Prince Rupert takes Cirencester**
21 February **Modbury taken for Parliament**
24 March **battle at Hignham** 12 April **Parliament takes Tewkesbury**
25 April **Royalists routed in Sourton Down battle**
16 May **Battle of Stamford Hill**
16 May **Battle of Stratton is won for the King**
5 July **Battle of Lansdown near Bath**
10 July **Siege of Devizes ends with Battle of Roundway**
26 July **Bristol falls to King, followed by**
Dorchester, Weymouth and Portland
3 August **Royalists siege Gloucester**
5 September **Gloucester is rescued for Parliament**

1644
19 January **Kings' forces win the battle of Braddock Down**
June **Siege of Lyme Regis**
23 July **Essex takes Tavistock for Parliament**
26 July **King arrives in Exeter**
2 August **Battle of Lostwithiel is won for King**

1645
11 March **Taunton sieged by King**
12 March **Royalists lose Trowbridge**
5 June **Clubmen uprisings in Dorset and Somerset**
29 June **Taunton freed**
July **Battle of Langport proves victory for Parliament**
July **Parliament takes Bridgwater, Bath and Bristol**
Led by Fairfax, Parliamentary forces sweep through South West
19 October **Tiverton is taken**

1646
12 January **Siege of Plymouth lifted**
19 January **Dartmouth** 26 January **Powderham Castle, near Exeter**
16 February **Battle of Great Toddington**
25 February **Launceston** 2 March **Bodmin** 14 March **Truro**
17 March **Falmouth is sieged**
21 March **Last battle of the war at Stow-on-the Wold**
25 March **victory procession through Plymouth**
17 August **Falmouth surrenders**

War and ideas

The English Civil War shook the foundations of belief that maintained society since feudal times. It stimulated a range of new and radical ideas.

Social contract
The debate over the nature of power and society sparked by the Civil War included the ideas of **Thomas Hobbes** (1588-1679) born in Malmesbury, Wiltshire. Hobbes wrote

Thomas Hobbes

Leviathan in 1651 that laid the foundation for much of Western political philosophy.

Hobbes questioned what life would be like without government where each person would have a right to everything in the world. This would inevitably lead to conflict and lives that are "solitary, poor, nasty, brutish, and short".

To escape this state of war, humans subscribe to a 'social contract' that underpins a civil, well-governed society. Hobbes believed that society is a population beneath a sovereign authority, to whom all individuals must give up their natural rights for the sake of protection.

He believed that given government, our peaceful and co-operative nature can be liberated. This made the case for a strong central authority to avoid the evil of discord and war.

Diggers by the Severn
The Civil War stirred radical political ideas. One group, known as Diggers, demanded the common ownership of land and equal treatment for all. They have been described as the first socialists. Their leader, Gerard Winstanley said:

> **The earth was made a common treasury for all.**

They were attacked by the local gentry who destroyed their cottages, drove off their cattle and beat up settlers.

A Digger settlement was established on Slimbridge Waste by the River Severn in Gloucestershire. Little is known of the community

Declaration by the Diggers in 1649 who saw themselves as 'True Levellers'

and it is likely that it was brutally suppressed.

The last stand of the Levellers
During the Civil War, Oliver Cromwell built the force for Parliament into a disciplined and faithful fighting machine known as the New Model Army. Yeoman farmers, tradesmen and skilled workers who joined up were a committed, thinking and intelligent force. Discussion and debate flourished.

There was support for a new, more democratic society without a monarchy. The followers of these ideas were know as Levellers.

The Levellers gained the support

Burford Church, where Levellers' leaders were executed

of the rank and file in the army for a declaration called *Agreement of the People* made in 1647. This contained a list of demands including:

- Annual parliaments, elected by equal numbers of voters per seat
- Votes for all men who worked independently for their living
- The right of recall of MPs by their electors
- Abolition of the House of Lords
- Election of army officers
- Complete religious tolerance
- Abolition of tithes and tolls
- Justices to be elected, law courts to be local and conducted in English, not French
- Land reforms

These radical ideas now threatened Cromwell's own power. John Lilburn, the leader of the Levellers was arrested but was smuggled out of the Tower of London.

In Salisbury there were two regiments of cavalry who supported the Leveller cause. They marched north to meet other groups from Banbury and Oxford. On 13th May 1649 they arrived in Burford on the Gloucestershire-Oxfordshire border.

Fooled by promises that Cromwell would listen to their demands, they were quickly over-run by a strong force loyal to Cromwell. The leaders were held in Burford Church until the 18th May when the three ring-leaders were taken out to be shot in front of their men.

A plaque outside the church commemorates **Cornet Thompson, Corporal Perkins** and **Private Church.** An annual rally is held in Burford each May to mark the anniversary of these events.

Levellers' Day March through Burford in 2007

John Locke

A Somerset-born philosopher with radical ideas was **John Locke** (1632-1704) who developed the works of Thomas Hobbes and others to become a founding father of the Enlightenment.

John Locke was born in 1632 in a small cottage by the church in Wrington. He spent his childhood in the nearby village of Belluton.

Locke studied medicine and became physician to Lord Ashley, 1st Earl of Shaftesbury who founded the Whig movement. Shaftesbury influenced his political views and Locke began writing.

Locke believed that human nature is characterised by reason and tolerance but was inevitably selfish. He argued that in a natural state, all people are equal and independent.

Everyone had a right to defend their "life, health, liberty, or possessions." but self-defence is not enough so people need to establish a civil society and government to resolve conflicts.

As population grows rules are required and people must delegate their natural or moral rights to government to deal with such things as the supply of land and the

John Locke's birthplace in Wrington

punishment of transgressors.

Human labour creates property, but it has limits to its accumulation through one's capacity to produce and to consume. According to Locke, unused property is waste and an offence against nature.

However he believed that to accumulate money was a right as it didn't harm anyone.

To achieve change, Locke advocated revolution not only as a right but an obligation in some circumstances. These ideas influenced the Constitution of the United States and its Declaration of Independence.

In 1683 Locke was forced to flee to Holland under suspicion of involvement in the Rye House Plot to assassinate King Charles II. Locke did not return until 1688 after the 'Glorious Revolution' when William of Orange took the throne.

John Locke

John Locke bust

Weston-super-Mare
Bristol
Belluton
Wrington
M5

Bideford witches

The Bideford witch trial in 1682 ended in the last ever hangings for witchcraft in England. A plaque at Rougemont Castle in Exeter marks the spot where four women were executed.

THE DEVON WITCHES
IN MEMORY OF
**Temperance Lloyd
Susannah Edwards
Mary Trembles**
OF BIDEFORD DIED 1682
Alice Molland
DIED 1685
THE LAST PEOPLE IN ENGLAND
TO BE EXECUTED FOR WITCHCRAFT
TRIED HERE & HANGED AT HEAVITREE
In the hope of an end to persecution & intolerance

Temperance Lloyd was accused of using magical arts, sorcery or witchcraft causing a local woman to become ill. It was claimed that she had been seen having "discourse with the devil in the likeness or shape of a black man."

Under arrest Temperance admitted her 'guilt' and was sent to Exeter for trial.

Mary Trembles and Susanna Edwards faced similar charges of causing illness. It was alleged that the Devil had carnal knowledge of Edwards including having "sucked her in her breast and in her secret parts."

Exile in Somerset

The tiny village of Culbone in West Somerset, with its small church, has provided home to a variety of troublesome communities. In the thirteenth century it was known as Kitnor. A group of monks had established a short-lived settlement.

A new community grew up of people who had been banished there by the church. They were a mixture of non-believers, the mentally ill and general trouble-makers. Some 40 people including children were sent to the isolated village and visitors banned.

Although litle is known of the outcast community, it was self-sufficient with members growing their own food and caring for one another. For some 40 years they maintained the village with little outside contact.

In 1385 Kitnor again became a place of exile, this time as a place of punishment for offenders. The 'crimes' ranged from minor theft to adultery. Separated from their families the group of about twenty men were unable to develop the sort of community as the previous outcasts. Some went mad or killed themselves.

The village again became deserted until 1544 when it became a leper colony for some 45 men, women and children. They were given no food or nursing and were forced to forage and scratch a subsistence for themselves. Despite the lack of support the small gathering coped remarkably well. The

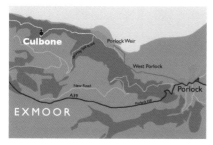

Culbone Church, said to be the smallest in England with its curious 'peep-hole'

small church contains a 'peep-hole' a feature that some believe allowed lepers to look upon the services.

The last leper died in 1622 marking the end of the colony and the village was empty again until 1715, although the old stone cottages were used by smugglers.

A new group of exiles moved in, this time of their own choice. Inspired by the vision of a shared, self-sufficient lifestyle. They built new cottages and cultivated the land for around fifteen years. They called the village Culbone but moved away to be replaced by yet another group of exiles.

A group of 38 East Indian men, taken prisoner by the British were banished to Culbone. They were able to trade charcoal for basic provisions and in 1751, after 21 years, 23 of them were allowed to go free but none made it back to India.

After this period, local landowners took possession of the village, including the Earl of Lovelace. Tied cottages were established as part of the estate. It was home to many of the Red family – a name changed to Ridd in the *Lorne Doone* novel.

The small church was renovated and in 1821 one of the six cottages became a pub, the Fox and Hounds.

Thanks to *Culbone a Spiritual Journey* by Joan Cooper 1978

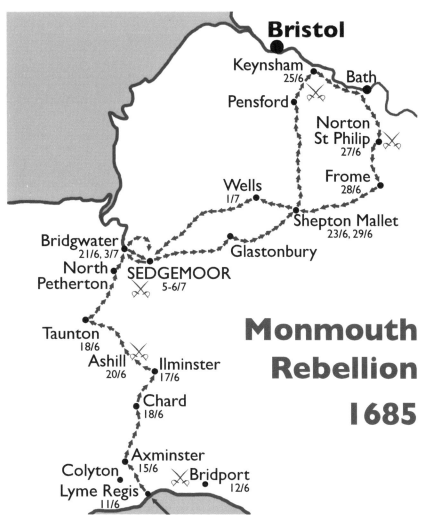

COLYTON-1685AD Rebel Town

CAR PARK

Monmouth Rebel

Colyton: now proud of its rebel past

Monmouth Rebellion 1685

Leveller green, confirming that their support was for religious and political freedoms. Girls from a local academy used their own petticoats to embroider some 27 banners for the rebel regiments.

Monmouth's troops of around 9,000

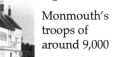

The White Hart inn used as a guard house, now the Lock Keeper Keynsham

The Duke of Monmouth was the illegitimate son of Charles II. In 1680 he toured the West Country winning friends and supporters. In 1683 he was banished to Holland.

On 11th June 1685, four months after the death of Charles II, Monmouth sailed with some eighty officers to land at Lyme Regis intent on taking the throne. The West Country was known to support the cause

of religious tolerance against new restrictions by the Catholic monarch, King James II.

The Duke marched his troops north, gaining support along the way. **Roger Satchell,** a yeoman in Colyton in Devon, recruited some 100 men to join the rebellion. The town today proudly claims to be the Rebel Town.

In Taunton, Monmouth was greeted by townsfolk wearing sprigs of

Sedgemoor Inn, Westonzoyland

Bridgwater pub sign

marched towards Bristol and on 25th June took up positions in Keynsham hoping to gather support. The White Hart Inn – now the Lock Keeper – was used as the guard house. Two forces of the Royal army attacked in bad weather. Taken by surprise the rebels retreated and the march to Bristol was called off.

In the hope of gaining more recruits in Wiltshire, Monmouth headed west to the village of Norton St Philip.

Headquarters were established in The George Inn and North Street was barricaded. The Duke was wounded by a shot while he was shaving in his room in the inn. The King's troops attacked but were driven back after losing 80 men to Monmouth's 18.

The site of the fighting is still known as Bloody Lane and the name 'soho' features amongst the houses after the Monmouth battle cry. His London residence was in Soho Square.

The rebels headed for Shepton Mallet and at what became known as 'Monmouth's Oak', Downhead they were joined by lead miners from the Mendips.

The rebel force withdrew south unable to gather enough support for their ambitious plans. The final

Sedgemoor Battlefield

Bloody Lane, named after the flow of Royalist blood as the King's troops tried to break the barricade in North Street, Norton St Philip.

North Street

The George Inn

St Philip and St Paul Church

Wellow Lane

Bath Road

Farleigh Road A366

Chevers Lane or Bloody Lane

North Street

Norton St Philip

Bell Hill

The George

Church

High Street

Wells Road

The George Inn

WADWORTH

battle took place at Sedgemoor just outside Bridgwater. Many were killed as Monmouth's force was crushed. The Duke fled, to be discovered later, hiding in a ditch in Dorset.

Monmouth was taken to the Tower of London. His execution was botched with the axeman taking five attempts and the use of a knife to sever his head.

Retribution against those who took part in the rebellion was severe. Brutal punishments were imposed by the infamous Judge Jeffrey and his 'Bloody Assizes'. Altogether 233 people were hung, drawn and quartered, the bodies being left until they decomposed.

The Taunton Assize took place in the Great Hall of Taunton Castle. Of more than 500 prisoners brought before the court on the 18th and 19th September, 144 were hanged and their remains displayed around the county.

Fourteen men from Colyton were executed of whom two were returned to their home town to face death in front of friends and neighbours. Twelve men were hanged from Hang-Cross Tree in Chard.

In Shepton Mallet a dozen men were hanged in Market Cross with their bowels burnt and heads and quarters boiled in salt. The Strode family of Shepton supported Monmouth and hid him after the battle of Sedgemoor. Edward Strode, however, was wealthy enough to escape execution and bought his pardon for £400.

Rebel heads were left to hang from the gateway of Cothelstone Manor on the edge of the Quantocks. Others were taken back to Lyme Regis and hanged on the beach where they first landed. This is now called Monmouth Beach and there are many other places named after the rebellion.

The Judge was later to be haunted by the vision of John Tutchin who he had sentenced to be flogged every fortnight for seven years.

High Street, Taunton: a plaque marks the spot where Monmouth was proclaimed King and where rebels were later hanged.

Taunton Castle

It wasn't just the infamous 'hanging judge Jefferies' that was so savage. Colonel Kirke killed many prisoners before they stood trial and one story tells of him sleeping with the innkeeper's daughter in Crewkerne on a promise that he would spare her father's life. When she awoke in the morning her father's corpse was hanging outside the window.

Some magistrates lined their pockets by transmuting the death sentence to transportation as slaves to the West Indies. They would be paid twice, once by the prisoners for allowing themselves to be saved from the noose and again by the slavers who shared the profit made on them.

The Monmouth Rebellion is sometimes called the Pitchfork Rebellion due to its poor arms. Although it failed it was just three years later in 1688, when King James was forced to flee the country to be replaced by Protestant William and Mary. Judge Jeffrey was arrested and imprisoned in the Tower of London where he died.

Grovely Wood rebels

Locals in Wiltshire villages around Grovely Forest have had the right since the eleventh century to gather wood (or estover). In 1603 the villagers' right was set down in a charter that stipulated that inhabitants must, on the Tuesday after Whitsun, go to 'Grovely Wood' at break-of-dawn and cut a bough of oak and stand the bough outside their houses for the whole of that day.

The Earl of Pembroke tried to stop the villagers' access and in 1820 four women from nearby Barford St Martin challenged him by collecting firewood.

The women were fined but refused to pay and were sent to prison. The villagers turned out to protest and, faced with local outrage, the women were released and the right to gather dead wood restored.

More disputes followed, leading in 1892 to the formation of the Oak Apple Club in the village, under the Labour banner 'Unity is Strength', to represent wood rights and customs and perpetuate the May celebrations.

Further disputes occurred and it wasn't until 1987 that a new accord was reached allowing the villagers their full rights. The Oak Apple Festival is held in Grovely Wood every 29th April where villagers from Great Wishford gather firewood to mark the traditional rights.

Great Wishford

Barford St Martin

West Country smuggling

Beer, in Devon, ideal for smuggling

Working people on poverty income levels had to survive on their wits and mutual support. In rural areas that often meant poaching for food, in coastal communities it was smuggling. In the 18th and 19th centuries rising duties on goods meant that money could be made from illicit trade.

Initially smuggling was in the export of wool, then prohibited to protect British weaving. With duties set on goods such as tobacco, tea, brandy, rum, silks, muslin and salt, smuggling became a lucrative if dangerous business. Communities would help hide the contraband and the smugglers. Sympathetic or

Jack Rattenbury

corrupt officials let the trade grow. Villages specialised: Sidbury dealt

with finance, Sidmouth with wagons and Salcombe with carriers.

Jack Rattenbury (1778-1844) was born in the East Devon village of Beer in 1778. He was fifteen at the outbreak of the war with France. Life was hard and getting harder. Beer relied upon fishing, farming, quarrying and lace making but its geography as an isolated cove made it an ideal smuggling base.

Rattenbury's life as a West Country smuggler (or fair trader as he preferred) is described in his own account written in diaries and published in a best-selling book, *Memoirs of a Smuggler*. He refers to

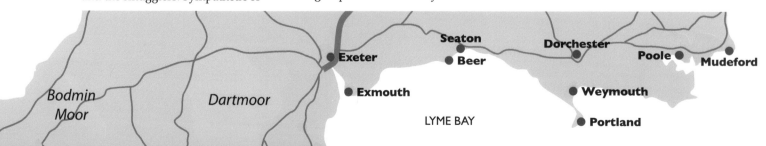

Bodmin Moor

Dartmoor

Exeter

Exmouth

LYME BAY

Seaton

Beer

Dorchester

Poole

Mudeford

Weymouth

Portland

himself as the "Rob Roy of the West". Rattenbury wrote of daring escapes – from the Navy, the press-gang, from privateers and from customs men. Hiding up chimneys, in cellars, on board small boats and in bushes, Jack evaded the authorities.

Jack Rattenbury retired from the smuggling trade with gout but in a surprising twist he became an adviser to the government on a proposal by the engineer Thomas Telford, to build a canal from the Bristol Channel to the south coast. Jack gave his views on the likely impact upon trade as well as sharing his knowledge of the coastal waters. It was never built!

Jack died in Seaton and is buried in the town's churchyard. His passing marked the end of the heyday of smuggling along the coast. The end of the Napoleonic Wars allowed normal trade with France to resume.

Poole Custom House
The coast around Poole was ideal for smuggling

Battle of Mudeford

A smuggling run from the Channel Islands was landed on 15th July 1784 at Mudeford Beach, near Christchurch, Dorset. Some 300 people were unloading the luggers when the Navy sloop *HMS Orestes*

intervened. Smuggler **John Streeter** ran for help from the locals at the nearby Haven House pub.

A fierce battle ensued killing one sailor and wounding many others. The smugglers retreated into the Haven House which was besieged for many hours. When the fighting ended some 120,000 gallons of spirits and 25 tons of tea had vanished.

Three men were arrested including **George Coombes** who was hanged, his body hung in chains from Haven House point until sympathisers cut it down for a decent burial. John Streeter escaped to continue his 'free-trading'.

Cornish smuggling

Cornwall was renowned for smuggling. The county was poor and food often scarce. The coastline made it almost impossible for the authorities to prevent the illicit trade and it was so common that Philip Hawkins the MP for Grampound bequeathed £600 to the King to compensate for the amount which his tenants had defrauded customs!

A nickname for Cornish people is 'Cousin Jack' probably based on smugglers' slang for cognac.

In 1750, Lieutenant-General Onslow received a letter from his agent in Cornwall, George Borlase, asking for soldiers because: "the coasts here swarm with smugglers."

King of Prussia

John, **Harry** and **Charles Carter** of Prussia Cove, Cornwall are amongst the best-known Cornish smugglers.

The narrow inlets, the caves and the secret passages around Prussia Cove made ideal conditions for smuggling

Haven House Inn, Mudeford from which smugglers fought off troops

and John Carter led a band of 'cove boys' in a sophisticated business operation.

On one occasion, officials came to the cove in boats and discovered hidden contraband from France. They impounded the cargo in Custom House, Penzance. John Carter had promised delivery of the goods and to honour his commitment he organised a break-in at the stores. Customs officials recognised the hand of John Carter because nothing else had been taken other than 'his own' smuggled goods.

The Carters were strong Wesleyan Methodists and banned swearing on their ships and held church services every Sunday. Harry Carter, nicknamed The King of Prussia,

Landing the cargo by F Brangwyn

wrote *An Autobiography of a Cornish Smuggler.*

Battling Billy, who ran the Halfway House Inn in Polperro used a hearse to hide kegs of brandy. He was shot

by excise men whilst driving the horse-drawn contraband.

Wreckers

Communities were always quick to seize opportunities presented by wrecks. But there is much mythology surrounding the setting of false lights to lure ships onto rocks.

> *Oh please Lord, let us pray for all on the sea,*
> *But if there's got to be wrecks,*
> *Please send them to we.*
>
> Wreckers' prayer

Fleet wreck

In October 1707 the Flagship *Association,* along with other ships in the Fleet, crashed into rocks close to Bishop Rock off the Isles of Scilly. Legend has it that when a sailor from the Scillies tried to warn the Admiral of the approaching danger because he could smell land he was hanged for insubordination.

The disaster took some 1,400 lives. Admiral Sir Cloudesley Shovell was washed up alive on Port Hellick beach on St Mary's island. When local woman, Mary Mumford found him she murdered him to rob his valuable emerald ring. His body was taken to be interred in Westminster Abbey. Mary Mumford confessed to the crime on her death bed.

Longitude

The disaster led to the Longitude Act in 1714 which offered a large prize for anyone who could find a method of determining longitude accurately at sea. James Harrison eventually won the prize with his accurate clock.

image: old post card, unattributed

Prussia Cove in 1905

Not Treasure Island but the Llandoger Trow in Bristol

Muslim pirates

Arab pirates used fast, light-weight ships to raid ports around the South West. The pirates – Barbary corsairs – captured 466 vessels between 1609 and 1616. 27 were caught off Plymouth in 1625.

Not just ships were attacked and there were several raids on Devon and Cornish villages. They took over Lundy Isand from where they raided passing ships.

Captives would be taken for ransom or as slaves. It has been estimated that in the 16th century, up to 20,000 European slaves were held in North African forts. Like British adventurers, they had the support of their governments.

Some of the Barbary pirates were caught and taken to Bristol to be drowned.

One Arab ship was wrecked off Salcombe in south Devon. It is believed that the Muslim sailors were killed and buried in unconsecrated ground on the beach, hence its name of Moor Sands. Large quantities of Moroccan gold have been discovered nearby.

Moor Sands, Salcombe

Bristol Pirates
Bristol had its share of smuggling and the famous Admiral Benbow Inn, the pirate haunt featured in Treasure Island is based on the Llandoger Trow in Bristol.

Blackbeard
One of the best know pirates was born in Stapleton in Bristol around 1680. There is some doubt whether **Edward Teach** was his real name but he enlisted on a ship bound for the West Indies after he nearly killed the landlord of the Guinea Tavern.

He quickly became a pirate. He was a big man and with his long black beard he cultivated his fiercesome image and new name, Blackbeard. If people would not give up their rings he would chop off their finger.

He plundered around 40 ships and was finally killed in 1718 during an ambush by the Royal Navy off Okracoke Island, North Carolina.

Rebel or villain?
The line between pirate and hero is a fine one. **William Dampier** was born in West Coker, Somerset. Sent to Jamaica he mastered map-making and sailed around the globe charting the seas.

After becoming ship-wrecked he became a 'free-booter' or pirate, returning home a wealthy man. He wrote a book about his castaway life called *A new voyage around the world* that became the inspiration for Robinson Crusoe.

Dampier was appointed by King William III to help chart Australia.

The battle of Hooks Wood

Smugglers needed trade routes to carry their contraband to lucrative markets inland. In March 1779, excise officers tried to intercept the movement of goods at Hooks Wood, near Farnham, Dorset. Having been tipped off that some twenty laden horses were on the move, excise troops confronted some 40-50 smugglers.

The dragoons shot one smuggler in the arm so badly it had to be amputated. Another was shot right through the chest and later died of his wounds. But the renegades fought back with clubs and managed to beat back the soldiers and escape. The next day two men were arrested but acquitted. The rest – with most of their goods – got away.

Revenue murder

In 1822 **William Lewis,** a seaman and smuggler of Weymouth was on board his ship the *Active* when it was approached by Revenue men. Ordered to lower her sails, the crew of the *Active* did so, but a shot was fired from the *Pigmy* and struck Lewis, killing him.

The inquest into his death concluded that Lewis had been murdered and that the shot had been "wantonly and maliciously fired".

Smugglers' Path leading to the White Northe in Dorset. The chalk headland was a famous landmark used by smugglers. It featured in the classic smuggling book *Moonfleet* by John Meade Falkner.

photo: Jim Champion from Wikimedia

Tea not blood

Smuggling communities felt justified to ply their illegal trade. **Robert Trotman** was killed in a shoot-out with troops on the beach between Sandbanks and Bournemouth. His grave in Kinson Church reflects local attitudes that he didn't deserve to die for a little tea.

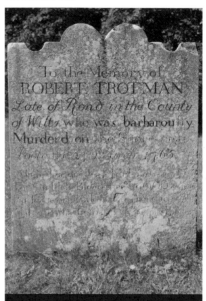

To the Memory of

ROBERT TROTMAN

Late of Rond in the County of Wilts who was barbarously Murder'd on the Shore near Poole the 24 March 1765

A little Tea one leaf I did not steal For Guiltless Blood shed I to GOD appeal Put Tea in one scale human Blood in to ther And think what tis to slay they harmless Brother

Gulliver's trade

Isaac Gulliver was born in Semington in Wiltshire in 1745 and became Bournemouth's most famous smuggler. His pub, the King's Head at Thorney Down, Handley became a centre for contraband. He moved to the White Hart Inn, Longham in Bournemouth where his smuggling operation grew to employ some 40 to 50 men. One story tells of Gulliver feigning death to escape capture. In a house in Kinson he whitened his face with chalk and lay in an open coffin under the stairs.

Kinson Church was used as a store and look-out. It became know as the Smugglers' Church.

As a wealthy man, Gulliver set up a wine and spirits business in Teignmouth and bought Eggardon Hill between Dorchester and Bridport. Although five miles from the coast, Eggardon Hill, at 820 feet above sea level, could be seen from off-shore. Gulliver planted trees to acts as a marker for his crews. The scheme worked well until the authorities realised the purpose of the plantation and obtained a government order to fell the trees.

The nearby Spyway Inn was on an old smuggling trade route north from the beaches of Swyre and Burton Bradstock.

In 1782 the government offered a pardon for those joining the Navy. It is believed that Gulliver paid £15 to 'buy' a substitute and thus clear his name.

Gulliver moved to Wimborne where he became warden of the Minster Church. He died in 1822.

Gulliver's Inn, Kinson

Eggardon Hill

Kinson Church, used to hide contraband, became known as Smugglers' Church

Spyway Inn

Temporary custodians?

The law of salvage has it that everything has an owner: ship and cargo. People rescuing goods from a wreck are 'temporary custodians' until they report the find to the Receiver of Wrecks.

The South West has had many such custodians over the years!

SS Minnehaha aground off the Isles of Scilly in 1910

SS Minnehaha

The *Steam Ship Minnehaha* was built in Belfast to ply the North Atlantic carrying passengers and cargo. In thick fog on 18th April 1910 she ran aground off the Scilly Isles. All the passengers and crew were rescued.

For the islanders this was an opportunity not to be missed. Farming and fishing were abandoned and school dismissed as the locals relieved the stranded ship of her valuable cargo. Cars and pianos came over the side. Sewing machines, clocks and furniture were salvaged. Bales of cigarettes and cheap American novels, wheels, typewriters, jewellery, oranges, apples, pencils and meat-skewers were some of the cargo rescued. It was said that the cargo was worth more than all of Scilly and Penzance put together. 224 cattle had to jump into the water to be saved. Ten cows were lost.

Two weeks after *Minnehaha* hit the rocks customs-house officials, police and salvage crews were working to save what they could and stop local opportunists. Islanders who had been slow to seize their chance now found it hard with one claiming that with so much protection "it is very difficult to smuggle anything and so far I have only managed a pencil!"

But the official process was not going well. George Pottie, the Superintending Engineer of the Atlantic Transport Line, sent to monitor the situation, reported on 24th April 1910 that "The salvage crew in my opinion at present have done nothing of any consequence."

Eventually the salvage proved successful and the ship was re-floated and steamed under her own power into Falmouth on 11th May.

Six members of the ship's crew were later charged with theft from the wreck and paid modest fines. No-one from the islands was arrested.

The Cita

On 26th March 1997, the *Cita*, on route from Southampton to Belfast ran aground at Port Hellick, Isles of Scilly. The ship's mate had fallen asleep during his watch. St Mary's lifeboat quickly rescued the eight crew.

The *Cita's* 200 containers carried a mixed cargo from toys to tyres, plywood to golf bags, tobacco to power tools. A department store had been washed up and the locals did not wait to go bargain hunting!

The Cita wreck

The islanders soon revived the old tradition of plundering the ship's treasure. Shoes were a favourite but finding matching pairs proved tricky. Groups were soon bartering odd shoes all over the islands. Polo shirts, computer mice, hardwood doors, toilet seats and much more were loaded into car boots, trucks, wheelbarrows and shopping trollies.

A constable confronted a well-known local councillor who was joining in the pillage. He explained that he was only doing his bit for the beach clearance campaign. Another police officer warned: "If I catch anyone with bald tyres after next week I intend to do them for laziness!"

When mainland police arrived they handed out *Receiver of Wreck* forms for people to declare their finds. They were surprised by how many locals shared the same name: Robert Dorrien-Smith (the lease owner of Tresco Island!)

Chains of people carried the cargo from the foreshore. Containers drifted to other beaches. Hardware? Over there; footware? Watermill Cove. Children's clothing? Porthcressa . . .

Few locals reported for work as they lost no time to save the goods from the fierce seas. It was the greatest take-away the Isles had seen and for many islanders struggling on low wages the free clothing was an opportunity not to be missed. The surplus was collected and sent to Romanian and African orphanages.

By 30th March the salvage firm had arrived to seal off the wreck. Soon after the sea had claimed most of the ship and any remaining contents.

The Napoli grounded off the Branscome beach.

Napoli is beached

On 18th January 2007, *MSC Napoli* suffered serious damage to her hull in severe gales. With the engine room taking in water the ship was sinking fast. Rather than lose her in deep water the ship was beached just off the Devon village of Branscome.

The *Napoli* had a wide range of good on board. Some 100 containers fell into the sea and were washed ashore. Early looters found BMW motorcycles and expensive car parts. Soon hundreds descended on the remote beach to collect wine casks, nappies, perfume, potatoes, pet food and other goods. TV films of the scene led to a scramble to grab anything of value before the cargo was lost to the sea.

Photos: Chris Rudge, who says he is happy to share them to show the environmental impact of the Napoli wreck.

The Floating Republic

Richard Parker (1767-1797) was the son of an Exeter grain merchant and baker. He joined the Navy but soon became a rebel. He challenged one of his captains, Edward Riou of *HMS Bulldog*, to a duel. On the ship *Assurance* he was court-martialed for insubordination in December 1793. As a result he was discharged from the Navy in 1794.

Richard Parker

He returned to Exeter but ended up in debt. With experienced sailors in short supply, he joined the ship *HMS Sandwich* in 1797. A few months later, whilst anchored at the Nore in the Thames Estuary, crew discontent spilled over into mutiny.

Richard Parker was voted 'President of the Fleet' by the sailors whose demands included:

- Equal treatment with the fleet at Portsmouth
- Time to see friends and families
- Payment of wage arrears before sailing
- No officer, turned down by any of His Majesty's ships shall be employed in the same ship again without consent of the ship's company
- Opposition to press gangs
- A more equal distribution be made of prize money to the crews.

Parker tried to represent the sailors' demands and those of more radical delegates who wanted wider social reforms.

On 6th June he organised a meeting of delegates with Lord Northesk. He handed him a petition and ultimatum that their grievances be addressed within a period of 54 hours, after which he warned "such steps by the Fleet will be taken as will astonish their dear countrymen".

But cut off from food and racked by internal disputes, the mutiny dissolved and Parker was arrested on 13th June.

Parker was executed on board the *Sandwich*. His body was not publicly gibbeted after death,

Richard Parker, handing the petition to Vice-Admiral Buckner on board HMS Sandwich.

picture: J.G. Bullocke, *Sailors' Rebellion*

contrary to the wishes of King George III.

Parker's wife Anne, who had worked tirelessly to prevent his execution, later managed to cut down and claim his body from the gallows.

Richard Parker about to be hanged

image: People's England

Dartmoor massacre

During the American War of Independence Britain used Princetown Prison on Dartmoor to keep prisoners of war in harsh conditions. Captured soldiers had to march the seventeen miles from Plymouth across the bleak moor. Many had to endure the cold even though they were almost naked.

On 24th December 1814, peace was declared but there was an argument over who was going to pay to return the prisoners to their homes in America. Money from the US Government to pay for clothing never reached the men.

On 4th April 1815 demands for bread rather than the poor biscuit meals led to a mutiny. Troops were summoned from Plymouth but by the time they arrived the 'rioters' had retired peacefully to bed.

Two days later the governor, Captain Shortland, discovered a hole in one of the walls. Suspecting an escape attempt he had the alarm sounded. The pealing of bells and beating drums sent prisoners rushing into the yard. They thought that fire had broken out. In the commotion, Captain Shortland lined up guards ready to charge.

Panic spread through the prisoners, men and boys. Shortland gave the order to fire and musket volleys were discharged into the defenceless crowd.

Seven were killed outright, another seven had to have limbs amputated, 38 were dangerously wounded and 15 slightly injured.

Inquiries that followed the massacre failed to address the real causes and Britain was now keen to return the prisoners to America. Lord Castlereagh, Home Secretary, offered to pay compensation to the widows and wounded by the US Government declined the offer.

Prisoners were despatched to Plymouth, some still barefoot. They remained angry at Mr Beasley, the US Agent, who had withheld the money due to them.

The real massacre was the ill-treatment in the prison. According to the *Prisoner's Memoirs* by Charles Andrew 269 American prisoners died on Dartmoor between 1813 and 1815.

I predict a riot

With no meaningful democratic process, local communities turned to riot to make their voice heard.

Starvation forced people to take desperate measures but 'riots' were often an organised reaction from communities struggling to survive.

There were many violent events across the South West especially over taxes, tolls and food prices.

An early recorded riot was in 1312 in Bristol when King Edward II introduced a shipping tax. Twenty men were killed and the King's officers had to take refuge in the castle. A toll on fish landed in the port caused civil uproar and the townsfolk, led by **John Taverner**, refused to pay.

The King was determined to end Bristol's militancy. Lord Thomas of Berkeley blockaded the city from the sea. Siege engines in the castle threw boulders at the blockades in Wine Street, breaking them down. Bristol was forced to submit. This brought fines of 4,000 marks to the town as well as arrears of all the duties due to the king. The ring-leaders were imprisoned and John Taverner and his son were banished.

In 1586 the West Country cloth trade was in depression and a poor harvest led to food shortages and high prices. Cloth workers were vulnerable as they had to buy most of their food rather than produce their own. But they were also more organised and able to fight back.

On 23rd April a ship loaded with malt was attacked at Framilode in Gloucestershire by up to 600 people. In 1595 corn was seized on the road from Warminster by angry cloth workers and in Somerset the next year a group of around 60 poor people hijacked a cart load of cheese.

Corn was the target for cloth workers from Seend, Warminster and Westbury in Wiltshire in May 1614 and there are accounts of other organised seizures involving large numbers of people.

A crowd of some 500 people seized corn bound for market in east Somerset in 1622.

Bristol turnpike markers

Popular uprisings were often led by organised groups such as miners.

In 1709 the price of food rose alarmingly. A bushel of wheat doubled in price from four to eight shillings. Two hundred coal miners from Kingswood marched into Bristol. They were promised a reduction in the price and dispersed.

The colliers in Bristol were persistent protesters along with miners in Somerset and the Forest of Dean.

Toll Tax Riots

Opposition to road tolls sometimes led to riots. There was a spate of incidents in Bristol and Gloucester in the mid-eighteenth century.

Miners of Kingswood led the opposition to the Bristol turnpikes. In 1727 Parliament established a Turnpike Commission for the roads leading to the city. Gates were erected and tolls were set at one shilling for a vehicle pulled by six animals and half-pence for a donkey laden with coal.

The Kingswood miners destroyed the gates. They refused to supply Bristol with coal, sending the price soaring. To stem the crisis, the colliers were exempted from the tolls.

In 1749 the turnpike trustees tried again to impose tolls. Several hundred farm labourers destroyed the gates at Ashton. Two of the rioters were hanged.

Bristol Bridge Riot

The main bridge into Bristol from Somerset was in need of replacement and in 1793 the new Bristol Bridge was opened. Local commissions had recommended that it be paid for from local taxes and duties but the city magistrates set a toll instead. This led to refusals to pay and riots.

On 30th September 1793 large crowds gathered and the Riot Act was read several times. Rocks and oyster shells

Bristol Bridge, scene of several riots

were thrown at the troops and those trying to collect the tolls. In the battle, ten people were killed and more than thirty wounded.

In the face of the riots, the tolls were abandoned.

Food Riots

Cornish tin miners were a prominent force behind food riots in Cornwall with recorded disturbances through the eighteenth and early nineteenth centuries. Food supply was a particular problem in parts of Cornwall due to the peripheral nature of the county and poor agriculture.

Sometimes riots erupted due to suspicion of profiteering. *The Cornish Miner* by AK Hamilton Jenkin described the situation in Penryn in 1748: "the tinners suspecting that some merchants had laid up vast quantities of corn for extortion, assembled in great numbers. Men, women and children broke open one of the cellars and took thence 600 bushels of wheat."

Disturbances were reported amongst cloth workers in Honiton, Topsham, Ashburton, Totnes, Okehampton, Chudleigh in Devon, Frome in Somerset, Bradford-on-Avon and Trowbridge in Wiltshire.

In 1752 some 900 miners and weavers entered Bristol to stem rising food prices. Troops quelled the rebellion but the mood of the population was shown through collections for the miners. No witness came forward to give evidence against those arrested. **Samuel Bonner**, a weaver, was given a token sentence due to his youth.

1766 Hunger Riots

1766 saw a wet summer and a dry autumn and the poor weather

blighted the corn harvest. The continent fared even worse and food prices soared. Trouble first broke out in the West Country in early August but rioting quickly spread across the South West and Midlands.

The government imposed an embargo on corn exports and lifted import duties on wheat. Those arrested were tried by special commissions held in December including in Salisbury and Gloucester.

In 1793 in Looe, Cornwall, miners marched to seized the cargo of a ship about to leave port. Trouble was averted by giving the demonstrators one shilling to buy grain.

1795 crisis

The war with France led to a soaring of food prices and plunged the poor into famine. Traders who tried to profiteer from the crisis faced attack. Violence started in Cornwall with tin miners preventing ships leaving with cargoes of barley. This spread to almost every port in the West Country. On 27th March some 300 women were involved in a riot in Exeter.

A tide-mill was attacked at Kingsteington in Devon. The miller was a naval supplier and thought to be the main cause of high prices. A huge crowd smashed their way through the mill and its machinery. The owner was injured and three men were indicted for the riot. **Thomas Campion** was later hanged near the scene of the crime.

In Plymouth the unionised dockyard was involved and some troops supported the townfolk. The arrest of a soldier led to a strike at Devonport.

On 30th October 1795 a party of

Skeleton and plough: an image used to highlight rural poverty

Forest of Dean miners captured wagons of barley and wheat on their way to Gloucester. The grain was taken to Drybrook where it was shared out amongst hungry locals. When another wagon was hijacked the following week, dragoons were called in to arrest the ring-leaders.

In November 1795 a ship was raided at Awre and flour seized. Five of the raiders were arrested and on 11th April 1797 **Thomas Yemm** and **Thomas Rosser** were hanged Eventually, the Crown distributed £1,000 worth of corn to the starving foresters.

1800-01 winter
The crisis of the 1800-01 winter was concentrated in the South West. Rioting spread across the region. Cornish Justices reported that: "almost every individual in the mining parts where the riots happened was more or less concerned in them."

People power
In many places the uprisings forced the authorities to limit prices. Early unions were involved in coordination and negotiations. In Totnes a 'Committee of the People' was elected to set prices and discipline farmers and traders

Bideford Potato Riots
When, in May 1816, a ship started to load potatoes at Bideford Quay, locals desperate for food protested. People were furious that farmers were sending food 'up-country' to sell for higher prices.

Rioting broke out and the parish constables arrested three men. The crowd attacked the lock-up and released them. The Yeomanry were called out and order was eventually restored, but the troops had to remain on duty for four days, patrolling the town and dispersing mobs, until they were relieved by a detachment of regular Dragoons sent from Exeter.

A similar riot occurred in Bridport when bakers were believed to be hoarding flour.

Hungry 40s
The 1840s witnessed depression and poor harvests and became known as the 'hungry 40s'.

In January 1846 *The Times* reported on a mass meeting in Goatacre in Wiltshire. One farm worker, who was one of about 1,000 people at the rally walked twenty miles to get there. He told of his struggle to provide for his wife and six children on eight shillings a week.

When he applied for parish assistance he was told to send one of his children to the workhouse. He was forced to chose which one.

With such hardship, locals resented food being hoarded or taken away for better trade elsewhere. In 1847 some 300 china clay miners marched through St Austell to the docks at Pentewan to prevent a ship leaving loaded with corn. There were 'bread riots' in Exeter and Torquay.

In November 1867, rioting broke out again. Women in Torquay threw stones. and it was reported that they "appeared to be the most active in inciting the rioters to deeds of violence". In Barnstaple a crowd, the local paper called "roughs and discontented of the lower order (not a few women), marched chanting: 'We want cheap beef and bread' and 'Let's have our rights'".

The Riot Act

The proclamation had to be read to any group of more than twelve people who were "**unlawfully, riotously, and tumultuously assembled together**".

If the group failed to disperse within one hour, then anyone remaining gathered was guilty of a felony, punishable by death. The passage that had to be read was as follows:

"Our Sovereign Lord the King chargeth and commandeth all persons, being assembled, immediately to disperse themselves, and peaceably to depart to their habitations, or to their lawful business, upon the pains contained in the act made in the first year of King George, for preventing tumults and riotous assemblies. God Save the King!"

Stogursey food price protest

An example of popular protest against food prices started in the Somerset village of Stogursey in 1801.

The disastrous harvest of 1799, the impact of the war with France and economic policies of the Pitt Government combined to leave corn in short supply and rising food prices. Troops were sent to the West Country to quell any protests and resist demands for price controls.

People often blamed farmers or suppliers for hoarding grain to push up prices. They looked to local magistrates to intervene.

In the Spring of 1801 about 100 people gathered in Stogursey to protest at food prices. They marched to Stowey where more joined in the demands for wheat to be sold at 10s a bushel, barley, beans and peas at 6s and potatoes at 5s a bushel bag.

They marched to seek the support of magistrates, Major Tynte and Mr Parsons but found that they had gone to Petherton to settle a similar dispute.

When they reached Petherton they were too late so the crowd

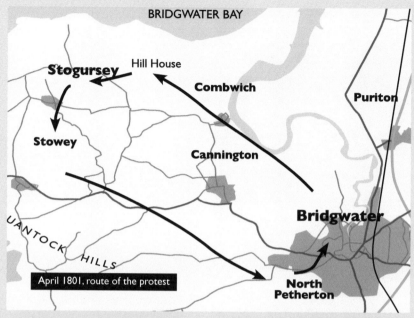

April 1801, route of the protest

marched on to Bridgwater gathering "snowball-like to the number 1,000" according to David Davis in a letter to magistrate John Acland.

The crowd confronted Justice Noller and when he refused to help a scuffle broke out and his coat was torn from top to bottom.

In fear of a violent revolt, the military were called who placed swivel guns to command Castle Street. David Davis describes the orderly behaviour of the petitioners: "I will not call them a mob. They protested to the inhabitants and to the soldiers that it was their intention not to commit any riotous act."

In their search for a sympathetic magistrate the protesters marched to Hill House to see Justice Everard. Perhaps closer to the Stogursey community or too isolated to resist, he showed his support to the point of tears. "He felt for their distresses and promised to exert his utmost to relieve them." said David Davis. With these assurances the crowd dispersed.

Days later the magistrates met the farmers and land owners. Prices were pegged and the crisis passed.

Stogursey

Kenn hanging example

In the early nineteenth century the authorities – in the face of mounting protests – were torn between granting minor reforms or falling back on more brutal repression. In one Somerset village they chose to set an example to workers who might resort to arson by hanging two labourers at the scene of their crime.

The riots that occurred later that same year showed that the tactic didn't work.

Capital punishment was given for many crimes including arson. Setting fire to farmers' ricks was a means of protest or revenge and when carried out at night the authorities found it difficult to gather enough evidence to prosecute.

In 1829 in the north Somerset village of Kenn trouble was brewing. An arson attack on three wheat mows belonging to farmer Benjamin Poole led to a practice not used for 30 years – hanging those caught at the scene of the crime.

Wages were very poor and prices high but village politics also played a big part in the events of that year. Petty pilfering and poaching had been increasing. Benjamin Poole's brother ran a beer house and didn't take kindly to William Wall opening an illicit cider house. After the arson attack

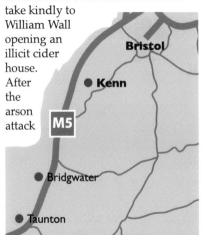

William Wall and two of his farm labourers: **John Rowley** and **Richard Clark** were arrested and held in Illchester Gaol. The high sheriff of Somerset presided over their brutal punishment.

In the summer of 1830 they were transported with their coffins the 42 miles back to Kenn for the last scene of crime execution in England. Thousands witnessed the event. Crude apparatus was hastily erected above a wagon. When the wagon was drawn away the youths remained suspended until death.

In Steve Poole's account of the hangings he explains that this was: "one of the most impressive and theatrical displays of judicial authority ever seen in the county".

This show of power by the authorities was just a few months before the Swing Rebellion set fires burning across the south of Britain. Colonel JM Muir, sent by Lord Melbourne to the West Country to deal with the Swing rebels felt that executions at the scene of the crime should be repeated as they: "would never be forgotten and prove a lasting and salutary warning."

In the end his retribution was muted and whilst a few rebels were hanged in gaol most of those convicted were transported into slavery in Australia.

The village of Kenn

Cloth battles

The cloth industry was a central part of the West Country economy in the 18th century. This highly labour-intensive process involved a variety of skills in homes and small mills. But incomes were meagre and livelihoods were threatened with the arrival of new machines.

Spinning Jenny

Wool was sorted, cleaned and sometimes dyed. Carding, brushing, scribbling and combing straightened the fibres ready for spinning to form a continuous thread, called a yarn. West Country scribblers made up a large male workforce that supplied women spinners working from home or small workshops.

Weavers, using a hand loom, would turn yarn into cloth. They were either journeymen who worked for a master weaver or those who owned their own loom at home. Weavers often relied on wives and children to help produce the cloth. The weavers would deliver the cloth back for fulling (cleaning and thickening) and finally for dressing or shearing (trimming the raised fibres).

Pay battles
At a time when unions were illegal cloth workers still organised themselves to protect their livelihoods. In 1717 a widespread combination of cloth workers in Devon and Somerset organised a dispute that led to disturbances in Exeter and Taunton. To show their loyalty they carried royal effigies while they attacked the houses of clothiers!

There were attacks against cheap imported Irish cloth in 1720 in Tiverton and at Crediton in 1725, when several hundred workers protested. When the town clerk tried to read the Riot Act, the weavers pulled off his hat and wig and put dirt on his head.

In November 1726 rioting in Wiltshire and Somerset accompanied a strike and in the 1730s there were riots in Tiverton and loom chains cut in Melksham.

In 1729, Stephen Feacham, a Kingswood clothier, cut the wages. Angry weavers marched to Feacham's house where he fired on them killing five people, including the sergeant of the guard with a wayward shot. Although he was found guilty of murder this was over turned by the government. Two weavers who organised the march were hanged for their part in the riot.

In March 1732, while Feacham was away on business the weavers made an effigy of the hated boss and paraded it through Lawford's Gate before hanging it on a gibbet in Lamb's Fields.

In 1738 a Melksham clothier, Henry Coulthurst, had his house and mills wrecked by weavers during a dispute over wages. Some of the rioters were tried and three were executed.

There were further riots in 1747 and 1750 and dragoons were sent to the town to help keep order.

But life for cloth workers was about to get a lot worse thanks to a series of inventions that revolutionised the methods of production.

New machines
The Spinning Jenny was invented by James Hargreaves in 1764. It could spin eight threads at once. There were claims that new gig machines could do the job of twenty workers.

Violent resistance was felt to be the only option for the cloth workers. In 1767 some 500 shearmen gathered on Corsley Heath to march on a mill in Horningsham, near Warminster and Frome, to pull down a new gig machine.

James May, a leading Wiltshire shearman, led the underground union in Warminster and Trowbridge. In 1769 the Master

Clothier of Melksham complained that journeymen had established an "unlawful and arbitrary combination".

In July 1776, a group of clothiers in Shepton Mallet introduced Spinning Jennies. Wool workers from neighbouring towns marched to protest at the 'trial' that threatened to devastate family incomes. They broke into the workhouse and destroyed the Jennies. A magistrate ordered the arrest of the ring-leaders and five or six were captured. The crowd coun-ter-attacked and the Riot Act was read. The troops fired on the crowd killing one person and wounding six.

In June 1781 Spinning Jennies were installed in a mill in Frome. On Whit Monday the crowd smashed the machines. In March 1790, Keynsham cloth workers joined with local miners to protest against their introduction.

The resistance took a tragic turn outside Westbury House in Bradford-on-Avon in May 1791 when some 500 cloth workers gathered to stop Joseph

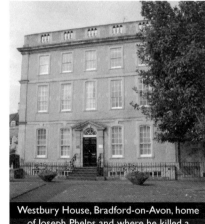

Westbury House, Bradford-on-Avon, home of Joseph Phelps and where he killed a protester.

Phelps, a prominent clothier, from introducing scribbling machines. Phelps fired on the crowd killing a man and mortally wounding two others. The coroner found a verdict of 'justifiable homicide' and Phelps was awarded £250 damages!

Troops were stationed in the main Wiltshire woollen towns to put down the rebellions but in August 1792 they were called away to break a strike amongst Mendip miners. Cloth workers seized their chance and smashed the machines and despite the troop intervention, the colliers won their pay rise.

More riots were sparked in Shepton Mallet and Westbury in 1794 over new scribbling engines. In December 1797, 200-300 Somerset shearers, with blackened faces and armed with bludgeons attacked mills near Frome.

Battle of Tiverton Fore Street

In 1749 wool merchants in Tiverton imported Irish worsted instead of using the cloth from local wool combers. A strike was called in protest but when funds ran out passions turned to violence. Strikers meeting at the Half Moon pub in the town's Fore Street fought with weavers using stones, clubs and bats. People were wounded on both sides. The mayor summoned troops and the Riot Act was read.

Many of the wool combers were forced to leave Tiverton in search of work.

Fore Street, Tiverton

TIMELINE

1776
Shepton Mallet attacks
One killed

1791
Bradford on Avon attacks
Three killed

1795
Food riots

1760s **1770s** **1780s** **1790s**

Spinning Jenny invented

machines arrive in West Country

few new machines are introduced

riots over new machines

Gloucestershire clothiers managed to introduce the new machines but not without some resistance. Paul and Nathaniel Wathen, a cloth firm in Woodchester, near Stroud, pioneered the use of the shearing frame.

On the night of 13th January 1800 there was an attack on their stock of cloths. The employers in the area offered a large reward and **Joseph Stephens** was arrested. The verdict was guilty and he was hanged. Before his execution Joseph expressed contrition and warned others not to attempt any revenge for his harsh punishment.

The turn of the century saw a down-turn in trade and fearful of competition from Gloucestershire, the Wiltshire clothiers stepped up mechanisation. In 1802 Warminster shearmen went on strike against gig mills. There was an attack on a cloth cart at Calstone Mills, near Devizes and Clifford Mill at Beckingham was burned down.

Wiltshire Outrages
Shearing was a highly skilled craft and better paid than most jobs in the wool trade. Since Tudor times, the work of the shearmen had been protected by law but advancing mechanisation and powerful mill owners

had weakened their rights. With inadequate poor relief the shearmen organised themselves in unions.

In the summer of 1802, Trowbridge Shearmen went on strike. Although unions were outlawed, the shearmen of Trowbridge had a closed-shop, their union cards said "Industry, Freedom and Friendship."

Damage done
Clifford Mill destroyed
Littleton Mill destroyed
Naish's workshops, Trowbridge destroyed
Six ricks burned
One barn burned
Two houses burned
One stable burned
Several outhouses and one dog kennel burned
Tree cut down
Windows broken and other property damaged

Gig mills in Wiltshire 1800-1802

Littleton Mill, near the town, was burned down with the cost put at £8,000. This was the most daring and successful attacks and forced the clothiers to back off from the threatened pay cuts.

The employers, however, were determined to break the power of the workers. James Read, a Bow Street magistrate, was sent to Wiltshire by the Secretary of State. He wanted evidence against the union and he arrested Thomas Bailey, a Trowbridge shearman. In gaol and under interrogation, Bailey cracked and told of the union committee and secret oaths.

James May, Secretary, **George Marks**, **John Helliker**, (elder brother of Thomas) **Samuel Ferris** and **Philip Edwards** were arrested and charged with administering an illegal oath.

They were held for seven months. The men claimed that they had been in the New Cross Keys pub, discussing the system of 'truck' payments – where employers pay in goods instead of wages. Thomas Bailey had accepted 'truck' but promised on a bible not to do so again. The explanation led to their release but **Thomas Helliker** was not so lucky.

Thomas Helliker was in the middle of his apprenticeship when new machines

1800s	1810s	1820s	1830s
1802 Helliker arrested	few new machines are introduced	**1822-23** riots in Frome and Warminster	**1834** Tolpuddle Martyrs
Wiltshire Outrages	few new machines are introduced	Combination Acts repealed / West Country cloth strike	**1830** Swing Rebellion

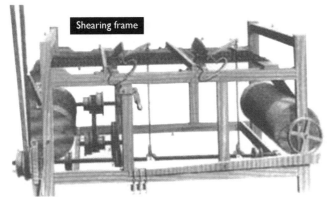

Shearing frame

arrived in Trowbridge. The wealthy magistrate and mill-owner, John Jones demanded an example be set and Thomas Helliker was arrested on suspicion of threatening a night-watchman with a pistol during the attack on Littleton Mill. Although protesting his innocence, he refused to betray a fellow member of the shearmen's union.

Heliker was tried and hanged on his 19th birthday in 1803 at Fisherton Jail, Salisbury. The shearmen carried his body over Salisbury Plain to be buried in honour in St James Church, Trowbridge. Girls in white dresses led thousands of mourners.

The violence subsided but the resolve of the shearmen was not broken.

John Jones continued to face the wrath of local people. In 1808 he was attacked as he rode home from Staverton. A gun shot missed. Four years later three shearmen were arrested for the attack but there was not enough evidence to make a case for attempted murder.

John Jones went bankrupt in 1812.

Further cases of illegal combination were brought before the courts at Bradford-on-Avon. Life for cloth workers in the West Country continued to deteriorate.

Employers reported that riots in Frome and Warminster in 1822 and 1823 were inspired by a union. The Combination Acts were repealed in 1824 and this brought a wave of industrial action.

A West Country-wide strike took place in 1825. Most employers quickly settled but the dispute dragged on amongst the water mills in Stroud. Riots broke out in Stroud and Chalford. In Wotton-under-Edge several people were wounded when mill owners opened fire on the crowd.

Strike leader **Timothy Exell** gained the title 'King of the Weavers' and the union was well organised. One meeting on Stinchcombe Hill claimed attendance of some 10,000 people. Strangely, Exell went on to argue against Chartism.

The battles were not a stupid attempt to stop the inevitable march of progress. The workers knew that mechanisation was coming but they argued that the benefits of machines should be shared.

Working people had little choice but resistance and rebellion or face poverty and destitution. They had to fight for their livelihoods and for their family incomes. Many retained a faith in the law to protect them and to uphold minimum pay and regulations against the impact of technology. But it was a legal system controlled by the employers and landowners.

The White Horse, Wiltshire Trades Union Council lay a wreath on the grave of Thomas Helliker in 2010

Falmouth Packet strike

The Post Office Packet service ran out of Falmouth Port from 1688. Pay was poor but sailors were protected from 'impressment' into the Navy and could supplement wages by taking unofficial cargo.

At the end of 1809 the authorities decided to enfore the ban on private trade. The clampdown led crews to ask for more money but the Post Office refused. On 24th October 1810 customs officers boarded two ships: *Prince Adolphus* and *Duke of Malborough* and confiscated illicit goods. The sailors refused to take the ships to sea unless their goods were returned. Captain Bull read a notice of impressment and seized the protestors.

The next morning a massive crowd descended on the Packet's office at Bell Court in Falmouth to demand the release of their fellow seamen. The Riot Act was read. Led by **Richard Pascoe** and **John Parker,** a mass meeting was called on the town's bowling green. It demanded the release of the men and a pay rise. Another meeting was summoned at the Seven Stars Inn at Flushing.

The Navy sent marines to arrest the leaders but the community sided with the sailors and the men escaped. Naval support ships arrived from Plymouth to escort the Packet vessels out of Falmouth and fearing the loss of trade the protest subsided.

Poor treatment

Throughout history, life for most ordinary working people has been hard and short. Children and parents were expected to care for each other. For the old, sick and unemployed there was little support. Authorities tried to differentiate between the 'deserving and undeserving poor'.

The Settlement Act of 1662, also known as the Poor Relief Act, allowed relief only to established residents of a parish; mainly through birth, marriage and apprenticeship. This reduced the mobility of labour and discouraged paupers from leaving their parish to find work.

In 1697 beggars were required to wear a badge of red or blue cloth on the right shoulder with an embroidered letter 'P' and the initial of their parish.

Not in our parish
Ways were devised to ease the burden on the local parish. The requirement for residency of over a year led employers to offer contracts of 364 days so that an employee could not become eligible for Poor Relief.

A pauper unable to prove 'settlement' would be removed to the parish nearest to the place of their birth. Some paupers were moved hundreds of miles.

Fathers of children out of marriage were required to pay the Parish for "the lying-in of the said woman and the maintenance of the said bastard child." Mothers were required to sign 'bastardy forms', naming the father.

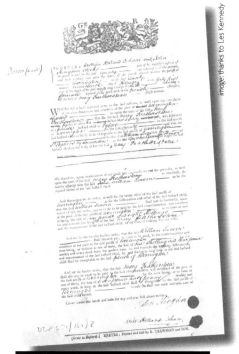

A Bastardy Form from Wenington, near Launceston

Speenhamland
Rising unemployment and falling grain prices after the French Wars (1793–1815) caused considerable pressure on Parish Relief. A group of employers and magistrates met in 1795 at the Pelican Inn in Speenhamland, Berkshire. Rather than pay for unemployment they devised a means-tested sliding-scale of wage subsidies. It became known as the Speenhamland System.

The effect was to establish a form of minimum wage, supplemented from Parish Relief. But employers cut wages as a result and the strain on Parish funds led to limits being applied.

Before it was destroyed: St Peter's Hospital, Bristol: formerly St Peter's Workhouse

Bristol Workhouse

In 1696, **John Cary**, a Bristol Merchant and Quaker, proposed a union of local parishes, that would generate enough income to run a workhouse where paupers could be put to work for their relief. The Bristol Corporation of the Poor was established.

Bristol's aldermen chose four of the "honestest and discreetest inhabitants" from each of the twelve city wards to serve as 'Guardians of the Poor'.

The first workhouse was in a building called Whitehall, adjacent to the Bridewell. It was to house a hundred pauper girls.

On arrival, the inmates were stripped and washed by the Matron and given new clothes. The diet included "Beef, pease, potatoes, broath, pease-porridge, milk-porridge, bread and cheese, good beer, cabage, turnips etc." Illness amongst the inmates was common with around twenty ill at any one time, suffering from measles, smallpox and "other distempers".

The girls worked at spinning for ten

and a half hours a day. They were hired out to local manufacturers.

In 1698, the Corporation bought the former home of sugar merchant Robert Aldworth and local mint.

At first it was called the Mint Workhouse but later became St Peter's Hospital. In 1699 a hundred boys moved in and were put to spinning wool and weaving. Boys were taught to read and to write.

The workhouse also took in children, the aged and 'lunatics'. Life was deliberately harsh. The work was hard and tedious in return for meagre food and shelter.

In his 1879 Report, Sir Frederic Morton Eden described life in St Peter's. "The number of inmates is 350, of whom 63 are in a pest house belonging to the Workhouse. The only work at present is picking oakum by which very little is earned. The house is infested with vermin, particularly bugs. To a visitor there appears on the whole to be a want of cleanliness."

The Bill of Fare was: broth, gruel, soup made of bullocks' head, pease soup, two days of meat and potatoes, bread and cheese.

Other cities followed Bristol's workhouse example, including Exeter in 1697, and Crediton, Shaftesbury, and Tiverton in 1698.

St Peter's was closed as a workhouse in 1865. In the 1920s and 1930s the building was a base for the Bristol Labour Party where aid was distributed during the depression. It was destroyed during the Blitz on Sunday 24th November 1940.

The Quakers established a workhouse

Oakum is a tarred fibre used in shipbuilding, for packing the joints of timbers. It was made from old ropes, painstakingly unravelled by workhouse inmates.

in 1696 for seven poor weavers and the instruction of children. It was so successful that in 1700 that new premises were built in New Street, St Jude's for the aged and feeble.

The premises incorporated an orphanage, a school and an almshouse, housing 24 paupers and ten apprentices.

The Quaker workhouse in Bristol

The Swing Rebellion

West Country rural life was hard but stable for generations. Towards the end of the eighteenth century, new methods and machines threatened the established order. Workers had no rights to oppose such changes and turned to riot and threat to defend themselves.

In *The Making of the English Working Class,* EP Thompson tells of a soldier, returning from the war against France who wrote to his MP in Bradford-on-Avon in Wiltshire to complain: "how many more they would employ were they to have it done by hand as they used to do. The Poor House we find full of great lurking boys."

He goes on to warn: "The burning of factories or setting fire to the property of people we know is not right, but starvation forces nature to do that which he would not."

In 1826 William Cobbett travelled through the countryside writing . He said of Wiltshire: "It is impossible for the eyes of man to be fixed on a finer country than that between the village of Codford and the town of Warminster; and it is not very easy for the eyes of man to discover labouring people more miserable."

An early threshing machine

By the early 1830s economic depression caused further rural unemployment and more pressure on the Poor Law system. Cuts to the levels of support were met with a variety of protests across the South West. In some places these amounted to church boycotts and walk outs. In Wroughton, Wiltshire the protest amounted to "smoking pipes in the cemetery."

Wage cuts hit particularly hard in areas already poorly paid such as southern Britain. The arrival of new threshing machines further weakened the position of farm workers.

The start of Swing

On the night of 28th August 1830, in East Kent, a threshing machine was destroyed by angry labourers. This was the start of a revolt that spread across the south involving machine breaking, arson and assaults on overseers and justices.

Actions often started with the posting of threatening letters in the name of Captain Swing, a fictitious character.

Knook Church in the village where one of the first attacks took place

The first recorded Swing disturbance in the South West was at Maddington in Wiltshire on 8th November 1830. A wheat rick on the farm of Mr Miles and a straw rick at John Thomas Smith farm in Wanborough were burnt down. 'Swing' letters had been received by farmers at Codford St Peter near Warminster and at Horton near Devizes. Wages in Wiltshire were notoriously low.

On 15th November a pea rick was burnt down in the village of Knook.

One of the most violent incidents took place at Pyt House in Tisbury, west of Salisbury. *The Times* reported that it began with quarry-men whose wages had fallen to 3½ shillings a day. But they were joined by some 400 labourers armed with bludgeons and crowbars determined to smash a large threshing machine. A troop of yeomanry arrived and in the battle that followed, **John Harding**, a labourer from Tisbury was shot dead and 25 others arrested.

Swing States

The rebellion swept though Wiltshire and Dorset in particular. Parts of Gloucestershire, Somerset and Devon also saw riots and burnings. Incidents in Puddletown and other Dorset

The rick-burner and the farmer

The entrance to Pyt House

British Museum

CITY of SALISBURY.

The **MAGISTRATES** having received Information that various **DISTURBANCES** and **OUTRAGES** have taken place in the Neighbourhood,--With the View of maintaining the **PEACE** in this **CITY**, particularly request the Co-operation of the **INHABITANTS**, and that they will **IMMEDIATELY COME FORWARD** and **ENROLL** themselves as

SPECIAL CONSTABLES.

The Magistrates will attend at the **COUNCIL-HOUSE** for that Purpose this Afternoon, at Half-past Three o'Clock.

Council-Chamber, Monday, Nov. 22, 1830.

Call for help to suppress the rebels

villages probably involved farm workers who were later to form a union led by the Tolpuddle Martyrs.

The response

Some employers agreed to raise pay or at least not cut it. There were even reports of farmers smashing their own machines to prevent attacks. Many attacks were headed-off with one-off payments or beer.

To stop the revolt, the farmers recruited special constables and turned to the militia to suppress the uprising. Marauding farm labourers were no match for armed soldiers and the ring-leaders were soon arrested.

The *Taunton Courier* claimed: "it cuts me to the heart to see honest husbandmen perishing by that worst of all machines, the

image: Devon Archives

Salisbury Guildhall

gallows – under the guidance of that most fatal of all leaders – Swing."

Retribution

Special courts dealt with hundreds of labourers arrested during the disturbances. Many were sentenced to hang but few were actually executed, being transported to Australia instead.

When the threat passed, many farmers cut pay again and the poverty faced by rural communities became even deeper.

Remember the rebels

The Swing Rebellion is a little known part of West Country history. A plaque was unveiled in 2009 in

Salisbury Guildhall to commemorate the turbulent events of 1830.

TO Mr. SWING.

From 'The Taunton Courier' of Wednesday, Dec. 8, 1830.

Taunton appeal to the Swing rebels

Salisbury Trades Union Council plaque to the Swing Rebels in Salisbury Guildhall

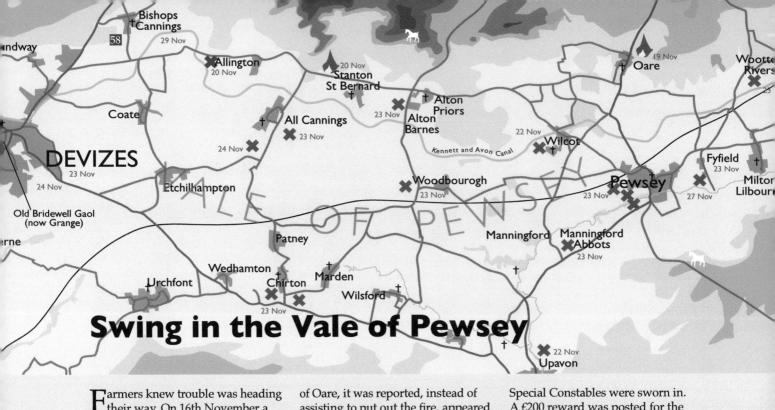

Map labels:
Bishops Cannings
58
29 Nov
ndway
Allington 20 Nov
Stanton St Bernard 20 Nov
Oare 19 Nov
Wootton Rivers
Coate
Alton Priors
Alton Barnes 23 Nov
23 Nov
All Cannings 23 Nov
Wilcot 22 Nov
Fyfield 23 Nov
DEVIZES 23 Nov
24 Nov
Kennett and Avon Canal
Pewsey 23 Nov
Milton Lilbour
24 Nov
Woodbourogh 23 Nov
27 Nov
Old Bridewell Gaol (now Grange)
VALE OF PEWSEY
Manningford
Manningford Abbots 23 Nov
rne
Etchilhampton
Patney
Wedhamton
Chirton 23 Nov
Marden
Wilsford

Swing in the Vale of Pewsey

Urchfont
Upavon 22 Nov

Farmers knew trouble was heading their way. On 16th November a suspicious-looking man on a fine horse was seen checking out ricks around All Cannings. The next night a rick of beans was burnt at Easton near Pewsey.

During the night of Friday 19th November, wheat, barley, beans and oats belonging to Mr Fowler of Oare were destroyed by fire. The labourers of Oare, it was reported, instead of assisting to put out the fire, appeared to take pleasure from the situation.

The next night farms in Stanton St Bernard were attacked, Joseph Perry's threshing machine in Allington was smashed.

On Monday 22nd November farmers met in the Dukes Arms in Marlborough to organise the defence.

Special Constables were sworn in. A £200 reward was posted for the conviction of the person responsible for the Oare attack.

Over the next week crowds attacked ricks, barns, and threshing machines. Money and beer were demanded.

The Vale of Pewsey

All Cannings

were breaking no laws by smashing the machines. Davis said: "We only wish that every man can live by his labour."

At this point Robert Pile arrived in haste to find some 200 men attacking his machine. He drew a pistol from his pocket and fired into the air. Mr Hare ran inside to get a shot-gun that he gave to Mr Pile. Suddenly as the men tried to wrest the gun from him it went off. James Love broke the gun against a tree and as Mr Pile tried to escape to the house he was knocked down. Charles Davis, despite having been wounded by a shot, stepped in to keep the crowd off as best as

In the early hours of Tuesday 23rd, **John Young** and another man led a mob to wreck the threshing machine of William Robbins at Chirton.

Magistrates met in Devizes and agreed to increase wages to ten shillings a week.

Men were going round the farms in All Cannings and Manningford persuading farm workers to join them in their demand for higher pay. At Manningford Abbots they met Sir Edward Poore who called on them to disperse but he offered to take up their grievances.

By mid-day the crowds had grown to about 300. They gathered at the Rose and Crown in Woodborough and **Charles Davis** took on a leading role and was called 'The Captain'.

They attacked John Clift's farm. He tried to buy them off with two half crowns and a five shilling piece. Mr Miller and Mr Neates had machines wrecked before the half-drunken men arrived at the Rectory at Alton Barnes.

Reverend Augustus William Hare refused to give them anything and

he followed them as they went off to Mr Pile's farm. More men arrived at the Rectory where Mrs Hare had bolted the doors. They told her that they meant her no harm but wanted money. Fearing the mob would break in, she threw coins from the window.

Reverend Hare rang the church bells in the hope of raising help but only curious women and children came.

While the men smashed Mr Pile's machine, Mr Hare spoke with Charles Davis who claimed they

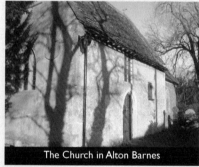
The Church in Alton Barnes

The Rectory in Alton Barnes

he could. Mr Pile got into the house with his head bleeding and his arm broken. Some of the crowd smashed their way into the house and made off after getting £10 from Miss Pile's purse.

The crowd continued their attacks at Stanton St Bernard and back to Alton Barnes.

The Old Bridewell Gaol in Devizes

The Bench in Salisbury Guildhall

Magistrates at Devizes were alerted and the Yeomanry was dispatched. They caught some of the crowd 'making merry' in the pub at Woodborough. As the troops escorted the 28 prisoners through Chirton there was a failed rescue attempt. Even more were arrested and taken to the Old Bridewell Gaol at Devizes.

The next day troops scoured the villages in search of rioters. They captured Charles Davis and he was taken to gaol.

On 5th January 1831, in Salisbury, he was tried for riotous assembly and attempting to demolish the house of Robert Pile. He pleaded 'not guilty'. He was acquitted but the next day faced a charge of wounding Mr Pile and stealing £10 from Miss Pile.

Fisherton Gaol, Salisbury

Charles Davis told the court that "I did not go into the house for money, I went to protect Mr Pile, as I had done before. I told the mob, before any money was asked for, to leave the house."

He was acquitted but was back in court on 7th January indicted for destroying Mr Pile's threshing machine and robbing John Clift. This time he was found guilty and a judgement of "death" was recorded.

On the 7th February Charles was taken from Fisherton Gaol and put on board the hulk *York* at Gosport. From there he was transported for life.

The York hulk for prisoners awaiting transportation

image: The Martyrs of Tolpuddle, TUC

Chalk and Cheese

Swing numbers

Between **1770** and **1830**

6,000,000

acres of common land were enclosed

4 months of protest in 1830

3 rebels killed in Wiltshire

1,976 arrests and trials

across **34** counties

in **90** courts

252 death sentences

19 people were hanged

505 protesters transported

Including **2** women

for between **7-14** years

but few could afford the return fare

The average age: **29**-years-old

HALF were married

644 were imprisoned

By 1835 **220** of those sentenced to

7 years' transportation were pardoned but few made it home

Until artificial fertilisers were developed, the fertility of the thin chalkland soils of Dorset and much of Wiltshire was poor. When agriculture was depressed it was these areas that were hit hardest.

The soil could be improved using the dung produced by sheep flocks. Wool and mutton offered some profit for farmers but the real value of sheep was their manure for the more valuable cereals such as wheat, barley and oats.

Other devices used in this area were the highly skilled job of managing water meadows. A thin layer of running water was kept over fields that protected the grass from frosts and brought valuable minerals. In early spring the land would be drained to allow the first new grass to grow.

In north Wiltshire, Somerset and Gloucestershire the soils turn to clay that can sustain rich grass for livestock and in particular the production of cheeses such as Cheddar and Gloucester. Thus comes the saying:

> *As different as chalk and cheese*

Farm wages in Dorset and Wiltshire were already amongst the lowest in the country and the slump in agriculture in the 1830s pushed pay even lower. So the Swing Rebellion tended to follow the contours of the chalk.

The map shows the Swing incidents: arson, machine wrecking and riots.

Chalk and Cheese pub in Maiden Newton, Dorset

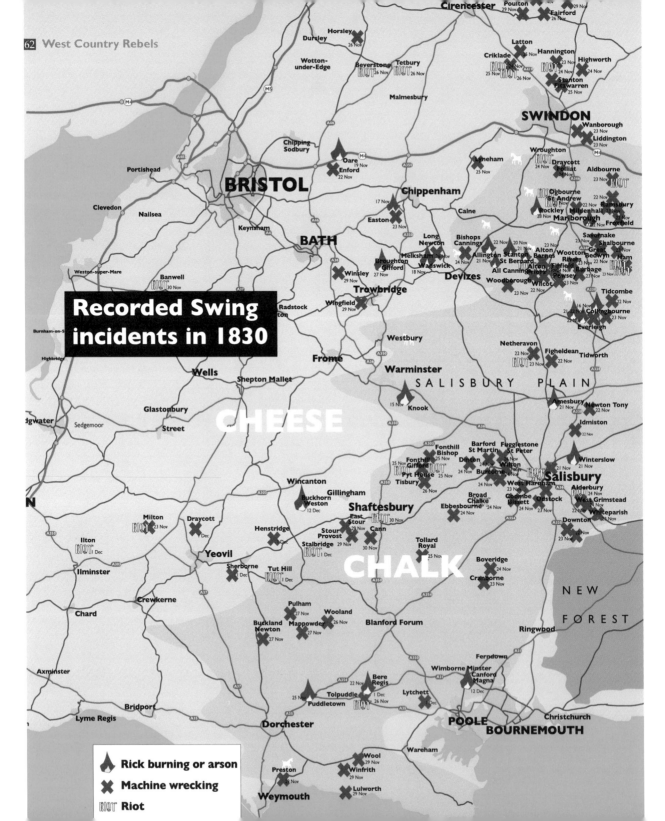

Recorded Swing incidents in 1830

Rick burning or arson

Machine wrecking

RIOT Riot

Trouble at inn

The Trouble House sign shows how the pub has lived up to its name

The Trouble House Inn, on the Tetbury to Cirencester road, was built around 1757. Formerly called the Wagon and Horses there are several versions of why the name was changed.

The pub was linked to events during the Civil War and is near an area prone to flooding known as the Troubles. Nearby gallows and stories of ghosts add to the turbulent history for the inn.

Swing trouble

The Trouble House played its part in the Swing rebellion that swept across the west. The uprising reached Gloucestershire on 26th November 1830. A threshing machine had been hired from a person in Wiltshire. When farm workers discovered the machine was being brought into the area they followed it to Newnton where they broke it to pieces at the side of the road.

The crowd of up to 200 people returned to Tetbury where they extorted money and beer before moving on towards Beverstone Special Constables were sworn in including Daniel Cole the Tetbury Parish Clerk.

John Tidcomb, a Tetbury farmer, tried to persuade them to go home. He reported that Elizabeth Parker said "Be d–d if we don't go to Beverstone and break the machine." John White said: "We want more work and more for doing it."

The Special Constables met the rebels about half-a-mile from Tetbury but they could not stop the mob, now armed with sticks, pick-axes and stone hammers. They went to the farm of Jacob Hayward where they smashed his threshing machine. Elizabeth Parker was witnessed wielding a sledge hammer.

More machines were smashed at William Robbins' farm and William Hart's farm at Chavenage, Mr Essex's at Colley Farm, Mr Saunders' at Upton Grove and Richard Kilminster's farm at the Grove in Cherrington.

Early that evening the crowd arrived

at the Trouble House for beer, bread and cheese. Two detachments of dragoons, stationed at Dursley and Wotton-under-Edge, surrounded the inn. 24 people were apprehended in the back room of the pub. They were then escorted to the gaol at Horsley.

Elizabeth Parker

Elizabeth Parker was one of only two women to be found guilty of being part of the Swing Rebellion.

She was sentenced to seven years' transportation for breaking Jacob Hayward's threshing machine worth £50 in the parish of Beverstone.

Evidence against many of the rebels was provided by Daniel Cole, the Tetbury Parish Clerk.

Daniel Cole felt cheated for his efforts. Magistrates had allowed £40 to be divided amongst the Special Constables less the fee to hire the chaise to take the prisoners to

gaol. It made £1/17 shillings each, "a very trifling remuneration for such services." Cole and his fellow constables appealed to the Treasury but the Lords refused to pay a reward.

Elizabeth Parker was taken ill after the trial suffering 'paralytick' attacks. The surgeon reported that her condition was "hazardous". She had problems speaking and lost the use of her legs and one side of her body.

In the circumstances she was shown mercy and given a free pardon. But she recovered and in March 1832 she was charged with stealing two £5 notes, five sovereigns and five half sovereigns from Daniel Cole. This time she was sentenced to be transported for life.

The connections or coincidences of this suggest that there is more to this story.

Elizabeth was taken to Tasmania on board *Frances Charlotte* and arrived in Hobart in 1833. Here she soon gathered a long list of offences: found out of hours, drunk, absent without leave, refusing to work, neglect of duty, indecently exposing her person, assaulting a constable and feloniously receiving a silk handkerchief.

On 5th October 1835 Elizabeth married Joseph Councel. He was born in Manchester and died aged 65 in 1875. Elizabeth died a year later in Victoria aged 66.

Calling time on the slow train

Back at the inn, Trouble House Halt, opened in 1959 and was the only railway station in England built specifically to serve a pub. Closed in 1964, the station was included in the song *Slow Train* by Flanders and Swann.

Nailsworth
Cherrington
Horsey
Avening
Upton
Trull   A433
Trouble House Inn
Chavenage
Upton
B4014
Beverstone
Tetbury
Newnton

Swing rebels attacked threshing machines on farms around Tetbury in Gloucestershire but were caught at the Trouble House Inn

Forest Rebels

image: Clifford Harper

The poverty and desperation felt by rural communities in the 1830s was compounded in the Forest of Dean by resentment against the loss of traditional rights of access to the Forest for wood, coal and grazing. The Foresters, known for their independence, fought back in the only way they could.

The Forest could sustain a family - just! The Dean's isolation meant settlers could build shack homes which led to the pattern of scattered settlements throughout the Forest. In 1668, in response to earlier uprisings, the King divided up the Dean into 'walks' each with a keeper to protect the crown's estate.

In a report into the Forest in 1834, the Commissioners found some 1,592 cottages held by 'encroachers' or squatters. Settlers tended to replant their boundaries outside of their former hedge thus enlarging their plots each time – a practice known as 'rolling hedges'.

Enclosures deprived people access to pasture and wood for fuel. To fight back, locals turned to breaking down fences and burning new saplings.

In 1803 Nelson visited the Forest of Dean and reported that "The state of the Forest at this moment is deplorable." He calculated that, properly cultivated, the Dean could produce some 9,200 loads of timber against 3,500 loads at the time. He described the poor state of the area and said: "There is also another cause of the failure of the timber: a set of people called the Forest free miners, who consider themselves as having a right to dig for coal in any part they please; these people, in many places, inclose pieces of ground."

Nelson blamed the inattention of the Forest on the authorities and demanded that "strong measures must be pursued." What Nelson saw as the poor state of the Forest was probably a sustainable way of meeting the range of needs of the local community.

The free-miners had long cherished rights to dig for coal but the legal standing was being challenged by authorities who wanted to encourage investment in new pits.

So-called 'foreigners' were bringing in cash and new ideas but they were also enclosing swathes of the woodland. The fences, designed to protect saplings, crops and stock prevented locals from living off the land as they had done for generations. Free miners were losing their independent 'self-employed' status as they were forced to work in the new, larger pits.

Forest free miner, **Warren James**, believed the enclosures only had temporary legal status and

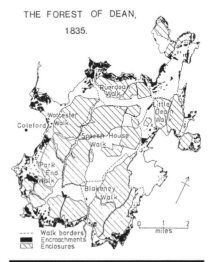

THE FOREST OF DEAN, 1835.

Forest of Dean in 1835, split into 'Walks' to help control the local population.

Small 'free' mines still operate in the Forest of Dean

dismantling of some 60 miles of banks and fences. Considerable effort was required to level earth ramparts and dig out gorse bush barriers. In his book *Warren James and the Dean Forest Riots,* Ralph Anstis recounts the report that the men were joined by around 80 women who "seemed even more intent on the work of destruction."

A squadron of dragoons arrived from Dorchester along with a detachment of 180 men from Plymouth to suppress the rebellion. Ring-leaders were captured including Warren James who was found hiding in a mine.

An etched glass in the Angel Hotel, Coleford showing the arrest of Warren James

demanded their removal. The authorities rejected his claims but by 1831 feelings were running high.

A meeting of Foresters agreed that notices be posted declaring their intention to open the forest and restore the "Right of Common".

On 8th June at Park Hill inclosure, Warren James led some 200 Foresters in starting to dismantle the banks and fences.

Although the Riot Act was read twice that day, the Deputy

Surveyor, Edward Machen and local magistrates could only look on, powerless to stop the crowd set about its task.

Troops from nearby Monmouth were summoned but they proved no match for the thousands of Foresters now united and determined in their cause.

This was not a 'riot' with a few fences smashed. Warren James led a disciplined and well organised

FOREST of DEAN.

Take Notice, that the FREE MINERS of the said Forest, intend to Meet on Wednesday next the 7th instant for the purpose of Opening the Forest, and their RIGHT of COMMON to the same, so long deprived of and All those Persons who may chance to have Stock thereon contrary to the Rights and Privileges of the Miners; are required hereby to remove the same forthwith otherwise they will have their Stock impounded without Further Notice.

Dated this 3rd day of June 1831.　WARREN JAMES.

The notice posted by Warren James declaring the intention to open the Forest and re-establish the Right of Common

The London press put the damage at £15,000 yet the final estimate by Edward Machen was £1,556 who was able to report that none of the trees in the enclosures had been damaged.

At his trial in Gloucester, Warren James was found guilty of felony and the judge condemned him to

Remains of old enclosures at Parkhill Inclosure where the 1831 rebellion began

Parkend

Parkend Walk

Whitemead
Park

Parkhill
Inclosure

Work or
Hang mine

Whitecroft

Bream

Parkhill Inclosure in the Forest of Dean,
where the uprising against enclosures began

death. 26 Foresters were tried, two sentenced to death. Others were transported, imprisoned and fined. Another 100 or so agreed to help repair the damage rather than face arrest.

The King commuted Warren's death sentence to transportation for life. Foresters organised petitions on his behalf and the arguments over the rights of free miners continued. Amongst those appealing for clemency was Edward Machen, Deputy Surveyor, and the man that read the Riot Act.

In 1836 – perhaps to pacify the community – Warren James was granted a free pardon. Whether he was unable to raise his fare home or whether he couldn't face a return to the Forest is not known but Warren stayed in Van Dieman's Land until his death in 1841 aged 49.

Something rotten in the land

In the early 1800s only people with large property rights and wealth could vote. So called Rotten Boroughs 'elected' MPs with only a handful of voters.

Rural landowners controlled the votes but the growing industrial cities demanded reform. For example Cornwall returned 44 MPs. The tiny hamlet of Bossiney, near Tintagel, had two MPs. The nine people eligible to vote were paid £150 each and the local aristocracy made a pact to carve up the seats beween them.

The vote for the Devon County seat in 1790 was the first election for 78 years. Another 26 years passed before the 650 electors were asked again.

The electorate was restricted to freemen, property owners or members of the local corporation. In Taunton only 'Potwallers' had the right to vote. These were men living within the ancient boundaries of the town and having a hearth on which they cooked their food. Only the mayor, masters and burgesses of Wells had the right to vote. In some seats over a quarter of the voters didn't live in the area.

Bath with a population in 1801 of 27,686 had just 30 voters. Bribery and corruption were common and elections were frequently challenged by petitions to Parliament.

Quilling and treating
Exeter had a reputation for lavish entertaining known as 'quilling' and 'treating'. Barnstaple was described: "If any one borough in the country is more corrupt than another it is

this." Candidates paid over £10,000 in bribes and costs.

Minehead was part of the estate of the Luttrell family of Dunster. Considerable sums of money were spent in entertaining voters with banquets and great quantities of drink. Those who opposed the Luttrell candidates were threatened with eviction.

Malmesbury MPs
Men of the Wiltshire town of Malmesbury who fought for King Athelstan in 939 were granted 'commoner' rights for themselves and their descendants. This small, exclusive Corporation elected two Members of Parliament.

Malmesbury Corporation had 13 voters

In the late 1700s, Squire Edmund Wilkins paid ten of the thirteen members of the Old Corporation an annuity of £30 for their votes for the MP of his choice. In return Pitt's government paid Wilkins £269.17s from a secret fund.

The 'price' of a Malmesbury MP increased to more than 500 guineas by 1818 when Sir Charles Forbes was elected. He complained when the cost rose further. The pro-reform *Morning Chronicle* claimed that it cost 12,000 guineas.

Old Sarum
The most notorious 'Rotten Borough' was Old Sarum in Wiltshire, the site of an Iron Age hill fort. Its population had moved out to nearby Salisbury but it still returned two MPs. At one time there were just five voters. Old Sarem was sold to ambitious politicians several times.

In 1801 the seat was 'owned' by the eccentric Lord Camelford. He placed friend, John Horne in the seat but he was declared ineligible due to him taking holy orders in his youth. Camelford threatened to "send a

The hill fort remains at Old Sarum

The plaque at Old Sarum to mark the reforms that ended the rotten borough

black man" referring to his servant, born in England.

The old elm under which MPs were 'elected' became known as the 'Parliament Tree'. A plaque now stands where the tree once stood.

Bad Manners in Ilchester

The Somerset seat of Ilchester had a reputation for bribery. A local inn-keeper said "damn me if Ilchester is worth living in without there are hang-fares and good elections." When Sir William Manners was thrown out of Parliament for bribery and treating he put up his brother John. It was a close run election amongst the 90 voters so Manners demolished a number of houses reducing the electorate to less than 60. He built a workhouse for the homeless.

In 1806 Manners was MP again and got a peerage. By 1818 local resentment with the arrogance of Manners led voters to ask Lord Darlington the 'Whig borough-monger' to stand candidates. Even Manners' chosen candidate, John Ward, declared: "His brutal, or rather insane, intolerance provoked the people of the place past all endurance so they sought a protector and found one in Lord Darlington. I am a victim of the defeat of the seat-selling, borough mongering system."

In revenge Manners evicted the inmates of the workhouse in mid-winter. The protest petition to Parliament in April 1819 was ignorned.

In the club

In towns and cities the contest was often between rival 'clubs'. In Plymouth the Shoulder of Mutton Club won a court case in 1803 to uphold the votes of freemen. In response the Corporation only allowed one apprentice per employer to become a freeman.

In Bristol in 1807, **Henry Hunt** challenged the control of clubs such as the White Lion Club and the Loyal and Constitutional Club. Tensions often spilled onto the streets in riot.

Growing demands

The demand for political reform grew. Earl Grey of the Whigs won a big majority in the 1831 election but the Reform Bill was defeated when it reached the House of Lords. This led to protest across the country, especially in Bristol.

A watered-down Bill only passed on the threat that hundreds of new peers would be created to force it through. It ended the worst of the voting abuse but many people were disappointed.

Voting was restricted to male house-holders living in properties worth over ten pounds a year. As a result, only one in seven adult males had the vote. The concessions didn't stop the growing demand for democracy.

Blandford vote protest

In October 1830, William Ponsonby, a whig reformer, lost by a slender vote at Blandford to Lord Ashley. In the belief that Ashley's agents had used corruption to steal the vote, locals came onto the streets in protest.

The rioting spread to Sherborne and Yeovil. On 21st October a crowd of over 100 chanting "reform and Ponsonby" attacked homes of solicitors who supported Ashley. The Riot Act was read but trouble continued until dragoons from Taunton arrived to disperse the crowd.

Twenty men were charged with riotous assembly, thirteen were imprisoned for between six days and eighteen months.

Blandford Forum

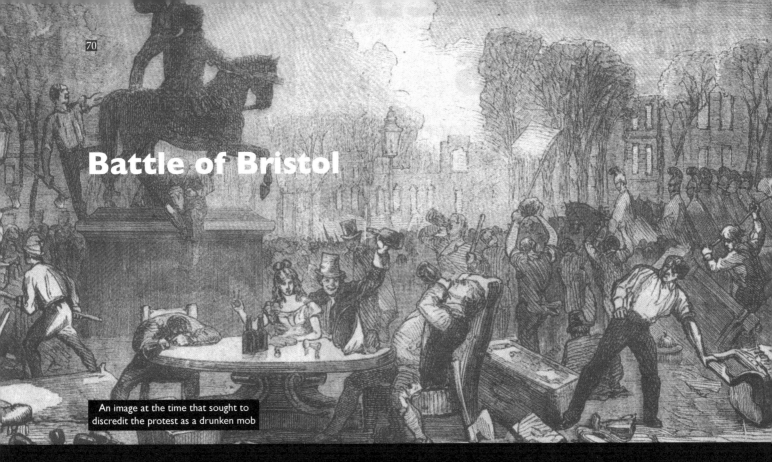

Battle of Bristol

An image at the time that sought to discredit the protest as a drunken mob

Queen Square, Bristol

In 1831 Bristol had a population of some 104,000 adults but only 6,000 people could vote. The campaign for electoral reform was growing and when the House of Lords overturned a modest reform bill, there was an angry reaction across the country, especially in Bristol. A fierce opponent of reform was Sir Charles Weatherall, the Bristol recorder. On 29th October 1831 – just after the Lords defeated the Reform Bill – his carriage was pelted with stones by protesters. The crowd grew and the rioting escalated.

The hated 14th Light Dragoons, known as the 'Bloody Blues' were called out. Their cavalry charge across Queen Square, in the centre of the city, killed one person. A furious crowd gathered

Old Gaol, The Cut, Bedminster, where the four rioters were hanged

the next day. The elegant Mansion House was burnt down and Queen Square was looted.

There was much anger at the way Bristol was run and city leaders went into hiding rather than take control. They posted notices telling people that Charles Weatherall had left the city in the hope that this might calm the riot. By the third day, the dragoons swept across the Square to brutally put down the revolt.

Twelve people were declared to have died as a result of the riot but some reports put the death toll much higher.

Four rioters were hanged and 88 transported or imprisoned. The hangings took place above the gate of the Old Gaol on the New Cut, Bedminster.

The local military commander, Lt Col Brereton, faced a court marshall for being too compassionate at the start of the rioting. He blew his brains out before the end of the trial.

The Battle of Bristol shocked the establishment and a new Reform Act was passed in 1832. This abolished the rotten boroughs but still left working people without the right to vote.

The mural on Bath Road to mark the Bristol Uprising of 1831

Union is strength

The growing demands for political reform went hand-in-hand with increasing trade union organisation. Outlawing combinations of workers didn't stop the growing union movement.

The Master and Servant Acts made a breach of contract by a workman a criminal offence and punishment was imprisonment. A breach by an employer, on the other hand, was a civil offence with no risk of imprisonment.

There are limited records of early unions but they existed across the West Country. There was a union of Devon and Somerset wood workers as early as 1717. The National Society of Brushmakers can be traced back to 1747 and a Bristol branch in 1782.

Tin box voices
Democracy in the Society involved a tin box. The secretary would write out the question and put it in the Tin Box. An out-of-work member would take it to the first shop for the 'Voices'. It would be passed around in secret and any shop holding the box for more than four hours would be fined. It could take a week to go around before the outcome was declared at the next meeting.

In 1800 the Combination Acts that made unions illegal failed to stop growing movement. A Parliamentary report

The arms of Bristol Brush Makers Society, 1782

found: "That the laws have not only not been efficient to prevent combinations of masters or workmen, but on the contrary have, in the opinion of many of both parties, had a tendency to produce mutual irritation and distrust, and to give a violent character to the combinations, and to render them highly dangerous to the peace of the community."

When the laws were repealed in 1824 unions began organising openly. Strikes became more frequent. Employers panicked at the rise of unions but the government feared that re-enacting the old Combination Laws would be too dangerous.

Amendments were passed in 1825 to make life harder for unions but still they grew. In 1833 there were several significant strikes and the Home Secretary was lobbied to re-enact the Combination Acts.

The Grand Union
The General Trades' Union was established, and on 7th September 1833 *The Pioneer*, a trades union magazine was published. A few months later the organisation became the Grand Consolidated National Trades Union. It grew rapidly with estimates of membership at around half a million.

Unions in the West
Reports showed that some 200 glove

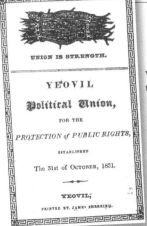

The symbol of the Yeovil Political Union was a bundle of rods for unity is strength

workers had formed a union and the radical Yeovil Political Union, established in 1831, was blamed for agitating the workers.

Workers would take an oath of allegiance and secrecy when joining the union. This was critical at a time when employers would victimise union members. The rituals included swearing on the bible and rites similar to those used in masonic practices. Wiltshire cloth workers took an oath when joining the union.

In January 1834 the *Western Flying Post* reported "considerable anxiety of the establishment of a trade union amongst the operatives." The newspaper went on to state that: "We sincerely hope . . . that every attempt of wicked and designing men to sow discord between them will be strenuously resisted."

Exeter Bricklayers
On 15th January 1834, a secret attempt was made to form a trade union of bricklayers in Exeter. **Daniel Gill** and **James Stoddart**, delegates of London bricklayers, who were on strike at that time, had been agitating for the union.

The Mayor discovered that 'assemblies of a secret kind' were to take place in the Sun Inn. The police hid in the next room and drilled a hole through the wall to spy on the meeting.

In his report to the Court, Joseph Cuthbertson, Captain of the Corps of Constables of the City of Exeter, said:

"When I came to the door of the club room, I found a man in a fustian jacket at the door. I asked for admittance which he denied me, on which I and those who accompanied me burst open the door. Upon entering the room we found a great number of persons present, I believe about sixty. We found also in the room the articles now exhibited which consisted of a figure of death with the motto, 'Remember thy latter end', two wooden axes, two drawn swords, two scabbards, two masks, two white garments, a Bible, the New Testament, a book marked 'A' and diverse papers.

"When the door was first broken, those inside attempted to keep us out but they failed in doing so. There were candles in the room but they were immediately put out.

"When I came into the room, several of the men - I saw three or four - appeared to have been blindfolded and I saw them pulling the handkerchiefs, with which they had been blinded, from their eyes."

Fifteen men were sent to the Assizes on a charge of 'combining and confederating themselves together for the purpose of effecting an unlawful object.'

Lord Denman, presiding, found the men guilty but he would not bring them up for sentence unless further complaints were made and they were discharged. This is in contrast to the Tolpuddle Martyrs who, just a few weeks later, were transported for seven years.

Lord Denman thought the public were much indebted to the authorities for their promptness which had: "prevented much mischief and had caused great benefit to the public as such associations could only tend to the injury of masters and servants."

Unions still organised in Exeter despite the court case. Lord Melbourne, the Home Secretary, wrote to the Mayor of Exeter on the 5th April 1834 saying he heard that secret combinations of workers continue to increase. He suggested that if things got worse, the mayor should go to the commanding officer in Plymouth for troops "rather than trust to the Yeomanry".

He wrote again on the 14th April congratulating the Mayor on his actions and saying he has arranged for two troops of Dragoon Guards to be stationed in the town.

It wasn't until March 1862 that the Operative Bricklayers Society was formed in Exeter.

The oath

image: WG Easton in The Martyrs of Tolpuddle TUC

The oath taken by the Tolpuddle farm workers matches that used in Exeter by the bricklayers

Strangers, within our secret walls we have admitted you,
Hoping you will prove honest, faithful, just and true,
If you cannot keep the secrets we require,
Go hence, you are at liberty to retire.
Are your motives pure?
Yes
After promising to keep the secrets:
Then amongst us, you will shortly be entitled to the endearing name of brother,
And what you hear or see here done, you must not disclose to any other;
We are uniting to cultivate friendship, as well as to protect our trade,
And due respect must to all our laws be paid.
Hoping you will prove faithful, and all encroachments on our rights withstand,
As a token of your alliance – give me your hand.

The stranger then reads the oath including:
I solemnly declare and promise that I will never act in opposition to the brotherhood in any of their attempts to support wages, but will, to the utmost of my power, assist them in all lawful and just occasions, to obtain a fair remuneration for our labour.

images: Clifford Harper

Tolpuddle Martyrs

In Tolpuddle, Dorset the labourer's wage in 1830 was nine shillings a week. In succeeding years it was reduced to eight shillings, then seven. In 1834 the farm labourers were threatened with a further reduction to six shillings a week.

Under the leadership of **George Loveless,** the workers of the village considered how they might defend themselves against these reductions in their wages. They tried to come to terms with their employers, using the vicar of Tolpuddle as an intermediary. Promises were made, but not kept.

The Tolpuddle workers turned for advice to the Grand National Consolidated Trades Union, led by **Robert Owen** which was then quickly winning members in industrial centres up and down the country. Two delegates of the union came to Tolpuddle and as a result the Friendly Society of Agricultural Labourers was formed.

At the birth of trade unionism in the village, the employers and the local magistrates took fright. The Squire, James Frampton, sought

guidance from the Home Secretary, Lord Melbourne. The result was that George Loveless and five of his fellow labourers were arrested, imprisoned in Dorchester and in March 1834 were sentenced to seven years' transportation.

There can be no doubt the 'crime' for which the men were punished was that of organising themselves and others in a trade union. But in law some other offence had to be found, for since an Act of 1824 trade unions were no longer illegal.

Many of the trade unions of this time still feared legal repression and retaliation by employers. The oath of loyalty required of new members was common practice in other organisations, such as the Freemasons and the Orangemen's Lodges. It was adopted by the Tolpuddle labourers.

Local magistrates posted a notice cautioning the labourers against joining "illegal societies or unions, to which they bind themselves by unlawful oaths".

Two days later the six men were arrested and held in Dorchester gaol. They were tried in the Crown Court of the Shire Hall on 17th March 1834, and two days later sentence of seven years' transportation – the maximum sentence – was passed.

Following their sentence, five of the men were sent to the hulks at Portsmouth, and in April 1834 set

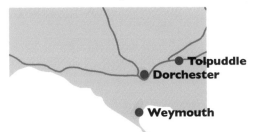

● **Tolpuddle**
● **Dorchester**

● **Weymouth**

sail in the convict ship, *Surrey,* for New South Wales where they landed in August.

George Loveless was too ill to travel and sailed later in the *William Metcalf* convict ship from Portsmouth in May 1834. He landed in Tasmania in September and remained separated from his five comrades until their return to England. The men had hard and harrowing experiences overseas. They worked in chain gangs and in penal settlements where their status was that of slaves.

As news of the sentence spread, the fledgling trade union movement organised a campaign for their release. On 24th March 1834, there was a Grand Meeting of the Working Classes, called by the Grand National Consolidated Trades Union on the instigation of Robert Owen. The meeting was attended by over 10,000 people: it was just the beginning. The agitation spread and grew. The London Central Dorchester Committee was formed to campaign for the men's pardon.

A vast demonstration took place on 21st April 1834. More than 30,000 people assembled in Copenhagen

CAUTION.

Guilty of Felony,

AND BE LIABLE TO BE

Transported for Seven Years.

CONVICTED OF FELONY,

And Transported for SEVEN YEARS.

Caution notice posted in Tolpuddle a few days before the arrests were made

Fields near King's Cross. Fearing disorder, the Government had troops at hand and 5,000 special constables had been sworn in. The agitation for the men's release was maintained. **William Cobbett, Joseph Hume, Thomas Wakeley** and other MPs kept the question constantly before Parliament. Petitions came from all over the country with over 800,000 signatures.

George Loveless refused to accept

compromises and after further pressure, the government agreed on 14th March 1836 that all the men should have a full and free pardon.

On their arrival home, great meetings were held to honour and to welcome the men. In London, an Easter Monday procession concluded with a dinner attended by 2,000 people.

The London Central Dorchester Committee, which had cared for the men's families while they were away, found themselves with enough funds to settle the men as tenant farmers in Essex.

James Hammett subsequently returned to Tolpuddle and got work in the building trade. In 1875 Joseph Arch presented to him an illuminated address and a silver watch on behalf of the National Agricultural Labourers' Union. Hammett died in 1891 and is buried in St John's churchyard, Tolpuddle.

The other five men went to Canada and settled on farms in the neighbourhood of London, Ontario. There they led peaceful, useful lives and were much respected citizens. **John Standfield** became Mayor of his district.

James Brine aged 25

Thomas Standfield aged 51

John Standfield aged 25

George Loveless aged 41

James Loveless aged 29

James Hammett

> *My Lord, if we had violated any law, it was not done intentionally; we have injured no man's reputation, character, person or property; we were uniting together to preserve ourselves, our wives and our children, from utter degradation and starvation. We challenge any man, or number of men, to prove that we have acted, or intended to act, different from the above statement.*
>
> George Loveless at his trial

The huge protest in Copenhagen Fields, London

The cottages' opening in 1934

effective organiser and was said to have achieved 90% membership of agricultural labourers in Dorset. He fought hard for better pay and conditions and built the union. On one occasion he organised a holiday to Plymouth filling 22 coaches with farm workers and their families picked up all over the county. He led a visit to Deep Duffryn mine, in Mountain Ash, South Wales, then a communist stronghold. A trip

Remembering the Tolpuddle Martyrs

Tolpuddle is a place of pilgrimage for trade unionists. In 1912 a Memorial Arch was dedicated by the Labour leader, Arthur Henderson. In 1934 it was visited by the Liberal leader Lloyd George.

Local agricultural union organiser **Fred James** organised an annual event and helped establish a rally for farm workers and trade unionists. The event included a procession of banners and laying of wreaths on the grave of James Hammett. Fred became a councillor in Dorchester and twice made Mayor. He became an Alderman of the town.

In 1934 the TUC decide to honour the story of the Tolpuddle Martyrs by building six cottages for retired agricultural workers. A massive rally was held, a new headstone for James Hammett unveiled, a medal produced and a centenary book published.

In 1945 **Arthur Jordan** (1918-2005) took over as the Dorset Organiser for the National Union for Agricultural and Allied Workers. He was a highly

Arthur Jordan

The speakers in front of the cottages in 1947

decline in agricultural labour also reduced the event. So the TUC widened its appeal by organising a festival of music, entertainment, camping, stalls and comedy alongside the traditional procession and speeches. As a result the event has grown considerably.

The front of the procession in 2006

photo: Simon Chapman

to the Forest of Dean attracted some 800 union members.

Despite his abilities as union organiser, his communist activities were hated by the right-wing leadership of the union. In 1952, the Labour Party leaders refused to come to the Tolpuddle Rally. Herbert Morrison was due to speak but refused to share a platform with communists, Arthur Jordan and **Jessie Waterman** the Dorset NAWU Chairman.

Just two days before Christmas in 1962, the union sacked Arthur Jordan, "for actions where he had not conformed to union policy." The list of complaints against him included several articles and letters he had written to various journals. Also on the list was that he had accepted an invitation to speak to Salisbury Trades Council before obtaining permission from the General Secretary.

Arthur Jordan died in 2005, aged 88, still a committed Communist Party member.

In 1984 Tolpuddle witnessed a massive rally to mark the 150th anniversary. The Labour leader, Neil Kinnock spoke to the crowd at a time of conflict with the Thatcher Government.

Through the 1990s the march and speeches began to lose their attraction and fewer people turned up. The

George Lansbury unveils the Eric Gill designed headstone to Martyr James Hammett in 1934

Museum

The TUC has a small free museum and shop to tell the story of the Martyrs.

Church Hill

Late 18th or early 19th century cottages.

Martyrs' Shelter

Erected in 1934 on land given to the National Trust by Sir Ernest Debenham.

Martyrs' Cottages

Built by the TUC in 1934 as part of the centenary celebrations for the Martyrs. Each of the six cottages is named after a Martyr. They are home to retired farm workers.

Sculpture

Created by Thompson Dagnall in 2000, it catches the moment when George Loveless has to wait alone to be transported.

James Hammett's Grave

JAMES HAMMETT
TOLPUDDLE MARTYR
PIONEER OF TRADES
UNIONISM CHAMPION
OF FREEDOM
BORN 11 DECEMBER 1811
DIED 21 NOVEMBER 1891

to return to Tolpuddle and died in 1891. The headstone was designed by Eric Gill in 1934. Each year wreaths are laid in the memory of the Martyrs.

Parish Church

St. John the Evangelist church dates from the 12th century.

Tolpuddle Village

Tolpuddle Hall

A vicarage has been on this site since the 16th century. Home of the Rev. Thomas Warren who refused to support the Martyrs at their trial despite an earlier promise.

Martyrs' Inn

Formerly known as The Crown Inn

Thomas Standfield's Cottage

Where the Martyrs met in secret and were betrayed. Built in the late 18th century.

Old Chapel

The original chapel where the Methodist Martyrs worshipped held its first service in 1818. A crowded service was met by "a rowdy mob of around a hundred persons . . . jeering and hurling stones."

Martyrs' Tree

The Martyrs met on the Village Green under the trees and discussed how to fight further wage cuts. The last remaining sycamore tree was planted around 1685.

Festival

In July each year, thousands march through the village to remember the Martyrs.

New Chapel

Built by William and John Hammett, kinsmen of James at a cost of £192. Local Methodists held their first service here on 1st January 1863. The arch was unveiled in 1912 by Labour leader Arthur Henderson.

Chartism in the West

Reform Place in Bridport built after the Reform Act

that had six key demands:

- ◆ Secret ballots
- ◆ Male suffrage, to be followed by female suffrage
- ◆ No property qualification to vote
- ◆ Payments for MPs to allow working people to stand
- ◆ Annual elections
- ◆ Equally sized constituencies

The first Chartist petition with 1.28 million signatures, gathered support throughout the West Country. The Whig Government rejected the demands and when supporters took to the streets the militia was called on to suppress the protests. Violent incidents took place in several South West towns and cities.

The 1832 Reform Act still left the majority of people without the vote. Chartism became a powerful force for democratic change and led to a massive campaign for a wide range of demands for social justice.

Henry 'Orator' Hunt (1773-1835) was a pioneer of working-class radicalism and an early advocate of parliamentary reform. Born in Upavon, Wiltshire, he developed a talent for public speaking in Bristol. He advocated annual parliaments and universal suffrage, and believed that 'mass pressure' could achieve reform. He earned the nickname 'Orator' after speeches to massive meetings across the country. He was influential on the Chartist Movement.

The People's Charter
Developing working class organisa-

tions sought to reform the voting system and to win political power through Parliament. The *People's Charter* was written setting out the demands for a more democratic society. The campaign became known as Chartism and had a number of key figures from the West Country.

William Lovett (1800-77) was born in Newlyn, Cornwall and became an apprentice rope-maker in Penzance before moving to London as a cabinet maker. He joined the protests for the Tolpuddle Martyrs and took up the campaign for electoral reform. He helped draft the *People's Charter* in 1838

William Lovett

Lovett's house in Newlyn

Plaque in memory of William Lovett

The Chartist cause attracted mass meetings across the region. **Henry Vincent** (1800-70) was born in Wotton-under-Edge in Gloucestershire. He chronicled some of the events as

Henry Vincent

he travelled through the West Country as a leading Chartist.

Henry Vincent established the *Western Vindicator* newspaper in Bath. He described speaking to hundreds of people in each town but in Devizes he met opponents who attacked him. He was knocked out and felt lucky to survive the assault.

He stood unsuccessfully as an independent Radical at Tavistock

in 1843 and Plymouth in 1846. A supporter of the anti-slavery movement he embarked on several lecture tours in America.

Chartism in the West
Chartist meetings were held from 1838 in Bradford-on-Avon, Trowbridge, Holt and Westbury. On 19th November 1838 a crowd of some 3,000 gathered at Trowbridge barracks by torchlight to hear Henry Vincent and **William Carrier,** a local worker, denounce the higher classes, the Queen and magistrates. Carrier is said to have promised "plenty of roast beef, plum pudding and strong beer by working three hours a day."

The government sought to ban such gatherings but the Trowbridge workers were too well organised. Eventually the militia gained control and Carrier was arrested and sentenced to two years' imprisonment.

The Chartists' campaign caused panic amongst some employers and authorities. In 1839, Richard Moyle, the Mayor of Penzance warned the Home Secretary of the "seditious and inflammatory language" of "a party of itinerant politicians, who style themselves 'Chartists'." The local meeting had attracted a lot of interest causing the Mayor to state: "The sensation which this meeting has occasioned in this tranquil part of the world is quite extraordinary. The upper classes of society are in a state of alarm and men have called on me urging me to do my utmost to suppress any such meetings in future."

Hundreds of Chartist leaders were imprisoned and strikers forced back to work. Despite widespread support,

The Bristol home of John Frost

the Chartist demands took more than 70 years to be realised.

68 Park Road, Stapleton, Bristol bears a Blue Plaque to **John Frost** (1784-1877). He settled in Bristol in his retirement. In 1839 he led miners

The headstone for John Frost, nearly hidden in Horfield Church, Bristol

in the Chartist Rising in Newport, South Wales. The protest ended in blood-shed. John Frost was arrested and sentenced to be hanged, drawn and quartered. Public outcry led to the brutal sentence being commuted to transportation to Van Diemen's Land. In 1856 he was allowed to return. He continued to write and campaign for democratic reform.

Many Chartists went on to create other pressure groups, friendly societies, educational institutes and took up roles in trade unions and local government.

Henry Solly (1813-1903) was a Chartist who went on to establish the Working Men's Club and Institute Union. He was the minister at the Unitarian Chapel in Yeovil, Somerset in 1840. Involvement with radical, working class politics was too much for some local Baptists and it became necessary for him to move to Tavistock.

Henry Solly was a keen teetotaller and was worried about the impact of drinking upon the welfare of families. He was also anxious about social polarisation and believed that people of different classes needed to meet. Socially and politically, he became identified with Christian Socialists. He felt that a more contained or moral version of capitalism offered the best chance of advancement and of harmony between classes.

John Arthur Roebuck (1802-1879) was a radical reformer elected Liberal MP for Bath in 1832. He wrote many pamphlets including one on the Dorchester Labourers and *Trade unions: their advantages to the working classes.*

Chartist activist **Thomas Willey** (1795-1861) was born in Bedminster, Bristol. He started a printing firm in the High Street, Cheltenham specialising in ballads. His work was popular amongst the domestic staff serving the wealthy visitors in the growing spa town. He chaired the local Chartist Land Plan meetings.

As only male land owners were allowed to vote, there was a Chartist campaign to provide modest plots of land to working class families. The Chartist Land Plan bought some 20,000 acres providing homes to around 5,000 families. The main land holding was on the Gloucestershire-Worcestershire border.

The land for the Chartist Land Plan in Gloucestershire

In 1846, on land near Redmarley in Gloucestershire, 45 Chartist cottages were built on plots of two, three or four acres of land – enough for a few animals and supposedly enough crops for self-sufficiency. The holdings were awarded to members on the basis of share ownership and ballot. Sale of surplus produce and a modest rent was set to make the project self-financing.

170 acres of land at Lowbands were bought by **Feargus O'Connor,** independent Chartist MP who was eager to see action but had little business sense.

The scheme began well despite opposition from some local farmers. The first winners of the ballot in March 1847 arrived at Lowbands supported by 5-6,000 people carrying flags and banners, headed by marching bands. A week-long conference attracted support from locals who wanted to learn more about the radical colony. In June 1847 268 acres of land at Snig's End were acquired for £11,000 and two years later, the allottees moved in to their new homes.

Many allottees couldn't grow enough food on the land to survive and the rents had to rise to cover costs. The company set-up for the initiative was never properly registered and in 1851 the scheme was wound-up.

The cottages remain as listed buildings and can be seen at Snig's End, Lowbands, Staunton and Corse.

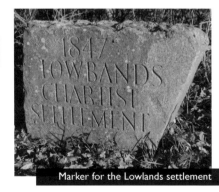

Marker for the Lowlands settlement

A sample of the Chartist Cottages in Gloucestershire

Chard Lace Riots

The winter of 1842-43 was hard. Demand for the bobbin lace made in Chard, Somerset had fallen. The employers cut the already meagre wages. By the summer of 1842 the situation was no better and on 15th August mill owner John Oram cut the pay further.

Oram's was the smallest mill in Chard but the workers decided to strike. As they spilled onto the streets Mayor Spicer ordered Tom Hutchins, the local constable, to read the Riot Act. The protest dispersed but the strike remained solid and news of the unrest brought **Ruffy Ridley** from London to Chard to hold a Chartist meeting.

The Mayor refused him the use of the Town Hall and so the meeting was held in the open-air in Market Place. Up to 1,000 people turned up and cheered

Ridley's message of unity and democracy.

By 22nd August the strike spread to Wheatley and Riste's, Chard's largest lace mill. After a mass meeting at Field Bars, the strikers marched to the Silk Mill where workers came out in support. The growing crowd went on to Holyrood Lace Mill where factory owner, James Hill, locked the gates. These were soon thrown open and more workers joined the dispute.

Mayor Spicer, alarmed by the escalating rebellion summoned troops from Taunton and even from the rival town of Ilminster. On 23rd August a small troop of Scot's Greys appeared but finding little disturbance rode off thinking it a false alarm. Meanwhile workers at Cuffs Mill joined the strike.

Armed gentlemen from Ilminster arrived to quell the growing unrest but the workers threw stones. Windows were smashed at the Mayor's large house on the High Street and the disturbances ran late into the night as more local constables were sworn in.

On 24th August Mayor Spicer agreed to meet

Chard Town Hall

a delegation and **William Holloway, Joseph Woodward** and **James Galpin** were elected to represent the workers. A large crowd marched towards the Town Hall where the meeting was due to take place. Troops blocked the road and a tense stand-off took place during which weapons were drawn. Seeing that the troops were making matters worse, councillors persuaded them to retreat to allow the meeting to start. Agreement was reached that the Ilminster Yeomanry leave Chard at but the strike remained unsettled.

Low paid workers couldn't afford a long stoppage and some roamed the countryside for food. Workers began to return to work and by 8th September the strike had collapsed.

The following year, John Oram, the owner of the mill where the strike started was declared bankrupt.

Ruffy Ridley had left Chard to continue the Chartist campaign and the next report of him was when he was locked up in Cinderford Gaol in the Forest of Dean.

Hollyrood Lace Mill, Chard

Boden Lace Mill, Chard

Radical Religion

The story of religion is dominated by the determination of the established church to retain power over the life of ordinary people. But new ideas and opposition to church officialdom run through the history of the West Country.

Worship and belief was strictly controlled by the church authorities. It was illegal not to attend church on Sunday and the Catholic authorities held considerable power over the state.

Lollards in the West

In the late 1300s Lollards followed the teachings of John Wycliffe and had strong following in Bristol in particular. They denied the superstition of the church such as purgatory and transubstantiation. They taught people the Bible and believed that faith was not reliant upon priests. They scorned the wealth built up by priests.

Lollards believed that things held in common were more important than that held by individuals hence the term 'communism'.

Sir John Oldcastle became a Lollard and was imprisoned by King Henry V. When he escaped in 1414 he called on Lollards to help overthrow the King. A large contingent from Bristol responded to the rebellion but it was quickly suppressed. Some 40 people were executed. Oldcastle went into hiding but in 1417 was caught and executed.

Lollardy remained strong amongst the cloth workers of Bristol. One follower, James Willis was a Bristol weaver who moved to the Chilterns where he led a Lollard revival.

The first English Bible

The Bible was only available in Latin or Greek which reinforced the power of the priests. Allowing the word of God to be read by anyone was considered heresy. William Tyndale, born around 1494 near Dursley in Gloucestershire, was determined to translate and publish the Bible in English. But he risked death by doing so. Tyndale's finished translation remains the basis of what we use today. In translating the bible from Greek, he interpreted the words in ways that further enraged the established church. For example he changed 'priest' to 'elder' and the church hierarchy became 'congregation'. 'Charity', implying the need to pay, became 'love'.

Tyndale's translation gave away his Gloucestershire roots. The Bible contained 'mizzle' a local term for light rain.

Tyndale's monument, North Nibley

He failed to win support for his mission in England and fled to what is now Germany. Luther had published a Bible in German and it had been a best-seller.

Tyndale worked in hiding to translate the Bible and used a printers in Antwerp to print copies to be smuggled across to England. Those caught distributing the English Bible were arrested and many burnt at the stake.

Even Henry VIII's break with the Roman Church didn't lift the ban

William Tyndale

on the English Bible but Tyndale managed to produce some 50,000 copies of his *New Testament*.

He was eventually betrayed in Antwerp and imprisoned by the Catholic authorities. In 1536, in the courtyard of Vilvorde Castle near Brussels, he was burnt at the stake. A mercy offer to strangle him first was botched and he re-gained consciousness as the flames caught hold.

In 1540, just a few years after his execution, Tyndale's Bible was accepted, even encouraged by the new Church of England.

Protestant Martyrs
The Marian Martyrs were persecuted by the Catholic Queen Mary I.

Exeter Martyrs
Thomas Benet moved to Exeter in 1524 after his home town of Cambridge became too dangerous for him. In 1530 he fixed a scroll to Exeter Cathedral door declaring "The Pope is Anti-Christ . . . we ought to worship God only, and no saints."

Exeter plaque showing Thomas Benet fixing a scroll to Exeter Cathedral door

Benet is burned at the stake in Exeter

He was arrested and after refusing to submit to the Pope was burned to death at Livery Dole in Exeter on 10th January 1531.

Exeter domestic servant, **Agnes Prest**, was inspired by Thomas Benet. She returned to her home county of Cornwall to marry. It wasn't a good match as her husband was an ardent Catholic. They had numerous children but when he tried to force her to take Mass she fled.

Agnes returned to her family but was arrested and held in Launceston gaol for three months. She was moved to Exeter but refused to give up her religion. On 15th August 1557 she was led outside the city walls to Southernhay where she was burned as a heretic.

John Hooper, the Bishop of Gloucester is said to have held steadfast to his Protestant faith during his execution in Gloucester on 9th February 1555.

Richard Sharpe, a weaver from Bristol and **Thomas Hale** a shoemaker were burnt back-to-back at the stake on 7th May 1557 in Cotham for their Protestant beliefs. **Thomas Banion**, a weaver, was burnt on 27th August 1557.

Outspoken rector
In 1616 **Edmund Peacham**, rector of Hinton St George in Somerset was arrested after sermon notes were found including "the people might rise in rebellion against these new taxes."

He was taken to be interrogated under torture in the Tower of London and then moved to Taunton Gaol where he died.

John Hooper statue in Gloucester

Salisbury Martyrs

Richard Spencer, John Maundrel, a farm worker, John Spicer, a stonemason and William Coberley, a tailor, suffered an agonising execution by fire in Salisbury. This was the price paid by many in the battle between religion, power and politics.

Keevil Church

In 1521 **Richard Spencer** left the priesthood to marry. He took part in putting on comedies and 'interludes'. But he fell foul of the Catholic authorities and was burned at the stake in Salisbury for heresy.

Born in Rowde, near Devizes, **John Maundrel**, got a copy of Tyndall's Bible and felt compelled to spread its word. He spoke against 'holy water' and was punished by having to walk around Devizes wearing a white sheet and carrying a candle.

Queen Mary I led a new attack against Protestants and when the three Wiltshire men questioned catholic practices they were caught by the brutal persecution. In Keevil Church they questioned the worship of idols and when the vicar prayed for souls in purgatory, John Maundrel heckled, knowing that no such place was mentioned in the Bible. He was supported by **John Spicer** and **William Coberley**.

The priest had the three held in stocks until they were brought before Salisbury bishops. In the interrogation they denied belief in the Pope, Catholic communion and Purgatory. They were taken from the gaol at Fisherton to Bemerton Field, near the current junction of Wilton and Devizes Roads. They were chained to stakes and burned to death.

The full horror of the execution was described by **John Foxe** who made an account of the martyrs. He described how William Coberley, chained to the stake: "was somewhat long aburning as the wind stood still.

"After his body was scorched with the fire, and his left arm drawn and taken from him, the flesh being burned to the white bone . . . blood and matter issuing out of his mouth. Afterward, when they all thought he had been dead, suddenly he rose up with his body again."

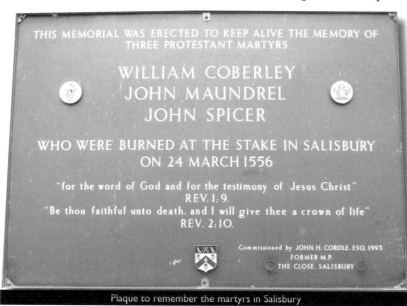

THIS MEMORIAL WAS ERECTED TO KEEP ALIVE THE MEMORY OF THREE PROTESTANT MARTYRS

WILLIAM COBERLEY
JOHN MAUNDREL
JOHN SPICER

WHO WERE BURNED AT THE STAKE IN SALISBURY ON 24 MARCH 1556

"for the word of God and for the testimony of Jesus Christ"
REV. 1. 9.
"Be thou faithful unto death, and I will give thee a crown of life"
REV. 2:10.

Commissioned by JOHN H. CORDLE. ESQ. 1993
FORMER M.P.
THE CLOSE. SALISBURY

Plaque to remember the martyrs in Salisbury

Dorset Martyrs

The religious troubles of the 16th and 17th centuries were felt in Dorset. Those killed for their Protestant faith are remembered with a sculpture and plaque in Dorchester.

This is the list of those who were connected with Dorset and who suffered in the religious turmoil of this period.

Dorset born **Alexander Briant** was hanged, drawn and quartered at Tyburn on 1st December 1581.

John Slade schoolmaster, born at Manston. Hanged, drawn and quartered at Winchester on 30th October 1583.

Thomas Hemerford priest, born at Folke. Hanged, drawn and quartered at Tyburn on 30th October 1584.

John Munden Dorchester and Netherbury schoolmaster. Hanged, drawn and quartered at Tyburn on 12th February 1584.

William Warmington priest of Wimborne Minster was banished from January 1585.

John Adams vicar of Winterborne St Martin. Hanged, drawn and quartered at Tyburn on 8th October 1586.

Thomas Pilcher Fellow of Balliol College and priest. Hanged, drawn and quartered at Dorchester on 21st March 1587.

John Hambley priest at Beaminster. Hanged, drawn and quartered at Salisbury at Easter 1587.

John Jessop companion to Thomas Pilcher died in Dorchester Gaol in 1588.

Helen Tremain wife of Samson died in Dorchester Gaol in 1588.

Morecock artisan died in Dorchester Gaol before 1591.

William Pike carpenter of West Moors, hanged, drawn and quartered at Dorchester at Easter 1591.

Eustace White priest arrested in Blandford Forum. Hanged, drawn and quartered at Tyburn on 10th December 1591.

William Pattenson chaplain at Chideock. Hanged, drawn and quartered at Tyburn on 22nd January 1592.

John Cornelius priest arrested at Chideock Castle, hanged, drawn and quartered at Dorchester on 4th July 1594.

Thomas Bosgrave arrested at Chideock Castle, hanged, drawn and quartered at Dorchester on 4th July 1594.

John Carey serving man, arrested at Chideock Castle, hanged, drawn and quartered at Dorchester on 4th July 1594.

Patrick Salmon serving man, arrested at Chideock Castle, hanged, drawn and quartered at Dorchester on 4th July 1594.

Hugh Green priest, arrested at Lyme Regis. Hanged, drawn and quartered at Dorchester on 19th August 1642.

Sculpture to remember the Dorset Martyrs in Dorchester

New religion

Quakers

The Quaker religion grew after the English Civil War and established a significant presence in the West Country. They believed in peace and an open, less formal approach to worship.

Quakers refused to observe social formalities such as removing one's hat in front of a 'social superior'. Meetings of Friends replaced formal church services and participants were moved to speak. They would sometimes interrupt church services, they encouraged ordinary people to express themselves and enhanced the role of women. This disturbed the clergy and gentry who saw the acts of Quakers as sedition.

George Fox (1624-91) was a travelling shoemaker from Leicestershire who believed that God's message came directly to individuals through their Inner Light. He formed the Friends of Truth that became known as the Quakers. In 1655 Fox came to the West Country to preach. He called it the "dark country" and spoke at Plymouth, Truro, Helston, Breage and Marazion. St Ives opposed his teachings and when he refused to doff his hat to the local Justice of the Peace he was imprisoned inside Launceston Castle. He was released without charge on 9th September 1656

George Fox

Quakerism came to Bristol by 1654 and included **Denis Hollister MP**. It was so popular meetings had to be held in the fields around the City as

James Nayler punished for his Bristol 'blasphemy'

there were no halls large enough.

James Nayler (1618–1660) was an English Quaker leader. He was born in Yorkshire. In 1642 he joined the Parliamentarian Army.

In October 1656, Nayler staged a demonstration in Bristol in which he re-enacted the arrival of Christ in Jerusalem that is commemorated on Palm Sunday, riding on horseback into the city centre. Followers sang "Holy, holy, holy" and strewed the path with garments. Nayler denied that he was impersonating Jesus and said rather that "Christ was in him".

On 16th December 1656 he was convicted of blasphemy in a highly publicised trial before the Second Protectorate Parliament. Narrowly escaping execution, he was instead punished with two floggings, branding of the letter B (for blasphemer) on his forehead, piercing

Come-to-Good meeting house near Feock, Cornwall. England's oldest Quaker meeting house

Horningsham. - The Oldest Free Congregational Church in the Kingdom.

1566

image: old post card unatributed

Horningsham Chapel the oldest nonconformist chapel in England

of his tongue with a hot iron, and two years' imprisonment with hard labour.

In 1658, three Marlborough Quakers were fined a hefty ten shillings each for being at a Meeting on the

A rare non-conformist grave for John Weire in a field near Watchfield, Highbridge, Somerset

First Day instead of in church. Quakers refused to pay tithes to the Church and this led to hundreds of convictions in Wiltshire alone. In 1670, **Dorothy Rawlings,** a poor Quaker widow was driven into extreme poverty by fines imposed for her hosting a meeting at Bromham, Wiltshire.

In 1681 there was a mass round-up of all members of non-conformist sects. The Friars Meeting House in Bristol was attacked. Unable to meet in their own rooms and chapels congregations met in the quarries around Bristol.

In 1685 100 Quakers were released from Bristol's gaols as part of an amnesty. The persecution eased and the sect adopted a less radical approach.

Quakers became leading business figures and established major factories in the region including Clarks in Street and Frys' Chocolate in Keynsham.

William Cookworthy (1705-1780) was an English Quaker minister, a successful pharmacist and innovator. He discovered china clay in Cornwall and devised a way of making porcelain.

Methodism

Led by **John Wesley** (1703-91), Methodism emerged as a powerful new form of Christian worship. It was particularly attractive to working people, disillusioned with the Church of England, controlled as it was by landowners and employers. Methodism offered a more open form of worship and the early movement was often linked to trade unionism, anti-slavery and other calls for social justice.

The key to Methodist organisation was the 'circuit' around which itinerant preachers would travel to hold services in

John Wesley statue in Bristol

New Rooms in Bristol

houses, barns, even outside. Wesley first preached outside to hundreds of local miners in 1739 on Hanham Hill, near Bristol. As the movement grew, simple chapels were built and they can be seen today all over the West Country. The oldest Methodist chapel in the world is the New Rooms in Bristol.

Methodists were often portrayed as political subversives. In the mid-

The beacon on Hanham Hill to mark the first outdoor Wesley sermon

eighteenth century they faced attacks on their property, personal abuse, sexual attacks and even murders. When Wesley went to Cornwall in 1743 the vicar of Illogan hired his church warden and a mob to chase him from the district. A month later he faced hostility in St Ives from the vicar and curate. The Methodist chapel was destroyed.

Later there were attacks in Exeter, Quethiok, St Germans and Mevagissy. The most serious was gunpowder placed under the doorstep of a Methodist meeting house in Wadebridge.

Other attacks were less violent but designed to deter worshippers. At St Mellion a goat was pushed into the congregation and at St Germans a fierce dog was let loose in the chapel.

But Cornish Wesleyans did not embrace demands for democratic reform or radical politics.

The more moderate Methodism became strong in Cornwall and outdoor services such as

1810 GWITHIAN METHODIST CHURCH

Gwennap Pit now and in 1911

those held at Gwennap Pit attracted hundreds of worshippers.

Tolpuddle Methodism

Five of the Tolpuddle Martyrs were Methodists and George and James Loveless were local preachers, as was Thomas Standfield occasionally. Next to Thomas Standfield's cottage in Tolpuddle was built a tiny cobb chapel. How radical such a development was is shown by the account in the *Salisbury Journal* of the chapel's first service on 13th October 1818. It reported that after the service: "a mob of about 100 persons were found assembled. These persons behaved in a most turbulent manner. A lady belonging to the Minister's party, before she could get into the chaise, was pushed down a bank into the road; the horses were much frightened by the tumult and noise and the driver was for a considerable time unable to proceed.

"For more than two miles, in a very bad road, the drivers, horse and carriages were pelted by the mob with stones, mud etc.; the windows of the chaise were broken and even the side of the chaise was pierced by a stone. One lady who rode by the side of the driver had a severe blow on her head and at Piddletown, the driver received a blow to his neck."

George Howell wrote of the attitude of the local gentry by describing Methodism as "Indeed, next to poaching, it was the gravest of all offences."

George Loveless later referred to the fact that men had been "persecuted, banished and not allowed to have employ if they entered the Wesleyan chapel at Tolpuddle."

When local wages were being cut yet again, George Loveless sought the support of the Church. The local vicar, Rev Dr. Warren, had been a witness to an agreement over pay levels and had promised to see it upheld. But Dr Warren went back on his word and denied the understanding. Four other clergymen signed the caution against forming unions and sat on the bench that dealt out the harsh sentences to the six farm workers.

This led George Loveless to strengthen his views on the official Church. On his return to England he responded to attacks on his character and cause by writing a pamphlet called *Church Shown Up*. It is a stinging attack on the hypocrisy and indifference of the Church. It is also a strident call for justice and democracy.

The old chapel in Tolpuddle

Secret services

Around 1653 the Baptist congregation in Kilmington village, east Devon sought refuge from persecution by meeting in the remote Lough Wood. Secrecy was critical and guards had to be set to warn of the approach of constables. The meetings would have taken place in the dense woodland of the time.

The Kilmington community were joined in worship by members from around Devon and Dorset and were amongst Baptists who were ostracised, ridiculed, imprisoned, transported and sometimes killed for their beliefs.

Huguenot refugees played a part and were given the nick-name 'French' which became adopted as a surname. The name is found frequently in the burial ground.

The National Trust now owns the chapel.

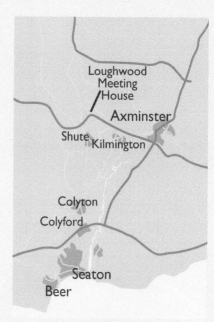

Loughwood Meeting House

Hindu reformer

The statue of Rajah Rammohun Roy outside Bristol Library

Rajah Rammohun Roy (1772-1833) was born in Bengal. In 1812 he witnessed his brother's widow cruelly forced to commit sati, the Hindu ritual death of widows upon the funeral pyres of their husband. Roy set his mind to abolish the practice.

He introduced the word 'Hinduism' into the English language in 1816.

In 1823, as founder and editor of two weekly newspapers, he organised a protest against British imposed censorship. This protest marked a turning point in Rammohun's life, towards political action. He advocated a more advanced system of education and justice to prepare India for the modern world.

In 1829 Rammohun Roy came to England on behalf of the 'King of Delhi', to petition the East India Company for an increase in the royal pension. The king granted him the title 'Raja'. Rammohun used the visit to lobby for reforms.

His health declined and on 27th September 1833 he died in Bristol and is buried in Arno's Vale Cemetery.

Mary Carpenter, in her book *The Last Days in England of the Raja Rammohun Roy* described him as "a man greatly before his age. He was a light shining in thick darkness."

Bristol now has a well-established Hindu community and a temple at Redfield.

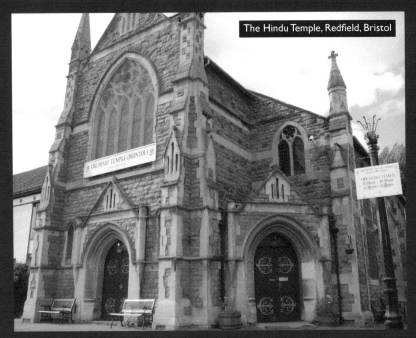

The Hindu Temple, Redfield, Bristol

Radical Cornwall?

The development of radical political movements and trade unionism was particularly strong amongst mining communities. Whilst these features were weak in Cornwall there are still examples of protest and resistance.

Cornwall's isolation from established structures including the Church attracted Wesley to promote Methodism. Radical opinions were focused within the development of the new religion rather than in civil society. Cornish Methodism was a powerful force in the county and fertile ground for Liberal politics but less so for trade unionism or socialism.

Although the author of the *People's Charter*, **William Lovett**, was born in Cornwall, the Chartist campaign struggled in the county. **Richard**

Spurr, (1800-1855) a cabinet maker from Truro, took up the cause and was arrested by police with drawn cutlasses on 16 January 1840 at the Trades' Hall, Bethnal Green whilst addressing a meeting of about 700 people. He emigrated to Australia in 1849 where he joined the growing campaign for democracy.

In 1839 **Duncan** and **Lowery**, Chartist missionaries in the region reported: "We find that to do good we will have to go over each place twice for the people have never heard of agitation and know nothing of political principles; it is all uphill work". (reported in *The Chartist Movement* 1918).

A Chartist meeting in Penzance caused panic amongst the authorities. **Mr J Skews** represented Cornwall at the Chartist Convention of 1845 and reported that "if the county were properly agitated it would be the best

Chartist District in the country." (*Northern Star*, April 1845)

The system of wage payments that treated workers as self-employed may have weakened collective activity and encouraged indivdu-alism. Yet the nature of food riots would seem to imply no lack of solidarity when required. There were many other examples of co-operation. Communities would pool their resources and skills to build chapels in almost every village.

In 1865 unemployed Cornish miners were recruited as strike-breakers in a bitter dispute in Cramlington in Northumberland. On 5th December 1865, a special train brought the Cornish miners to the pit village where they were put up in the empty houses of the evicted strikers. About 150 men accepted an offer from the union of 10 shillings each for them to return home. But more arrived to break the strike.

There was some solidarity with the northern workers. In 1867 some 400 Cornish miners met in the Temperance Hall in Liskeard and voted to stop at home until the dispute was settled.

Although not welcome by the locals many stayed because there was no work in Cornwall. It took many years for them to be accepted.

Remains of Bottallack Mine

More Cornish families moved north in search of work. Hundreds were settled close to the mine at Roose in Cumbria. In the 1881 Census 70 per cent of the population had birth-places in Cornwall and became known as a 'Cornish village in Furness'. Before the arrival of the Cornish miners Roose was pronounced with a hard 's', as in goose; now it is pronounced 'Rooze', due to the Cornish accent.

There were some strikes in Cornwall: 1831 at the Lanescot Mine and over an attempt to form a union at the Consolidated Mines near Redruth in 1842. The development of early agricultural unions also struggled in the county. In 1873 the National Union of Agricultural Workers had some 86,000 members in 982 branches but none in Cornwall.

Miners led a surprise victory in 1885 when **Charles Augustus Vansittart Conybeare** (1853-1919) was elected as a radical Liberal MP for Camborne. He lost his seat in 1895. Cornwall was restored to its more moderate Liberal politics.

In 1894, **Charles Robert Vincent** set up a branch of the Marxist Social Democratic Federation. He was a bookseller in Truro but was persuaded to become an organiser for the new Workers Union.

In the early 1900s, Beatrice and Sidney Webb claimed that there were only 600 trade unionists out of a workforce of some 125,000.

In 1906 **Jack Jones,** a docker, was the first socialist candidate in Cornwall. He won just 1.5 per cent of the vote in the mining constituency of Camborne being overwhelmed by the Liberal landslide.

Remains of Blue Hills Mine

Jack Jones was an organiser for the Gasworkers and General Labourers Union but it was the Workers Union that led the 1913 Clay Strike (see later).

Although defeated the strike boosted the Cornish Labour Movement.

Cornish emigration

Between 1814 and 1914 around a quarter of a million people sought a better life by emigrating from Cornwall.

The potato famine hit Cornwall in the 1840s and the crash of copper and tin prices forced families to leave. The crisis amongst Cornish mining communities halted the fragile development of trade unionism just at the time of its growth in areas such as South Wales.

Cornish emigration poster

The development of mining around the world that created a demand for the particular 'hard rock' skills of Cornish tin miners.

The irony is that many emigrés were amongst the leaders of trade union actions in the mines of Australia. Cornish miners were involved in the Eureka Stockade in 1854 where many died fighting for voting rights.

A series of strikes in South Australia's Moonta and Wallaroo copper mines proved successful for the Cornish migrant workforce and a Miners' Association was established. This was to establish the United Labour Party of South Australia and in 1891 its first MP was **Richard Hooper** a Cornish Methodist trade unionist. As was **John Verra** from Gwennap in Cornwall who became the Australian state's first Labour premier in 1910.

A statue stands at Bendigo, Australia, in honour of the Cornish miners, with an inscription thanking those miners "who created the economy from which grew a beautiful city".

In Cobre, Cuba in the 1840s and the Morro Velho Mine in Brazil in the 1870s, Cornish miners were involved in strikes.

Tom Mathews and **James Farquharson Trembarth** were Cornish migrants who became pioneers of the labour movement in Johannesburg and Kimberley in South Africa.

The massive emigration from Cornwall meant many families became reliant on wages earned overseas. In 1898 the *West Briton* reported on the rush on the banks after the arrival of mail from South Africa where many Cornish miners were working. By 1910 some 7,000 miners were in South Africa sending back up to a million pounds a year to Cornwall.

Following the Boer War, the British Government sought to restore South Africa's mining industry by recruiting up to 60,000 Chinese workers. This policy caused considerable disquiet in Cornwall as some opposed the prospect of the Chinese taking 'Cornish' jobs.

The Cornish Diaspora spread around the world. Latin America, Canada, Australia, South Africa and America all have strong Cornish links. At one time it was estimated that in Grass Valley, California, over 60% of the people were Cornish.

The silver mining town of Pachuca in Mexico is known as Mexico's Little Cornwall. Cornish miners brought football with them, and the town has many examples of Cornish archi-tecture and is famous for its pasties, after the Cornish pasty.

South Crofty, the last working tin mine in Cornwall, struggled to remain commercially viable. There was a big campaign in the county to save the pit. The Thatcher Government pumped in cash to keep it going but it closed in 1998. There are still hopes that mining will return to Cornwall as mineral prices rise.

Kitty Mine, St Agnes now houses other businesses

The sad state of South Crofty

A Cornish question in 1998: When the fish and tin are gone what are the Cornish boys to do?

White Country disputes

China clay country

Although a big employer, the china clay industry fought to keep unions out. There were some local disputes such as the strike in 1872 by 200 clay workers at Thomas Stocker's West of England Clay Works. They won big pay rises of 25-50 per cent but by 1875 a trade slump led employers to try to cut wages.

A strike at the Martyn's clay works began on 2nd July. The workers marched from pit to pit gathering support. A mass meeting in St Austell heard strike leader **Joseph Matthews** appeal for a disciplined, peaceful dispute.

Some employers backed down but when a strike deputation met the clay merchants they warned the workers that they had large stock piles and would win the dispute. When the strike held firm, the employers gave in and restored pay levels.

After this success, Matthews set up the St Austell China Clay, China Stone and Surface Labourers' Friendly Union. Even with 'Friendly' in its title the Cornish bosses were determined to kill off this union before it took hold. Matthews and other activists were sacked.

A strike was called and some 2,000 workers came out. The dispute quickly turned nasty with clay captains threatening workers and reports of violence against strike breakers. 150 police were called in from Plymouth.

Early morning raids saw union leaders: **Rundle** and **Hawkey** arrested for intimidation. They were gaoled for six weeks and fined £50. Matthews was also caught and given ten weeks' hard labour.

The strike dragged on through Christmas and with no money

coming in workers were forced back to work on 22nd January. Northern unions were reluctant to give cash support as Cornish miners had a reputation as strike breakers.

In the early 1900s the new Workers' Union started organising clay workers. **Joe Harris, Matt Giles** and **Charles Vincent** led the campaign. **Julia Varley,** an organiser from the Black Country came down to rally clay wives.

1913 Clay Strike
In 1911 they pressed for improvements in their harsh conditions. Their

March through St Austell in support of the strike

image: Workers Union Annual Report 1914

The 'Cornish Alps'

demands were:

♦ An eight-hour-day

♦ Wages paid once a fortnight

♦ An hour a day lunch-break

♦ A rise of five shillings to £1.25s a week

The clay companies rejected the demands and on 21st July 1913 the workers at the Carne Stents Pit near Trewoon walked out. The dispute quickly won the support of almost all clay miners. A few strike-breakers were reportedly beaten up

and at Nanpean a can of dynamite exploded on the window sill of a shift manager's house.

On 2nd August a procession through St Austell was led by the **Rev H Booth-Coventry** and Matt Giles. A meeting of some 2,000 miners held at Bugle in August 1913 was warned by the Deputy Chief Constable. "I don't want you to get into trouble," he declared. The workers marched on the engine house in Karslake. They made their protest and walked back singing hymns.

China clay water cannon

The 200-strong police force realised they were out-numbered. 100 Welsh police from Glamorgan were brought in along with 60 from Bristol and 30 from Devon. Some had been trained to break up strikes and were considered less likely to be swayed by the local community.

As the strike dragged on the miners ran out of money. They sold what they could, including family treasures, to survive.

In October the Glamorgan police seemed set on a fight at Bugle. **Julia Varley,** was pushed to the ground, batons were drawn and when the police charged some of the miners were wounded.

In a poll of the workers 2,258 voted to continue the strike but the strain was being felt. Pickets attacked Halviggan

The Cyclist Section of the Cornwall Police were able to reach various parts of the strike area 'very rapidly' before the foot police could arrive.

engine house and teenager, Howard Vincent shot PC Collet, a local police officer, in the thigh.

On 5th October a conference in the Public Rooms in St Austell voted to return to work.

Despite the defeat spirits were remarkably high and the strike helped bolster trade unionism across Cornwall.

With nowhere big enough for members to meet, on 1st January 1914 a Union Hall was opened by Joe Harris in Nanpean, built for £100. A few months later another hall was built at Foxhole. It was opened by Rev Booth-Coventry. By 1933

the wooden hut was replaced and became the offices for the Transport and General Workers Union.

Joe Harris became a popular Labour leader in Cornwall and union membership grew.

In February 1914 there was a new three-year pay deal that actually gave more than the 25 shillings claimed in the strike.

The dispute politicised the workforce. When war broke out many clay workers refused to volunteer to fight. The strike hero, Rev Booth-Coventry was even booed when he appealed for the workers to support the war effort.

Stocker's Copper

A TV *Play for Today* called *Stocker's Copper* was shown in 1972 telling the story of the strike. Written by Tom Clarke, the play focuses upon the relationship between clay striker and police officer.

In the film, Manuel Stocker, one of the striking miners, is forced to earn cash by taking in a lodger, Herbert Griffith, a police officer from Glamorgan. Their friendship starts to grow but the tension of the strike increases.

The film ends as the police read the Riot Act and break up the picket-line to smash the strike and the relationship between the two men.

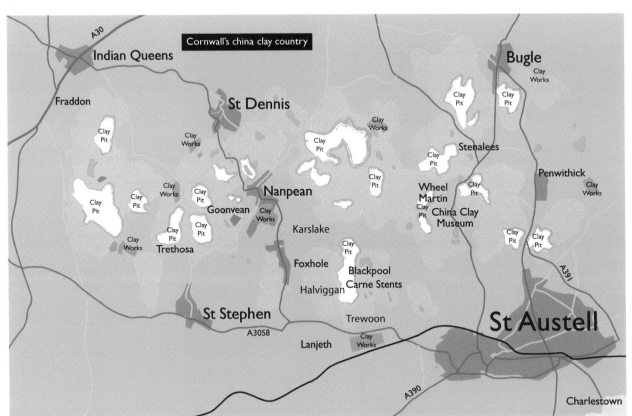

The Cornish Clay Strike

Perhaps it's interesting, and I guess that you would like
to hear an account of the Cornish Clay Strike:
Well, the men at Carne Stents first to down tools,
And for taking that action were counted as fools.

But as you see their policy proved a blessing in disguise,
and has proved to the world that they really were wise,
Virginia men were next, and they had the nerve
and around the Fal Valley they all did serve.

To Kernick and Trethosa their course then they took
and down in those pits the crowd did look;
But the men were ignorant of the union resolution.
The great problem to them simply had no resolution.

Well then, friend, I think that they passed by Goonvean
and held a great meeting at the bottom of Nanpean.
The organisers went there the strikers to meet
They stood on the hedge and the man on the street.

At Foxhole we settled next morning to meet
The old scheme of wages we had to defeat;
For wages at present only just keep us alive
and now we are determined to reach 'twenty-five'.

The course we then took was a place called Lanjeth,
And when we got there we were just out of breath,
But whilst waiting there a kind of friend we found,
Who opened his gate and in the field we sat down.

By the leaders, on the ground, some speeches were given,
And by the time they had done, the clock struck eleven
After some consultation as to the course we should take
The men were unanimous for Blackpool to make.

In the China Clay area the motors are near flying,
To starve out the men the employers are trying,
But the Cornish are solid and determined to fight
To get the twenty-five shillings which they think is their right.

The world is now watching with an anxious eye,
To help these gallant claymen we hope you will try.
There is just one word more and then I have done –
Please give a donation to the Strike Relief Fund.

It is my pleasure, dear friends, to write part number two
of the China Clay Strike, which we have passed through.

Well after a month's struggle it commenced to rain
So the employers did their utmost to get back their men.

For these heavy showers helped fill in the pits
And just frightened the poor fellows into fits
Then the next move was to import some hundred of police
Who would have us to believe they were sent to keep peace.

So all through the dispute ran the spirit of peace
Until it was broken by the Glamorgan police
Who I imagine fell in love too much with the barrel
And then John Barleycorn soon induced them to quarrel

The Glamorgan police were all watching their tricks,
And demanded the pickets to give up their sticks,
When they caught a small number down in a by-lane,
They acted like demons or men gone insane.

Poor Vincent, our leader, was the first they attacked,
Was truncheoned and batoned and his poor head they cracked;
I suppose they then left him by the roadside for dead
But they couldn't kill his spirit though they opened his head.

Well, six weeks had passed, and I would just like to note
That we decided to ballot and let the men vote;
The men were out against their will was the constant report,
So we wanted to the public 'twas a false report'.

After taking their vote proved twasn't so;
To go to work two-thousand two-hundred and fifty-eight said
"No".
To go back on the old conditions this was the best,
One five hundred and sixty-eight voted yes.

Well, after ten weeks of hard fighting, we decided to retreat,
But some may claim it to be a defeat,
We are not downhearted, boys, no not yet,
For an advance in wages we hope soon to get.

So boys join the workers union
And win the victory next time,
And if you'll promise to do so, why then I'll end my rhyme,
To see you all in the union is just what we would like,
Then we could settle by arbitration and thus avoid a strike.

Written by an unknown striker

Newquay Headland Riot

Silvanus Trevail was a Cornish architect and property developer. He built several major coastal hotels including King Arthur's Castle at Tintagel, Carbis Hay Hotel in St. Ives, Housel Bay on the Lizard, the Pendennis Hotel in Falmouth and both the Atlantic and Headland Hotels in Newquay. Other examples of his work can be found across Cornwall.

It was Silvanus Trevail's development of the Headland Hotel in 1897 that caused controversy with local fishermen and farmers. He planned to build on the coastal land where they dried their nets and grazed cattle.

It was on 31st August 1897 that the riot occurred. Fearing for their livelihoods, the locals tore down the wall and construction site office, throwing the planks over the headland. When Silanus Trevail arrived to see the damage he was pelted with eggs and apples.

Five men were convicted and fined for assaulting Trevail and 21 were convicted and fined £2 each for their part in the disturbances.

In a letter now on display in the hotel, William Pearse, Secretary to the Board of Directors, states that the "disturbances originated in the ill-advised attempt of the Directors of the Atlantic Hotel to fence in a portion of the land."

But the directors brushed aside any potential challenge by the Commons Protection Society and committed to "push on the building with all possible speed."

The Headland Hotel is now a prominent feature on the Newquay coastline.

The Headland Hotel being built

Bodmin Moor

● **Newquay**

● **Truro**

photos: on display at Headland Hotel

The morning after the riots

Headland Hotel, Newquay

Newlyn Riots

In May 1896 fears over loss of trade to east coast fishing boats spilled over into violence. There was tension between the communities over fishing on the sabbath. The new quays built at Newlyn had opened up the port to larger drifters from Yarmouth and Lowestoft. Sunday fishing meant that they could land their catch sooner than the local boats. On Monday 18th May an angry crowd boarded the east coast boats and threw their catches into the harbour. Attacks continued over the next few days with fishermen from St Ives, Mousehole, Porthleven and the Scilly Isles supporting the Newlyn cause.

300 Royal Berkshire soldiers were dispatched to Penzance and Navy ships sent to keep order. A pitched battle ensued at Larrigan River but faced with formidable numbers of troops the crowds dispersed.

The east coast boats switched to Plymouth. Eight Newlyn men were charged and after short sentences they returned home in triumph, met by bands and bunting. But younger generations of Newlyn fishermen soon started fishing on Sundays.

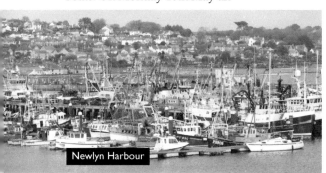

Newlyn Harbour

Memorial to Newlyn fishermen

Coffin ships

Greedy ship owners would often overload ships to maximise their profits. But such ships were dangerous and more liable to capsize in rough seas. Sailors often took matters into their own hands and refused to sail such ships even if this meant imprisonment.

In 1855, a group of sailors calling themselves 'The seamen of Great Britain' wrote to Queen Victoria complaining that courts had found them guilty of desertion for refusing to go to sea in dangerous ships.

Around the same time, an inspector of prisons reported that nine out of twelve prisoners in the jails of South West England were sailors, imprisoned for twelve weeks for refusing to sail in so-called 'coffin-ships' they considered to be unseaworthy.

In 1866, several crews were jailed, one after the other, when they refused to set sail in an old ship named *Harkaway*. The sailors complained that even at anchor on a calm sea, the ship took in water to a depth of more than a metre each day. The *Harkaway* finally set sail for the West Indies with its loaded cargo after it had taken on board its fifth crew.

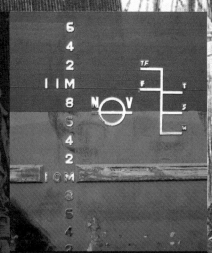

Plimsoll Line

In 1875 the *Sunbeam* put into Plymouth Sound with its crew refusing to cross the Atlantic due to the ship's poor conditions. In court the sailors claimed that the ship was utterly rotten and that they preferred prison to an untimely death. Found not guilty of mutinous conduct the fifteen men were freed. In support, the Plymouth Co-operative Society gave them £5.

Plimsoll Line

After a long campaign to make ships safer, **Samuel Plimsoll** MP was successful and the Merchant Shipping Act of 1876 made load lines compulsory. The basic symbol, of a circle with a horizontal line passing through its centre, is now recognised worldwide.

When a ship is loaded, the water level must not go above the 'Plimsoll Line' with variants displayed to take into account temperature, saltiness, season and location.

SAMUEL PLIMSOLL
BORN 1824 – DIED 1898
ERECTED BY THE MEMBERS
OF THE NATIONAL UNION OF
SEAMEN, IN GRATEFUL
RECOGNITION OF HIS
SERVICES TO THE
MEN OF THE SEA
OF ALL NATIONS

Statue to Samuel Plimsoll erected in London by the National Union of Seamen

Early refugees

The history of the West Country includes people and influences from all over the world. The stories of early migrants are often hidden or lost.

Huguenots and Walloons

French and Flemish Protestants faced with persecution on mainland Europe sought refuge in Britain including across the West Country. They brought new ideas especially in textile production and silversmith techniques as well as non-conformist religion. 'Flemings' appear in registers of Dartmouth, and Walloons came to Plymouth in the 16th century.

The Huguenot community settled in Stroud and helped establish the woollen industry in the town.

In October 1685, Louis XIV of France declared Protestantism illegal with the revocation of the Edict of Nantes. The exodus of Protestant Huguenots deprived France of many of its most skilled and industrious individuals, who would from now on aid the country's rivals in Holland and England.

Many Huguenot asylum seekers escaped by hiding in bales of goods and heaps of coal. Some came in empty casks using only the bung-hole to breathe. As a result they tended to arrive in and settle around South West ports. Huguenot congregations were formed in Barnstaple, Bideford, Dartmouth, Exeter and Plymouth.

Miss Boursiquot came to Barnstaple where she married fellow refugee **Jacques Fontaine**. The register of St Peter's parish church entered her name as Bazzacott! Jacques Fontaine wrote of their experience: "the good people of Barnstaple were full of compassion, they took us into their houses and treated us with the greatest kindness. Thus God raised up for us fathers and mothers in a strange land."

Barnstaple gained from the new arrivals. They introduced innovations in the wool trade including new methods of manufacture and dyeing for which the north Devon town became famous. The region's cloth trade was boosted by the Huguenots such as in Shepton Mallet, Bradford-on-Avon, Corsham and Trowbridge.

Around 500 settled in Bristol, about 2.5 per cent of the city's population. The **Bonnets** were one family from France who hid their two small children in panniers slung on their donkey. When a soldier stopped them he thrust his bayonet into one of the bags. The distraught parents had to wait until it was safe to check. Luckily the child was only stabbed in the leg.

St Mark's chapel, on College Green, was provided by Bristol Corporation for the Huguenots to use.

The refugees were not welcomed by everyone. Sir John Knight, the Tory MP for Bristol spoke out in parliament against "the naturalizing of foreigners". He warned that such arrivals would "sacrifice our English liberties to a number of mercenary foreigners."

He claimed that the migrants were

The Flemish Weaver pub in Corsham, Wiltshire

those "who can work cheaper than the English." And that: "the profit will be theirs and not England's". He asked: "will not the new-made English (yet foreigners still) return to their country and friends with their gain?"

"Should this Bill pass, it will bring as great afflictions on this nation as ever fell upon the Egyptians."

He compared the French to a plague of frogs and speaking against proposals to support the refugees, he said: "Let us first kick the Bill out of this house and then the foreigners out of the kingdom."

The Huguenots were well-organised, educated and well-connected. Not only did they bring new skills and techniques but they helped ports such as Bristol develop international connections.

Beer Spaniards
A Spanish ship was wrecked off the south Devon coast near Beer.

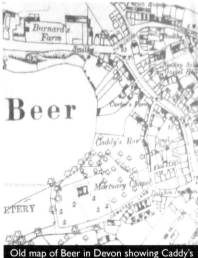

Old map of Beer in Devon showing Caddy's Row (formerly Cadiz Row after the Spanish that lived there

St Mark's chapel, Bristol used by the Huguenots when they first arrived in the city

The village had lost over half its population in the plague and so the crew stayed and settled. Beer folk became know as the Spaniards.

Black people in the West
In 1688 when William of Orange landed in Brixham, Devon to take the English throne, he brought with him some 200 blacks from the plantations owned by the Netherlands. There is an account of them marching through Devon on their way to London.

As a maritime, trading region, the West Country was the first encounter for many foreign sailors and travellers. Some settled here and became part of their local community.

Early records of black people in the West Country, however, are most often associated with the slave trade.

Campaign against slavery

The West Country continues to live with the legacy of the part it played in the trans-Atlantic slave trade.

Sir John Hawkins from Devon sailed the first English ship to transport Africans as slaves to the Americas in 1562.

His early attempts to exploit West African slaves were not especially profitable. Hawkins faced fierce resistance despite having superior weapons and some help from local rulers. On one raid he lost seven men and only captured ten slaves. In the Caribbean he faced further problems selling slaves to the Spanish.

Slaving voyages were limited until the massive growth in the trade in the 18th century.

Bristol, in particular, grew wealthy on the back of the trans-Atlantic slave trade. Ports around the South West were involved in the triangular route that took ships with goods to buy slaves in Africa, transported them in horrific conditions to the plantations of the West Indies and back to Britain with profitable sugar and tobacco crops.

In Dorset, the Drax, Pinney and Hallett families made their fortunes from the slave trade. In 1699, Richard Hallett brought black servants back to his estate in Lyme Regis.

The most well-known slave brought to the West Country is **Scipio Africanus**, whose real name is not known. He was servant to Charles William, Earl of Suffolk and Brandon, who married one of the Astry family

Scipio, one of the first slaves in the UK, buried in St Mary's Churchyard, Henbury, Bristol

of Henbury House. Scipio Africanus died in December 1720 at the age of 18. The verse on the stone at Scipio's feet refers to him becoming a Christian and the benefits of his Christian belief.

Another of the early African slaves was **Pero** who is remembered by Pero's Bridge in Bristol. Pero was the personal servant of John Pinney (1740-1818) a very rich Bristol merchant.

Of African-Caribbean origin, Pero came to England in 1783 as a slave. It is likely he was born in the tiny Caribbean island of Nevis. Pero's parents were black slaves and probably African-born. When Pero was twelve-years-old, he and his younger sisters: Nancy, who was eight, and Sheeba six, were sold to John Pinney. He was taught how 'to shave and dress hair.' and how to pull teeth.

Pero's Bridge, Bristol

PERO'S BRIDGE
THIS BRIDGE IS DEDICATED TO THE MEMORY OF PERO AN ENSLAVED MAN OF AFRICAN ORIGIN WHO WAS BROUGHT FROM THE CARIBBEAN ISLAND OF NEVIS TO BRISTOL IN 1783. HE WAS A SERVANT OF THE PINNEY FAMILY WHO LIVED IN WHAT IS NOW THE GEORGIAN HOUSE MUSEUM IN GREAT GEORGE STREET. HE DIED IN THE CITY IN 1798.
March 1999

When John Pinney returned to live with his family in Bristol, he brought Pero with him but left Pero's sisters behind, sold to Charles Huggins, a man known for his cruelty. Pero died in 1798, aged 45, in Ashton, Bristol.

The bridge, built in 1999, was the first significant project in the city to mark the sacrifices made by slaves and to recognise the role of slavery in the history of Bristol.

Olaudah Equiano

was a slave who gained his freedom and wrote about his experience. His work had a powerful influence on the growing campaign for abolition. He first landed in Cornwall as a slave. In his book, *Interesting Narrative* he describes his visit to Falmouth in 1757 when he was aged twelve:

Olaudah Equiano

"At last the ship arrived at Falmouth, after a passage of thirteen weeks. Every heart on board seemed gladdened on our reaching the shore, and none more than mine. I was very much struck with the buildings and the pavement of the streets in Falmouth; and, indeed, any object I saw filled me with new surprise."

He describes seeing snow for the first time, thinking it to be salt.

The Life of Olaudah Equiano

"I was astonished at the wisdom of the white people in all things I saw; but was amazed at their not sacrificing, or making any offerings, and eating with unwashed hands, and touching the dead. I likewise could not help remarking the particular slenderness of their women, which I did not at first like; and I thought they were not so modest and shamefaced as the African women."

When Olaudah returned in 1777 he arrived at Plymouth as a freeman. He wrote about "pious friends" in Plymouth and Exeter.

The Navy employed Equiano as Commissary for Stores but he was sacked when he uncovered corruption and waste at Plymouth. The Navy later paid him £50 for his work.

West Country slaves

During this period some West Country sailors were enslaved by North Africans. Some were captured within sight of the South West coast. Ransoms were paid by those with the funds but more died overseas.

Bridgwater petition

The first town to petition Parliament for the abolition of the slave trade was Bridgwater in Somerset in 1785. Some believe it was because of the legacy of local men transported into slavery in the West Indies following the Battle of Sedgemoor. 612 Somerset men sailed in eight ships. Many died on the voyage or on the quayside awaiting auction. After four years, survivors were pardoned but only a few made it home to tell of their lives in bondage.

South West abolitionists

In September 1830 there was a meeting in Illfracombe calling for the abolition of slavery and a Devon and Exeter Society for the Abolition of Slavery was reported in 1832. **William Davy**, from Exeter, was one of the counsels who defended James Somerset, a re-captured slave.

Exeter painter, **Benjamin Robert Haydon,** did a painting of the World Anti-Slavery Convention in 1840.

Anti-slavery campaigner, **Thomas Clarkson** (1760-1846) is commemorated with a blue plaque at Seven Stars Inn, Thomas Lane, Bristol. In 1787 Mr Thompson, the publican, helped Clarkson find out about the horrors of the trans-Atlantic slave trade. Clarkson interviewed sailors and other crew members to find out about conditions on board the slave

Thomas Clarkson

Seven Stars Inn, Bristol

The Stroud Arch and associated plaque

conditions including cruelty and bullying, especially towards black sailors. There was a tremendously high death rate – it was normal for up to a quarter of any crew and its prisoners to die from disease during a voyage.

Rev Henry Bleby who fought against slavery in the West Indies was born in Winchcome, Gloucestershire. He witnessed the slave revolt led by Samuel Sharp that brought forward the end of slavery. It was 1831 when the rebellion swept through Jamaica involving around 60,000 slaves. Despite Britain's opposition to slavery, British troops were used to quell the uprising. Hundreds were executed as plantation owners tried to regain control. Henry Bleby gave his account of the massacres to the Anti-Slavery Society and wrote books on his experience.

Henry Woolcombe was a Plymouth anti-slavery campaigner. He is said to have rescued 737 slaves by Naval patrols off the West Indies.

The Stroud Arch

Henry Wyatt (1793-1847) was a wealthy local business-man and Stroud MP. The Stroud Anti-Slavery Society in 1832 put pressure on the newly-elected MP for the abolition of slavery in Parliament. A petition, whose signatories constituted a roll call of non-conformist tradesmen and manufacturers of the Stroud area, urged immediate and entire abolition without compensation.

This proposal was too radical for the new Whig government; in 1834 the Emancipation Act paid the slave owners £20 million; the slaves got no compensation. However Henry Wyatt was moved to erect an arch

ships. Many crew members were frightened to talk to him because they might not get any further work if they told how bad conditions were.

Clarkson was threatened and beaten up on several occasions during his investigation. He found that conditions on the ships were appalling. The enslaved Africans suffered the most, and were treated in a very brutal manner in order to try to break their spirit and crush any potential resistance.

Even the crews faced dreadful

at the entrance to his carriage drive. Inscribed "Erected to commemorate the abolition of slavery in the British Colonies the first of August AD MDCCCXXXIV". It is a unique monument of this size in Britain.

Another Bridgwater petition

In 1846 **Frederick Douglass**, a runaway slave from America gave a lecture in Bridgwater about his experience and the campaign for abolition. His accounts of how slaves were branded with hot irons and nailed to the walls by their ears led to another petition being gathered amongst the people of the town. Some 1,200 people signed the demand to end slavery that was sent to Bridgewater in Massachusetts. An exchange of letters followed in which Bridgewater explained that slavery was no longer practiced in the state.

Hannah More (1745-1833) was educated in Bristol. She was the most influential female member of the Society for Effecting the Abolition of the African Slave Trade.

More helped run the Abolition Society and wrote *Slavery,* a poem to promote the cause. She worked closely with William Wilberforce and spent the summer of 1789 holidaying with him in the Peak District.

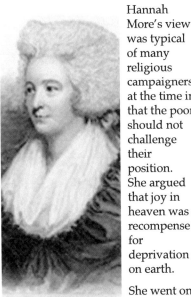

Hannah More's view was typical of many religious campaigners at the time in that the poor should not challenge their position. She argued that joy in heaven was recompense for deprivation on earth.

She went on to establish Sunday

Hannah More

Schools in the Mendip Hills. She earned nearly £30,000 from her books making her one of the most successful writers of her day.

Hannah More helped **Ann Yearsley** to publish anti-slavery poems. Ann began work selling milk but by 1785 her poems brought her fame although the two women fell out. Ann became known as the 'Poetical Milk Woman of Bristol'.

Mary Carpenter (1807-1877) campaigned against the slave trade. She was born in Exeter, the daughter of a Unitarian minister. In 1835 she helped organise a Working and Visiting Society, to provide education to working class families. She was its secretary for the next twenty years. She supported the setting up of so-called Ragged Schools including one in Lewins Mead, Bristol to which she added a night-school for adults.

Mary Carpenter wrote about the need for good free day-school and reformatory schooling for juvenile delinquents. She opened the country's first reform school for girls in Bristol – in what is now the Red Lodge Museum.

Dorset

Thomas Buxton was a Dorset abolitionist and was President of the Anti-Slavery Society.

In 1833 Buxton wrote of the abolition support in Bridport: "Almost everyone seemed ready to give their names with their whole hearts. Many who could not write seemed as if they thought the blood of all the Negroes would be on them if they did not make their mark."

Elected as the MP for Weymouth from 1818 to 1823, Buxton was a Quaker, along with fellow Dorset campaigner **William Foster** who reported on the horrors of slavery.

James Stephens was born in 1758 in Poole. He became a lawyer specialising in trade. He worked with William Wilberforce in the drafting of the 1807 Abolition Act.

William Stephens was from Bridport and possibly a relative of James. He was an active abolitionist as was the **Reverend John James** who was born in Blandford in 1785.

The 'ladies of Lyme Regis' and 'female inhabitants of Charmouth' sent petitions to Parliament against slavery and in May 1833 towns of West Dorset petitioned for abolition.

Thomas Lewis Johnson (1836-1921) settled in Bournemouth in the 1890s and wrote about his life as a slave in Virginia. He spoke at events all over the country and became a British citizen in 1900.

His book, *Twenty-eight years a slave: the story of my life on three continents* was published in 1909.

Thomas Lewis Johnson

Bristol's slavery connections

Much of the centre of Bristol had an association with the Trans-Atlantic slave trade. Grand houses, churches and theatres were built using the profits of slavery. Bristol lost its importance as a port when bigger ships used Liverpool rather than navigate the narrow Avon Gorge.

1 The trail begins at the @Bristol exploratory and Millennium Square and takes about an hour and a half to complete.

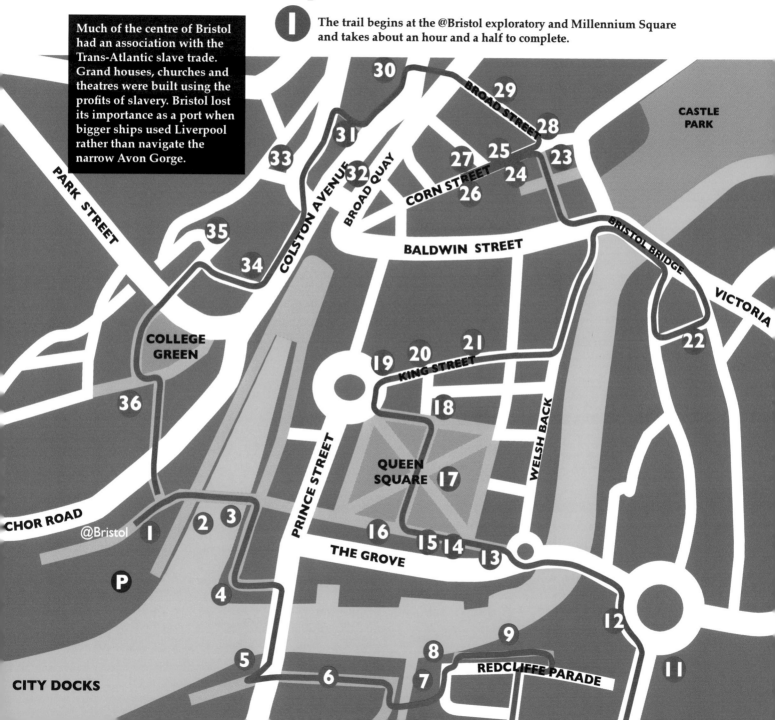

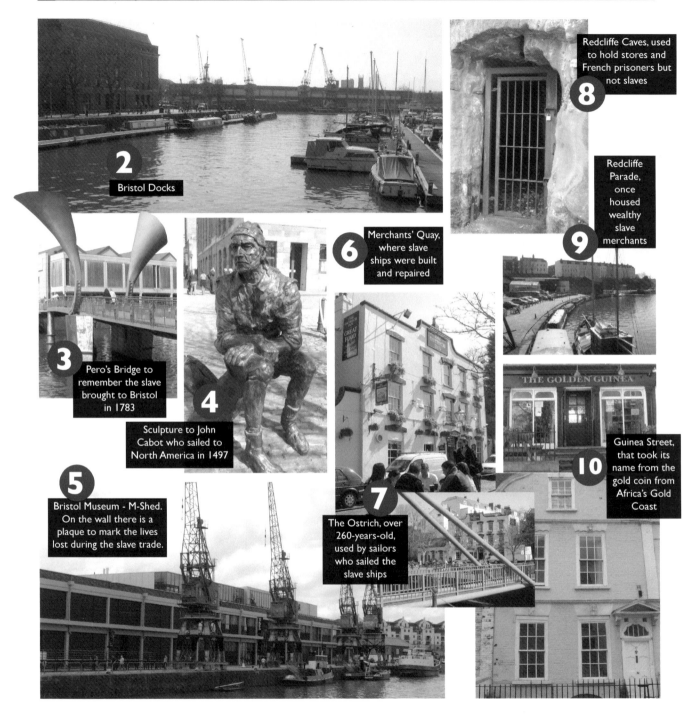

2 Bristol Docks

3 Pero's Bridge to remember the slave brought to Bristol in 1783

4 Sculpture to John Cabot who sailed to North America in 1497

5 Bristol Museum - M-Shed. On the wall there is a plaque to mark the lives lost during the slave trade.

6 Merchants' Quay, where slave ships were built and repaired

7 The Ostrich, over 260-years-old, used by sailors who sailed the slave ships

8 Redcliffe Caves, used to hold stores and French prisoners but not slaves

9 Redcliffe Parade, once housed wealthy slave merchants

10 Guinea Street, that took its name from the gold coin from Africa's Gold Coast

11 St Mary Redcliffe church, grew to be one of the largest parish churches in Britain from the wealth of the slave trade

19 Offices of the Merchant Venturers and next door, their alms houses. The Society started in the fourteenth century. It lobbied government to gain access to the lucrative 'African' trade and grew rich on slavery.

20

12 Quaker Burial Ground. Quakers campaigned against the slave trade

13 Hole in the Wall, named after the spy hole used to warn sailors of press gangs

15 WOODES ROGERS 1679-1732 Great Seaman, Circumnavigator, Colonial Governor Lived in a house on this site

21 The Old Vic, built in the 1760s by wealthy slave merchants

14

Queen Square, built for the richest slave traders: such as Woods Rogers, described as "Great Seaman. The first American consulate and the Custom House are in the Square

17 **18**

16 IN A HOUSE ON THIS SITE THE FIRST AMERICAN CONSUL IN GREAT BRITAIN WAS ESTABLISHED IN SEPTEMBER 1792

22 Seven Stars Thomas Clarkson, who exposed the horrors of slavery, was based here

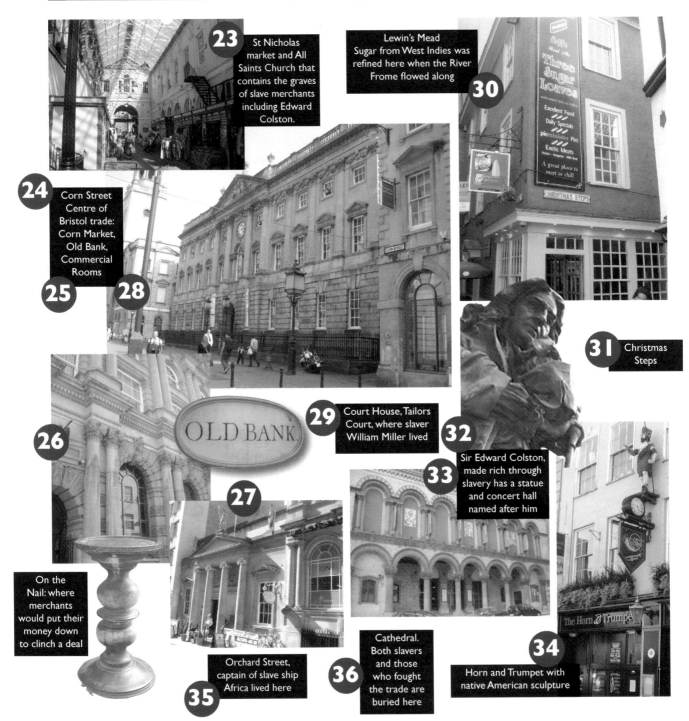

23 St Nicholas market and All Saints Church that contains the graves of slave merchants including Edward Colston.

Lewin's Mead Sugar from West Indies was refined here when the River Frome flowed along **30**

24 Corn Street Centre of Bristol trade: Corn Market, Old Bank, Commercial Rooms

25 **28**

31 Christmas Steps

26

OLD BANK

29 Court House, Tailors Court, where slaver William Miller lived

32

Sir Edward Colston, made rich through slavery has a statue and concert hall named after him

33

27

On the Nail: where merchants would put their money down to clinch a deal

Orchard Street, captain of slave ship Africa lived here **35**

Cathedral. Both slavers and those who fought the trade are buried here **36**

Horn and Trumpet with native American sculpture **34**

Working class education

Working class children were largely denied education until the industrial revolution exposed the need to have a labour force that could be trained. Social reformers were moved by the plight of uneducated youngsters and religious campaigners saw schooling as a way to bring people to the Church.

Robert Raikes House in Southgate Street, Gloucester

Bluecoat schools

Bluecoat schools date back to Tudor times and were a type of elementary school maintained by voluntary and church contributions for teaching poor children to read and write.

The schools provided clothing and education freely or at little charge. Blue was a favoured colour for charity school children because it was the cheapest available dye.

Statue to Exeter Bluecoat School

Sunday Schools

Robert Raikes (1736-1811) started the Sunday School Movement. He was the publisher of the *Gloucester Journal* based in Southgate Street. But he is best known for his work to help poor boys. The best available time for education was Sunday as boys were often working in the factories the rest of the week. The first

Robert Raikes memorial in Gloucester Park

Sunday School began in 1780.

Raikes used his newspaper to promote the school and bore most of the cost in the early years. Later, girls attended and within two years, several schools opened in Gloucester.

By 1831, Sunday schools in Britain were attended by some 1,250,000 children, some 25% of the population. These schools are sometimes seen as a forerunner to the current English school system.

State Education

The Elementary Education Act 1870

Mount Charles Elementary School in St Austell, Cornwall. The first built under the 1870 Education Act

began the process to providing schooling for all. It set up School Boards and paid for children whose parent could not afford the fees.

By 1880 the law insisted on compulsory attendance from 5–10 years and the Free Education Act 1891 provided for the state payment of school fees up to ten shillings per week.

Workers Education Association

Every year thousands of adults take up learning with the Workers Education Association. They run courses from learning about the internet to local history.

The Association is over 100-years-old and was formed by **Albert Mansbridge** (1876-1952) who was born near the India House in Barton Street, Gloucester. His father was a carpenter and his mother an active member of the Women's Co-operative Guild.

Albert wanted "workers to have their share of the kingdom of the mind," according to biographer Mary Stocks. He was working as a clerk for the Co-op when he sought to win trade union support for his mission to bring education to working people.

Albert became a teacher and in 1903 established the Association for Promotion of Higher Education for Working Men, later to be re-named the WEA. He wrote a book called *An Adventure in Working Class Education* in which he said: "Every living person is potentially a student."

Albert helped found the South West Co-operative Housing Association and was chair between 1944-48 when it set out to provide homes after the war. A road on the Society's estate in Totnes, Devon is named after him.

He died in Torquay in 1952 and is buried in Gloucester Cathedral.

Swindon education

In 1843 fifteen workers from the Great Western Railway set up a modest library with 150 books. The next year, with the support of the company, a

Swindon Mechanics' Institute

Mechanics' Institute was established with the object of 'disseminating useful knowledge and encouraging rational amusement'.

Reuben George was a strong supporter of adult education in Swindon. George came to Swindon from Gloucester as a young man and worked there as agent for the Wesleyan and General Insurance Company. He supported the WEA and ran university extension lectures.

George was also a key figure in the formation of the Swindon Labour Party in 1916 and he was one of the first three Labour candidates to stand for Parliamentary election in Wiltshire. He was a Swindon Town Councillor and mayor in 1921-2.

Bristol Socialist schools

In Bristol there were attempts to establish a Socialist Sunday School in rooms rented to the Bristol Socialist Society facing the Horsefair, and known as "The Socialist Centre".

Ben Tillett opened one of these schools in 1894.

These paved the way for the Independent Labour Party's successful Schools at the Kingsley Hall, and the Socialist Guild of Youth Movement.

Radical voice

Swindon's first newspaper was founded by **William Morris** (1826-1891) in 1854. *The Swindon Advertiser and Monthly Record* was printed on a hand press in Wood Street. Morris acted as journalist, editor, printer and distributor. The paper often advocated progressive and controversial views. Morris became well known for his scathing editorial comments often aimed at Swindon's rich and powerful. He wanted to create a newspaper, "that would act as a mouthpiece for the poor."

His comments landed him in court on a number of occasions as he was forced to defend the paper against libel charges.

In 1861 he attacked local landowners who had held an extravagant feast at Coate Water. While the local poor starved they roasted a whole ox and used lumps of meat as footballs on the frozen lake.

The gentry were furious with Morris and even burned an effigy of him in the market square, along with as many copies of the *Advertiser* they could find.

The criticism didn't stop the newspaper from flourishing and later that year Morris moved production to Victoria Street and printed it on steam-powered presses made at the Great Western Railway works.

Daily publishing began in 1898, with it being renamed the *Evening Advertiser* in 1926.

Forest radicals

Isolated between the Severn and Wye rivers, the Forest of Dean has held on to old customs and traditions. People of the Forest are renowned for their independent spirit.

Sir Charles Dilke (1843-1911) was the Liberal MP for the Forest of Dean. He began his political career as MP for Chelsea and was destined for high office until a sex scandal ruined his chances. He was described as the "lost prime minister". He moved to the Forest of Dean where he became a champion for local people especially the miners.

Even after the birth of the Labour Party and strong support for socialism in the Forest of Dean, Charles Dilke continued to curry local favour. At a Socialist meeting in Cinderford Town Hall, the chairman, **Mr HC Hallam** of Littledean, declared that the Liberal MP "was one of the most helpful friends of practical Socialists in England. Socialists hoped that Sir Charles Dilke would continue to represent the Forest of Dean and when at last the inevitable time came he would be succeeded by an Independent Labour member."

When the local hospital was built, funded from subscriptions from local miners, it was named the Dilke Hospital.

After Charles Dilke, **James Wignall**, a trade union organiser for copper sheet rollers, was elected in 1918 as the first Labour MP for the Forest of Dean. He served until 1925.

David Organ (1876-1954) was President of the Forest of Dean Miners' Association. He helped lead the poorly-paid mine workers through the strike in 1920, the lock-out in 1921 and the General Strike in 1926.

Charles Dilke

Frank Hodges was a Forest of Dean miner who became Secretray of the Miners' Federation of Great Britain and Chief Negotiator with Lloyd George.

Charles Dilke encouraged **Morgan Philips Price** (1885-1973) into politics. At the age of 27, Price was adopted as the Liberal candidate for Gloucester but didn't win. He joined the Labour Party and for a few years the Communist Party.

He was the *Manchester Guardian's* correspondent in Russia and covered the 1917 Revolution. He left the paper but his support for the Bolsheviks was expressed in reports for the *Daily Herald.*

In 1923 Price went to Munich and saw first hand the threat of Hitler. His writings led some to describe him as one of the twentieth century's greatest journalists.

He returned home to the Forest of Dean and was elected MP in 1935, a post he held until his retirement in 1959.

Dilke Hospital in the Forest of Dean, opened in 1923

Leckhampton Riot

In 1894, Cheltenham music dealer Henry Dale, bought land around Leckhampton Hill near Cheltenham. He was keen to develop the land and refused to recognise any of the traditional rights of way. He obstructed footpaths, fenced off a large area and even built a house, 'Tramway Cottage', for the foreman in an old gravel pit beside Daisybank Road, right over the main footpath and on the very spot where on bank holidays people from all around would gather.

On several occasions crowds destroyed fences which Dale had erected. In July 1902 four ring-leaders were charged with obstructing the police – **Walter Ballinger, Charlie Burford, Leonard Luce** and **John Price.** They were acquitted, which encouraged as many as 2,000 people

Locals demolish Tramway Cottage

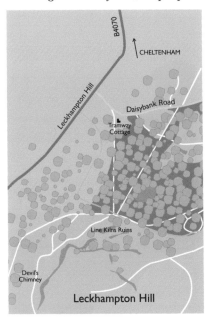

to stage a march. They made for Tramway Cottage, which they dismantled until hardly a stone was left standing.

The court found in favour of Dale's enclosure and only three paths were granted as public rights of way. Dale then rebuilt the cottage exactly where it had been.

Local resentment smouldered, more marches were held, but the last battle was on Good Friday 1906. A crowd again gathered at Tramway Cottage. The police read the Riot Act. The crowd dispersed and arrests were made. At a trial in Gloucester sentences of 4-6 months' hard labour (reduced on appeal) were handed down to **Walter Ballinger, Charles Barrett, William Heaven, Leonard Luce, William Sparrow, Henry Wallace, James Williams** and **Ernest Young.**

Francis Mourton was Chairman and **George Townsend**, Secretary of the Stalwarts committee, whose

unofficial HQ was at the Wheatsheaf Inn. George Townsend wrote *The Ballad of Leckhampton Hill* and *The Writ* about the events.

By 1929, the quarry company had gone out of business and Cheltenham Town Council purchased the 400-acre estate, so that people could walk freely over it once more.

Tramway Cottage today

Woods open for ever

From the middle ages, pilgrims and drovers walked through St Anne's Woods, Brislington in Bristol to a ferry to cross the River Avon. In 1884 James Sinnott, a solicitor, bought St Anne's Estate and installed locks on the gates at each end.

One man, who lived in Brislington and worked at Bristol Wagon Works in Lawrence Hill, had to walk an extra three miles to work.

Outraged at the action of Sinnot, he appealed to the Bristol and District Footpath Preservation Society to re-open the route. The Vice-Presidents of the Society included Rev Canon Ainger, the Lord Bishop of Bath and Wells, and Archdeacon Wilson.

In January 1891, after a campaign lasting six years and long trial, the mediaeval right of way was "declared open for ever".

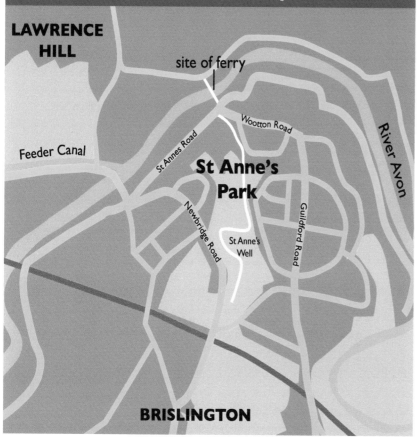

LAWRENCE HILL

site of ferry

Feeder Canal

Wootton Road

St Annes Road

St Anne's Park

River Avon

Newbridge Road

St Anne's Well

Guildford Road

BRISLINGTON

Walter Morrison

Walter Morrison (1836 -1921) was elected Liberal MP for Plymouth 1861-74. He was a supporter of the co-operative movement and women's suffrage.

In 1872 he proposed the Proportional Representation Bill but was defeated.

Rev Ben Parsons

Benjamin Parsons (1797-1855) was the minister of Ebley Chapel near Stroud for 28 years. He was a Chartist preacher who believed that the Bible was a radical book to promote social justice.

Parsons helped build local education including Ebley British School opened in 1840. In sermons and speeches he spoke out against slavery, land enclosures, the Corn Laws and Church Rate which non-conformists still had to pay. He advocated rights for women, strict observance of the sabbath, peace and temperance.

When he died in 1855 a granite monument was erected in the church yard with the help of public subscription.

Miners' mutual

In 1866 two non-conformist preachers in Cornwall, **Arthur Bray** and **Henry Cliff,** started the Miners' Mutual Benefit Association. Although mainly a provident society its benefits included strike pay.

Employers sacked anyone joining and a strike was called. Troops were called out and despite support from the Stone Cutter and Excavators Society the strike collapsed.

Cornish Bal Maidens

Women and children worked down or around mines from the earliest times. In Cornwall, they were called Bal Maidens, from a Cornish word for mining place.

The growth of industry boosted demand for Cornish copper. By the 1690s fleets of ships were taking the metal to Gloucestershire and onwards to the new factories of the Midlands. Women were used to 'dress' and 'pick' the copper. This was a process of washing the ore and picking out the good stones. It was casual and low-paid work. They would also do the cleaning, cooking and laundry at the pit head.

At the Delabole slate quarry women carried slate up to the storage yards and looked after the donkeys. A few worked as 'slitters', the most skilled job.

In 1736 Rev William Borlase complained at the difficulty of obtaining female servants because they could get better paid jobs in the mines.

In 1800 some 2,000 women were employed in Cornish mines and over 6,000 by 1851, a third of the workforce. Half of all women in Illogan and Gwennap worked in the mines. By the early 1900s women had all but disappeared from the mining workforce. Some women returned to the mines during the First World War.

Bal Maidens at work

Josephine Butler

Josephine Butler (1828-1906) was a social reformer who campaigned against the sexual exploitation of vulnerable women and children. The daughter of John and Hannah Grey, Josephine was born in Northumberland and is best known for her work in Liverpool but she lived for a period in Cheltenham.

She married George Butler and had four children. The family had strong radical views including support for the Union in the American Civil War.

When Eva, her six-year-old daughter, died after falling from the banisters at the top of the stairs Josephine became grief-stricken. She threw herself into feminist causes. She campaigned for higher education for women and for legislative reform to provide prostitutes with some degree of protection, equality and justice.

Josephine Butler led the campaign to repeal the Contagious Diseases Acts. Under the law magistrates could order a genital examination of women and those found to be infected with venereal diseases could be interned in locked hospitals for three months.

Josephine Butler's practical work fed into her own writing including: *The Education and Employment of Women*, and *Women's Work and Women's Culture*.

image: Clifford Harper

Agricultural unionism

The South West farm labourer was amongst the poorest in the country. **George Bartly** in his report, The *Seven Ages of a Village Pauper* (1874) described Dorset, Wiltshire and Somerset as competing to be the worst. The South West generally was a region of "wholesale neglect'.

Housing conditions were appalling. In the 1860s **Canon Edward Girdlestone** described the typical Dorset cottage: "built of mud, with a thatched roof. Many have only one bedroom. Enter one: a more dreary place it would be difficult to imagine." He wrote of the wretched rooms full of acrid smoke.

In 1867 **Dr Aldridge** spoke at a meeting of the Farmers Club in Dorchester where he described the cottages at Fordingham as being so bad "he would not put animals in such places".

Mr Selby, an agent of the Agricultural Labourers' Union, gave evidence to the Royal Commission on the Housing of the Working Classes in 1884. He spoke of cases in Wiltshire of seven and nine persons sleeping in one small bedroom.

Attempts to organise farm workers were made. In January 1846 a meeting of 1,000 workers was held in Goatacre, Wiltshire. But despite the inspiration of the Tolpuddle Martyrs it wasn't until the 1870s that agricultural unionism was established.

In 1872 **Joseph Arch,** a Methodist lay preacher, founded the National Labourers' Union to improve the lives of farm workers. He travelled the country to build and sustain the union through difficult times for rural communities.

Arch was often in the West Country. Farm workers were vulnerable to down-turns in the market for food but also to employer 'lock-outs' and

Farm worker evictions in Wiltshire

evictions. Families were often evicted for trade union support.

The growth of new unionism generated much debate about how far industrial power could change the lives of people. Joseph Arch knew that farm workers needed political influence too. In 1880 on his way to Salisbury, he was persuaded by the local Liberal Party to stand for Parliament for Wilton, the former county town of Wiltshire.

His election campaign included demands for land reform and opposition to Tory landlordism. One topical issue he felt strongly about

was to end flogging in the army. The short election campaign saw rowdy public meetings. Employers threatened workers, who had the vote, not to support Arch.

The result was 818 to Sidney Herbert, the Tory and brother of the Earl of Pembroke, and 397 for Arch. It didn't put Joseph Arch off and in 1885 he was elected as MP for North West Norfolk.

The union didn't fare well and by 1894 it had 1,100 members and accounts of just £2. In 1896 the union was dissolved but it paved the way for a much stronger union.

One from the plough
George Mitchell (1826-1901) was

born into poverty in Montacute in Somerset. He worked from the age of six and when he was nineteeen got a job in the stone quarry. He learnt the trade and became a successful businessman. But he didn't forget the hardships of the quarry and farm workers that he grew up with. He became known as *One from the plough*.

Mitchell became a key figure in the development of agricultural trade unionism. He called a meeting of farm workers on 3rd June 1872 in his home village of Montacute. The union branch was formed with 58 new members.

In 1877 George Mitchell organised a mass meeting at Ham Hill, near Yeovil. Farm workers marched accompanied by local brass bands. Some 20,000 people came to hear George Mitchell and Joseph Arch.

The event became an annual gathering of farm workers until 1892 when Mitchell spoke for the last time.

Bert Wellstead was a leading figure in building the union in Dorset along with **Fred James**. Bert was elected to

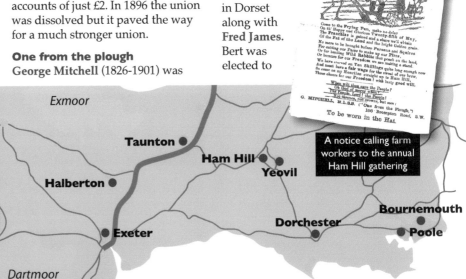

Mass meeting on Ham Hill in 1877 with Joseph Arch in centre

A notice calling farm workers to the annual Ham Hill gathering

Exmoor

Taunton ●

Ham Hill ●●
Yeovil

Halberton ●

Dorchester ●

Bournemouth ●
● Poole

● Exeter

Bodmin Moor

Dartmoor

Ham Hill

the National Executive and became a local Justice of the Peace. His father, **Harry Wellstead** was the last Dorset member of Arch's Union.

Gloucestershire

With the bad harvest of 1871, life for farm workers got even harder. By early 1872 families were starving.

Miners in the Forest of Dean formed a relief committee and workers realised they needed to get organised. In March a meeting was held in the Feathers Hotel in Staunton. **Thomas Strange**, a Primitive Methodists school teacher formed the Agricultural Labourers Improvement Society. A local branch was formed chaired by **Mr Barnes** with **John Stafford** as Secretary. More meetings were held in Stroud. They called for 15s a week instead of the 10-12s paid in the county.

William Yeates, a mechanic from Stroud helped build the union that merged with Arch's. He stood down after he mishandled money on a scheme for Brazilian emigration.

In 1874 there was a strike in Northleach. **James Spencer** organised meetings and services in local villages and said that "A true union spirit has taken the hearts of the agricultural classes in all the villages of the Cotswolds Hills."

3,000 workers met in Cirencester to hear Joseph Arch. Students from the agricultural college, called the 'blockheads', tried to disrupt his speech.

John Charles Ellicott, Bishop of Gloucester and Bristol hinted that farmers might find the village horsepond invitingly near when union organisers were around. Despite his retractions he was dubbed 'the horsepond bishop'.

Plymouth Joiner Leader

Devon-born **John Prior** became an apprentice carpenter and joiner in Plymouth. He led the local Joiners' Society and demands for better conditions led to a lock-out. His handling of the dispute enhanced his reputation and he was elected to the General Council of the Amalgamated Society of Carpenters and Joiners. He became General Secretary 1871 to 1881 after which he became HM Inspector of Workshops and Factories.

Canon aid

In 1863 the Rev Edward Girdlestone became rector of Halberton in north Devon. Canon Girdlestone came from Lancashire and was shocked by the conditions in which Devon labourers lived.

The cider was sour and meat scarcely ever on their tables. Dark, damp cottages caused premature arthritis. Labourers might earn 7s to 8s a week with nothing in kind and a wife's work was often included.

> *Labourers did not live in the proper sense of the word, they merely didn't die.*
> Canon Girdlestone

During the cattle plague (rinderpest) of 1866, Girdlestone told local farmers that it was a visitation from God because they were treating their labourers worse than their cattle! Local farmers were furious, as were other clergy. Only the Wesleyan minister sided with him.

Girdlestone helped some four to five hundred families move to the north west where he knew conditions were better.

Girdlestone was a pioneer of the agricultural labourers' trade union. By 1880 wages in the area had risen by 50 per cent and Halberton school had doubled the number of pupils since families could afford the fees.

Mural on Stapleton Road Station, Easton in Bristol depicting Ben Tillett, union leader

FORMER EASTON WAIF UNIONISES NATION'S UNSKILLED WORKERS

Easton & Bristol News

WORKERS' UPRISINGS FOR EMPLOYMENT REFORMS

GREAT LONDON DOCK STRIKE INSPIRES BRISTOL WORKERS

BEN TILLETT

New unionism

In the late 1800s saw the growth of 'general' unions. Not just skilled workers got organised but dockers, miners and factory hands. "New Unionism' was born and West Country workers were part of this movement.

British trade unionism had been dominated by craft unions. They were able to use their skill and labour control as means to increase their bargaining power. They matched friendly societies, offering a range of services such as funeral benefits and support during sickness and unemployment.

Unskilled workers were difficult to organise. They were often employed on a casual basis and in contrast to craft workers, could be easily replaced.

Women workers

The development of so-called 'new-unionism' was marked by the successful strike by women match workers in Bryant and May in London.

Emma Paterson (1848-1886) founded the first women's trade union: the Women's Protective and Provident Association in 1875 in Bristol. The union represented a wide range of workers including dressmakers,

upholsterers, bookbinders, artificial-flower makers, feather dressers, tobacco, jam and pickle workers, shop assistants and typists.

She went on to become the first woman member of the TUC General Council.

Emma Paterson

DEDICATED TO THE MEMORY OF EMMA PATERSON, 1848-1886 PIONEER OF TRADE UNIONISM, and FIRST WOMAN DELEGATE TO THE TRADES UNION CONGRESS in 1875.

Ben Tillett

Amongst the leaders of this new movement was **Ben Tillett** born into poverty at 8 John Street, Bristol in the shadow of the Easton Coal Pit. His mother died when he was a child and a succession of step-mothers treated him badly. He ran away from home as a child and found work as an acrobat in a circus. He also worked as a shoemaker but at the age of thirteen he joined the Navy. In 1876 he was wounded and left the service.

Tillett moved to London and after marrying Jane Tompkins he settled down in Bethnal Green and had nine children.

Ben Tillett became a Christian Socialist and joined the Temperance Society. He joined the Tea Operatives and General Labourers' Association and in 1887 was elected as General Secretary.

In 1889 Tillett's union was involved in the London Dock Strike. The dockers demanded four hours continuous work at a time and a minimum rate of sixpence an hour. During the strike Tillett lost his speech impediment and became one of the labour movement's greatest orators. After five weeks the employers granted all the dockers' main demands.

After the successful strike, the dockers formed the General Labourers' Union. Tillett was elected General Secretary and Tom Mann became the union's first President. In London alone, 20,000 men joined this new union. Tillett and Mann wrote a pamphlet together called *New Unionism,* where they outlined their socialist views and explained how

Ben Tillett

their ideal was a "co-operative commonwealth".

Tillett was one of England's leading socialists, a member of the Fabian Society and one of the founders of the Independent Labour Party.

In 1898 he met opera singer Eva Newton on a union visit to Australia. She was from a wealthy Sydney family, and he was fascinated by the theatre and by her different life-style. She became pregnant in 1899 and came back with Tillett to London. Their affair lasted thirty years or more and their four children were sworn to secrecy about their father's identity.

Tillett was one of the founders of the Labour Party but did not get on with its two main leaders, James Keir Hardie and Ramsay MacDonald. In 1908 he attacked the leadership in his pamphlet *Is the Parliamentary Labour*

Party a Failure? and soon afterwards left to join the Social Democratic Party.

In September 1910 Tillett helped to establish the National Transport Workers' Federation, an organisation of 250,000 workers. He became the leader of the union and in 1911 it won a national strike. However, the following year, Tillett's union suffered a defeat at the hands of the Port of London Authority. It was during this strike that Tillet helped found the trade union newspaper, the *Daily Herald.*

After a term as MP, Tillett retired from the House of Commons in 1931 and died in 1943. Tom Mann later retired to Wiveliscombe in Somerset.

In 2000 a Living Easton Time-Sign to Tillett was unveiled by Bill Morris, General Secretary of the Transport and General Workers Union.

Time-sign in Easton

Bristol trade unionism

The growth of general unions in the South West was centred around the large urban centres. Labourers in the building industry formed a Bristol Branch that had 800 members by 1873. The boot and shoe workers got organised with more than 3,000 members in Bristol and Kingswood.

A new militant mood came to life in the autumn of 1889 in Bristol. That year the Gasworkers branches of London and Bristol amalgamated. On 9th October they went on strike in support of a wage improvement. The company hired 120 scabs from Exeter but despite police escort failed to get them through the picket-lines. The employer agreed to the union demands.

The Bristol Trades Council organised a celebration attended by around 10,000 people. 2,000 dock workers then went on strike for more pay and after that struck again for a closed-shop.

With the support of the gasworkers and others, women cotton workers in Barton Hill Mill went on strike for better pay and conditions. On 26th October a huge procession through Bristol of some 15,000 people was addressed by Ben Tillett.

On the Strike Committee were **Helena Born** and **Miriam Daniell** from the Marxist Bristol Socialist Society founded in 1885.

Helena Born was born in Devon in 1860 and attended Hatherleigh School in Taunton. She loved music, and when the family moved to Bristol she sang in the choir of Oakfield Road Unitarian Church.

An artist and poet friend was Miriam Daniell, whose studies had led her to embrace socialism. Both had similar tastes. They explored nature in the course of long rambles and Miriam shared her enthusiasm for humanitarian causes.

They reflected links between the working class and middle class intellectuals but also between industrial and political ideas.

Helena and Miriam threw themselves into the work of the strike organising committee. They addressed meetings, led parades, helped collect strike funds and distribute relief. They gave up their comfortable quarters in Clifton to live in Louisa Street, St Phillips, a house that became a hive of socialist activity.

Miriam Daniell wrote a pamphlet on why equality between the sexes must be the hallmark of new unionism. Miriam and her lover, **Robert Allan Nichol**, wrote *The truth about chocolate factories or modern slavery, its cause and cure*. Nichol was named as co-respondent in the divorce in 1893 and after she fell pregnant the couple emigrated to Boston, America. The child, Eleanor, was called 'Sunrise'.

They were involved with the radical Boston Liberty Circle but Miriam died suddenly in 1901 in San Francisco.

The month-long Barton Hill strike attracted massive public support. The women settled after some modest concessions from the employer who had threatened to close down the works if the strike continued.

Sander's White Slaves
Enid Stacey (1868-1903) was a young middle class socialist active in the city of Bristol. Her father, Henry

Sharlands
The Sharland Brothers in the early 1870s with their mother, top row: James, John, Thomas; bottom row: Richard, their mother, Robert, William.

Active socialists in Bristol, they helped form the Social Democratic Federation and Labour League in the City.

Enid Stacey

Bristol gas workers' banner: No.1 Branch, now part of the GMB

Stacey was an artist and one of the leading socialists in the area. He painted the No.1 branch of Bristol Gasworkers' banner.

Enid became honorary secretary of the Association for the Promotion of Trade Unionism among Women. When her participation in strikes resulted in clashes with police she got fired from her job as a tutor.

When the women at Sanders Sweet Factory, Redcliffe Street, came to Enid for help in 1892 she told them to join the Gasworkers' Union.

The 300 women workers worked excessive hours, suffered large fines and were locked in the factory during dinner breaks! They revolted when the employer extended their hours of work by an hour-a-day and abolished their 15-minute meal-break! The nickname 'Sander's White Slaves' was well earned!

Bristol Strikes

Sarah Edwards, one of the women who had first talked to Enid, was dismissed. All of her workmates walked out! The strike began in early October 1892. The women went around Bristol every day with collecting boxes.

Gasworkers and dockers regularly marched with the women. In the same month, the dockers were locked out by the employers anxious to smash the Dockers' Union. Regular processions all added to a sense of crisis in the city.

From the start the police hounded the women and pickets. Following complaints in the press about begging, magistrates and police became increasingly hostile.

On 18th December 1892 the authorities banned an evening torch-light parade. The women accepted the ban and instead collected funds in the Horsefair. During the evening the police and militia charged them with batons, swords and lances! Miraculously no-one was killed although many were injured.

Black Friday

On Friday 23rd December 1892 another huge demonstration was organised. It was to be a peaceful lantern parade to collect money for the strikers and locked-out workers. The organisers agreed to police requests to ban the penny 'Chinese' lanterns but there was no agreement on the route.

Some 200 mounted troops tried to restrict and split the march. At Bristol Bridge there was a confrontation during which several people were hurt.

A meeting of members of the Liberal Reform Club, Brunswick Square, which was held that same evening, passed a resolution that appeared in the press next morning.

It condemned: "the dastardly conduct of the authorities for instructing the military and police to charge the peaceful and orderly meeting of citizens held in the Horsefair this evening."

Ben Tillett was arrested for 'inciting crowds to riot'. The trial that followed saw protests involving up to 30,000 people. The case was moved to London where he was acquitted.

In January 1893 the Sanders' strikers and the dockers joined forces and in drizzling rain five or six thousand paraded through the city to the Grove where two mass meetings were held.

A great demonstration was organised for Saturday 9th February 1893. The procession took a long route: West Street, Stapleton Road, Seymour Road, Newfoundland Road,

Bristol Bridge, scene of the 1892 Black Friday clash

Union Street, Bridge Street, Baldwin Street, and the Quay to the Grove. The marchers walked up to twelve abreast and the procession about a mile-and-a-half long. Fifteen bands of music were in attendance, and a wealth of banners displayed.

Support for the strikers grew and financial aid rose dramatically. Strike pay was now higher than the actual wages paid by Sanders!

The strike lasted until mid-1893. The employer conceded improvements in terms and conditions and the strikers returned to work. All of the sacked activists were placed in new jobs. The strike was hailed a success.

During the strike a total of 25 women were arrested and taken to court. In every case the union successfully defended them.

After the dispute Enid Stacey became active in the formation of the Independent Labour Party, becoming a travelling speaker for them in 1895. She spoke and wrote of her vision for socialism and women's rights. Enid died from an embolism aged just 29.

Bristol Hall of Science

In 1840 the Bristol Hall of Science was opened near Broadmead. It was to play host to music, theatre and lectures. Its first event was a debate on Socialism and the Utility of Public Institutions with Robert Owen as one of the speakers.

Called the "temple of Satan" by *Felix Farley's Journal*, the Hall could seat 3,000 people and in 1875 it became Broadmead Rooms.

THE MARCH OF THE WORKERS
FRIDAY, DEC. 23rd,
BIG LANTERN PARADE
OF THE
Locked-Out Deal Runners,
Sanders' White Slaves,
And the GENERAL ORGANIZED TRADES.
The PROCESSION will assemble at the GROVE, at 7 p.m. sharp.
FINISHING WITH
A MONSTRE MEETING
In the HORSEFAIR.
The Christmas Bells are ringing, the sky is clear and bright
Your masters pray for peace, but are compelling you to fight.
Labour to the Front.
Away with Politics.

Friday 23rd December 1892 became known as 'Black Friday'

Robert Gray Tovey

Bristol's first Labour Councillor

In 1886 the Bristol and District Labour League took on the City's Mayor, Charles Wathen in the St. Paul's ward. Robert Gray Tovey of the Clothiers Cutters' Association and Secretary of Bristol Trades Council was selected at a public meeting.

The League advocated municipalisation of water, lighting and tramway undertakings and the abolition of unnecessary sub-lettings of Corporation contracts.

Despite a dirty campaign during which Robert Tovey was called an atheist and a drunkard, he lost by just 18 votes in a shock result: 584 to 566.

The following year, Robert Tovey was successful, becoming the first Labour Councillor in Bristol.

Bert Alpass

The 1894 Local Government Bill created elected parish councils. In Berkeley, Gloucestershire in March 1895, **Joseph 'Bert' Alpass** a shop-worker, was elected to the Parish Council of Hamfallow and topped the poll for the Parish of Hinton in Sharpness of the Thornbury Rural District Council. Alpass was said to be the youngest parish councillor in England, with a keen desire to serve the poor and oppressed. He was a supporter of the Independent Labour Party.

The *Gloucester Citizen* for 17th May 1897, reported: "Berkeley Market Place was the scene of much commotion and rowdyism. The Berkeley and Sharpness Independent Labour Party had arranged the first public exposition of socialist principles in the town. The meeting was opened by the singing of a socialist song."

The report went on to describe attempts to disrupt the meeting. A "noisy interrupter was waving a union jack surrounded by a few farmers and local celebrities. *Rule Britannia* and the *National Anthem* were sung. The crowd listening to the socialist speakers became exasperated and the flag was wrestled away and the singer hustled into a public house. The opposition began throwing rotten eggs, one hitting a speaker on the socialist platform. From this point onwards a regular melee ensued and excitement ran high."

Bert Alpass, undaunted announced that they would hold another meeting next Saturday night. "Cheers were given for the Independent

Bert Alpass

Labour Party and socialism, and the crowd, one of the largest seen in Berkeley for some time, dispersed."

On another occasion, at Cam, Alpass was knocked down as farmers smashed the chair he was standing on. But he told them he would return the following week and hold another meeting.

In 1898 Alpass decided to take on Colonel Salmon county councillor for Almondsbury. Clarion Cyclists rode out from Bristol to support him and the result was Salmon (Conservative) 448, Alpass (Labour) 447.

Bert Alpass went on to fight the Parliamentary seat of Thornbury in 1922 and Cirencester and Tewkesbury in 1924 but was unsuccessful. He was elected as Labour MP for Bristol Central in 1929-1931 and for Thornbury 1945-1950.

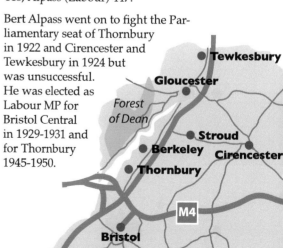

The right to strike

Pete Curran (1860-1910) became famous for his victory in the Plymouth Intimidation Case. He was organising local dock workers in his role as Secretary of the National Union of Gasworkers and General Labourers.

Curran and two others were fined £20 each in October 1890, for intimidating a coal merchant of Plymouth by threatening a boycott if he did not stop employing non-union labour. When Curran took the case to the appeal court, the case aroused national attention.

The coal merchant, Treleaven, sued him, claiming that the strike threat was intimidatory. The Plymouth courts ruled that the strike was simply to damage the employer. *The Times* claimed the verdict "decides in effect that every strike organised for the purpose of crushing free labour – that is to say, the majority of the strikes undertaken by New Unionism – is illegal."

The case revolved around the unloading of four ships with non-union men hired by Treleaven. At the appeal Curran's barrister, argued that if the ruling was not over-turned: "The mere warning of the employer that there was to be a strike would be an offence, though the strike itself would be legal." The Plymouth court's verdict was overruled.

Had it not been so, then the history of 19th century trade unionism might have been very different. The case would have set a legal precedent against the right to strike.

Curran's triumph in Plymouth pushed him to prominence in the labour and trade union movement. *The New Age,* a socialist review said: "Mr Curran's name is known to the labour movement throughout the empire."

Curran worked with Keir Hardie and Ramsay MacDonald in preparing the inaugural conference of the Labour Representation Committee in 1900. He became the MP for Jarrow in 1907.

But in February 1909 he suffered the indignity of a court appearance for being drunk in the street.

His liver couldn't take the drinking and on 14th February 1910, Pete Curran died at his home in London. At his funeral, thousands followed his hearse to Leytonstone Cemetery amid what *The Times* described as "thick lines of sympathising spectators".

Thanks to Neil Young and his article in the *Western Morning News* of January 2008

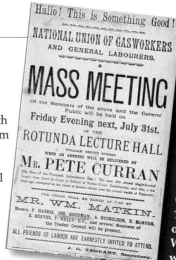

Pete Curran "The hero of the Plymouth Intimidation Case"

Swindon rail workers

On 11th January 1890, the local branch of the General Rail Workers Union was launched at the Corn Exchange, Old Swindon. 800-900 men attended, although the organisers were said to be disappointed with the turnout!

The *Swindon Advertiser* reported the meeting and the mood for trade unionism: "They had seen the good result of the movement in Bristol," it explained.

The rail union grew fast across the country, recruiting almost 60,000 in the first two months. In February 1891 the fledgling union organised a mass march and rally in Swindon. Over 1,000 people marched from the Great Western Railway to the Corn Exchange.

The meeting supported the motion proposed by Mr C Keene, the Secretary, that the union press for a 10 per cent pay rise and the abolition of overtime.

Ben Tillett supported the campaign and the *Swindon Advertiser* said: "We are somewhat at a loss to know why Mr Ben Tillett and his conferees are so sweet in stirring up ill-will in Swindon."

First Labour Day

The 1889 International Congress called for demonstrations of workers in all countries on May Day 1890. This followed riots in America in 1886.

In Bristol, trades unionists and socialists, accompanied by bands and with banners and flags, left the Ropewalk to march up Old Market Street, Castle Street and Clare Street. **Samson Bryer** described the event in *An Account of the Labour and Socialist Movement in Bristol* "At the Drawbridge, a strong reinforcement of dockers and sailors and firemen joined. Proceeding via Park Street and Whiteladies Road the public followed, and it was a procession of considerable dimensions that reached the Downs. There, huge crowds surrounded the two platforms."

A resolution was carried: "…that the long hours of labour…is the chief cause of the unemployed; believes in reducing the hours of labour to a maximum of 48 per week.

A section of Bridgwater Trades Union Council banner

Bristol radicals

At the turn of the nineteenth century, Bristol had a number of free-thinking and radical activists. There were individuals who stood up for working people and the poor.

Norah Lillian Fry (1871-1960) was a member of a Bristol Quaker Fry family of Fry's chocolate.

She was born and educated in Clifton, Bristol. She campaigned about the lack of proper schools for disabled children and the shortage of housing for people with learning difficulties.

In 1918 she was elected the first female councillor in Somerset.

For over fifty years she was a member of the Court of Bristol University. She gave the university money to set up the Department of Mental Health. The Norah Fry Research Centre is named after her.

Mr E Watson was a forceful speaker, who drew large crowds for the Bristol Socialist Society. He wrote pamphlets, poems and songs such as *Song of the Miners:*

> Lo! The Worker's Day is dawning!
>
> Cowards pale at Freedom's warning,
>
> Glorious breaks the gladsome morning,
>
> And Labour marches on.

Shoemaker poet, **John Wall** (1855-1915) born in Bristol, went to Castle Green Day School until aged thirteen when he became an apprentice 'clicker' learning to cut the 'uppers' in the boot and shoe trade. He used his factory experience to write short stories, poems and songs.

He became involved in trade unions and was elected Secretary of Bristol Trades Council in 1883. He organised seminars and evening classes for working people. The Trades Council paid scholarships for the University College of Bristol. Attracted to the idea of 'co-operation', he founded the Bristol and District Co-operative Society and its first small store in Houlton Street in November 1884.

He realised that strong trade unions and socialism were needed to obtain a more equal distribution of wealth and leisure. His poem of 1893, *The Labour-Greed Conflict* reflects his growing belief in the class struggle:

Plaque to John Wall in Croydon Street, Easton, Bristol

> Now he finds, to his dismay,
>
> He's betrayed, reviled, at bay;
>
> So he slowly turns his sleeves up for the fight.
>
> What're your weapons, simple one?
>
> Justice? Right? Hush! 'Tis begun!
>
> The death duel between Greed and Labourite.

John Gregory was born in Bideford, Devon in 1831 and died in 1922. The son of a Wesleyan lay preacher, he settled in Bristol after spending some time in Wales. By trade a shoemaker, he was a lifelong supporter of the labour movement. He was a free-thinker, humanitarian, and an open-minded philosopher.

He wrote poetry from a very early age on a variety of subjects. His books included *Idylls of Labour, Song Streams, Murmurs and Melodies, My Garden, A Dream of Love in Eden* and *Star Dreams*. He sold some of his poems to raise money for working class struggles.

John Gregory

He became leader of the Organising Committee of the Bristol Socialist Society in 1885. He established the Boot and Shoe Rivetters' and Finishers' Society in 1874 and the Bristol Co-operative Boot and Shoe Manufacturing Society in 1889. He helped found the Social Democratic Federation and the Bristol Co-op. As a representative of Bristol Trades Council John Gregory was invited to help organise farm workers in Somerset and was a friend of Ernest Bevin.

He was against the monarchy and wrote a pamphlet in 1887 called *The Jubilee Humbug* attacking the expense of Queen Victoria's celebrations.

Dan Irving worked for the Midland Railway Company, he was a foreman shunter but lost a leg in a serious accident. Irving was a radical Liberal won over to socialism. He became a prominent activist in the city until he moved to Burnley as the Secretary of the Social Democratic Federation. He was elected MP in 1918, retaining the seat until his death.

Frank Sheppard lived in Cairns Crescent, Ashley Road in the 1890s.

He was Secretary of the Bristol Socialist Society and was elected both as a City Councillor and a Guardian of the Poor. He became the first Labour Lord Mayor of Bristol in 1917.

Tom Phillips was a working shoemaker who became one of the finest speakers in the local movement.

JA Cunningham, a bank clerk was one of the earliest Labour members of the Board of Guardians, where he served for twenty years. He was a member of the School Board and Education Committee.

Harry Jarvis, a carpenter, became President of the Trades Council and the Socialist Society, and chaired the Social Democratic Party's very

Bristol socialists also devoted their energies to poetry and song.

successful conference in the Shepherds' Hall, Bristol, 1909.

Walter Fare fought several Municipal contests and became District Organiser of the National Union of Distributive and Allied Workers.

John Curle was a long-standing Secretary of Bristol Trades Council and Labour's first city magistrate.

Ada Vachell (1866-1923) was a champion of the poor and disabled. She founded the Guild of the Handicapped in 1895. There is a Blue Plaque on the house in which she lived at 130 Hampton Road, Redland, Bristol.

The Guild established a centre in Braggs Lane, St Judes as the Guild for Brave Poor Things, later changing its name to Guild Heritage.

Guild Heritage building in St Judes

Hobson's the choice

Samuel George Hobson (1870-1940) was the only Independent Labour Party candidate in the South West in the 1895 General Election. He stood in Bristol East and got a respectable 1,874 votes, 31 per cent.

Born in County Armagh, Hobson had a Quaker education in Saffron Walden and then Sidcot, Somerset. He became a socialist when he moved to Wales, joining the Fabian Society and then becoming a founder member of the Independent Labour Party (ILP).

He began writing for the ILP newspaper, *Labour Leader*, and in 1900 was elected to the Fabian Society's executive.

During his time in Bristol he was a member of the Bristol Socialist Society.

From 1906, Hobson developed a theory of a socialism based on guilds, a form of workers' self-management. He left the Fabians in 1910 and began writing for the magazine, *The New Age*. He coined the term 'guild socialism,' and in 1914, wrote *National Guilds: an Inquiry into the Wage System and a Way Out.*

He tried unsuccesfully to organise a builders' guild. Hobson wrote a memoir entitled *Pilgrim to the Left - Memoirs of a Modern Revolutionist* in 1938.

Bridgwater brick strike

There was a strike amongst Bridgwater brick workers in 1864 but it was in 1896, when the most significant dispute occurred. Workers asked for a sixpence rise but the employer, Henry James Major, refused to talk. On 26th May 1896 the strike began.

On 8th June, there was a rally in Cranleigh Gardens and marches through the town kept the dispute alive. The town's mayor, Henry Pollard tried to intervene but Henry Major still refused to negotiate.

On 23rd June the mass picket at Barham's Yard on the East Quay was attacked by the police. Three workers were arrested and charged with intimidation, receiving heavy fines.

Dockers leader, Ben Tillett, addressed a mass rally at Cranleigh Gardens.

A cart carrying tiles was seized by the strikers and 26 were arrested.

Hostility and tempers ran high and more police were called in. They charged the strikers in an attempt to recover the cart. But angry strikers hit back using tiles as missiles and the police had to take shelter in the Town Hall.

Troops from the Gloucestershire Regiment arrived. Local hotels and inns refused to billet the soldiers. Local sympathy was clearly with the strikers.

The mayor, read the Riot Act and the troops dispersed the crowd. Injuries were high and Bridgwater felt like it was under military rule.

A ballot voted to continue the strike but the financial strain on the workers was too much. On 5th July, the strikers voted for a return to work.

The following year, wages were increased from 12 to 15 shillings per week and the working day reduced to twelve hours.

A beehive kiln at the former brick yard in Bridgwater

photo: Pat Morley

West Country trades councils

The growth of unions to represent both skilled and semi-skilled workers led to the need for bodies to bring them together at local level. Trades councils were launched across the region.

Bristol

A Council of Amalgamated Trades was launched in Bristol in 1868 but didn't survive. On 26th January 1873 a small group of trade unionists met in the Cork and Bottle on Castle Green to set up Bristol Trades Council to aid "the industrial classes in the West of England to organise themselves." Affiliated societies included those representing rope and twine makers, saddle and harness makers, stone masons and corn porters.

John Cawsey was the first Secretary of Bristol Trades Council but the early years were hard. It relied upon a few craft unions but in the 1880s the Council grew. It was invited to join an investigation by the Bishop into Bristol's poor.

In 1885 it gave up its political neutrality and established a Local Labour League to put up candidates. The next year Trades Council Secretary **Robert Tovey** was elected councillor for St Paul's.

Cheltenham

On 6th November 1875 375 building workers met in St George's Hall and agreed to form Cheltenham Trades Council with **George Skey** as President. It didn't last but on 5th July 1894 the inaugural meeting of the Cheltenham and District Trades and Labur Council was held in the Rose and Crown Inn. **Charles Fisher,** stonemason was President.

Gloucester and Bath

By 1890 Gloucester had a Trades Council followed the next year by Bath Trades Council.

Exeter

A strike amongst carpenters and joiners in Exeter ran on for many weeks in 1890. It won public sympathy but it exposed the need for inter-union solidarity. The dispute turned nasty when a strike-breaking foreman was jostled by a large crowd on Exe Bridge. **Charles Gray** was accused of threatening to throw the man into the river and was subsequently fined.

Exeter Chamber of Commerce suggested that a little forbearance by the masters could end the dispute. The unions needed a collective response and on 25th July 1890 the inaugural meeting of Exeter Trades Council was held in the Phoenix Inn, Goldsmith Street (now the Guildhall Shopping Centre).

The carpenters returned to work with a settlement reached through arbitration and the value of the Trades Council was established. Carpenter **Bro O Kenshole** was elected Secretary and joiner **Henry Loram,** President. Eight shillings was collected to meet initial costs.

The new council began to press the town council on issues such as public health and education.

Swindon

1891 saw the birth of Swindon Trades Council. General or 'new' unionism was on the rise. A public meeting in the town to launch the Rail Workers Union attracted some 900 people.

Plymouth

Tom Proctor was an activist with the Amalgamated Society of Engineers and the Social Democratic Federation. He worked with the Plymouth leaders of the Gasworkers' and General Labourers' Union to form the Trades Council. It quickly set about a variety of local campaigns including a cooperative coal society and a 'Labour Register' for the unemployed. Tom Proctor was Chairman and **Charles Simmons,** Secretary but within two years the council ran into trouble.

The Gasworkers had succeeded in organising mill workers at Buckfastleigh but a demand for higher pay was met by a lock-out. Re-employment was conditional on dropping union membership and the gasworkers' organisation was almost ruined. The impact was felt in the Trades Council but it was political differences over supporting a Labour candidate that caused its collapse.

Some unions wanted to maintain their relations with the Liberals – there were 23 Liberal trade unionists in Parliament. Exeter Trades Council learnt from this experience and remained neutral in the 1892 General Election. **Albert Dunn,** a young lawyer was a radical Liberal active in the town at the time. He presided at a railwaymen's meeting and declared that: "Although the struggle between classes and the masses has in days gone by given victory to the former, that verdict must and will be reversed in the cause of time." He was beaten by the Conservative MP but went on to become the MP for Camborne in 1910.

Plymouth tries again

By 1897 a building workers' strike in Plymouth involved flying pickets going to Torquay and Newton Abbot. There was a need to re-form the Trades Council and on 26th May delegates from the 'three towns' of Plymouth met in the Borough Arms with **Bro Salter** of the Tailors' Union in the chair and George Canniford, Brushmakers' Union as Secretary.

The new Trades Council persuaded the TUC to hold its conference in

The proud list of bodies that delegates from Bath Trades Council attended

Plymouth and in 1899 Council delegate **WJ Vernon** of the Lithographic Printers' Society in Plymouth proudly opened the Congress in the Guildhall.

During strikes trades councils brought unions together and formed Councils of Action and Strike Committees.

In the 1960s around 60 West Country trades councils were recognised as a local voice of working people. Through the councils, representatives were elected to serve on a variety of civic bodies and advisory groups.

Trades councils have helped build trade union solidarity at community level and campaign for progressive change.

Living the Whiteway

In the autumn of 1898 Samuel Veale Bracher, a Quaker, and other Tolstoyans established a small 'colony' at Whiteway, near Shepscombe in Stroud.

It occupies forty one acres of communally held land. The colonists burnt the property deeds on the end of a pitchfork in a symbolic rejection of property. The socialist ideals inlcuded sharing provisions and living off the land.

Mohandas Gandhi visited Whiteway in 1909. Residents have included immigrant anarchists, conscientious objectors and refugees from the Spanish Civil War. For a period the anarchist newspaper Freedom was produced in Whiteway.

In the 1920s the authorities sent a husband-and-wife team in to spy on the colony. They claimed to have witnessed "promiscuous fornication", but were unable to prove it.

Cheltenham

Whiteway

Stroud

Working class representation

George Odger (1820-1877) stands, proudly wearing the silk hat made for him by the Hatters' Trade Union. The photograph comes from the 1870 parliamentary by-election campaign in Bristol. Odger was from the Labour Representation League, set up the year before to promote working class MPs. Also in the photograph are Odgers' supporters from Southwark: (left to right) H Chenery, William Stafford and J Andrews, a pork butcher.

George Odger, the Secretary of the London Trades Council, came a close second, winning 4,382 votes to the Tory's 4,686.

The hat is still in good condition and is in the People's History Museum.

photo: TUC Library

Clarion calls

Rambling and Propaganda Society

The Bristol Socialist Society formed a group "to take rambles and excursions for physical and intellectual recreation, to promote social intercourse amongst its members and do propaganda work in the rural districts." For a dozen years or more it ran fortnightly Saturday afternoon and holiday time rambles.

Frequently a hundred or more members attended. On occasions Will Sharland's choir performed and the walks were enlivened by the singing of socialist songs.

Clarion Cyclists

In 1895 the Socialist Ramblers united with the Clarion Cyclists to establish a socialist presence in Bath.

They held open-air meetings in the Sawclose. One meeting was stopped by the police. The following Saturday more attended, determined to uphold free speech.

The police arrested the chair, **William Baster.** He contended that he had a right to speak, and was freed. He immediately returned to the Sawclose to hold another meeting. A few days later, the Bath Socialist Society was formed.

A delegation from Bristol cycled all the way to the Clarion Conference in Bakewell, Derbyshire in 1896. They arrived at 2am with one riding an 'ordinary' bicycle otherwise known as a 'penny-farthing.

On Sundays in 1896 cyclists visited Radstock, and with the aid of a few colliers and shoemakers established a socialist group there.

The Clarion Cyclists also visited some other places in Somerset and horse-drawn Clarion caravans toured the countryside hosting socialist lectures.

In 1907 there was another battle in Bath over free speech. On Moorland Road, Oldfield Park, religious bodies held open-air meetings but when socialists met on the same spot the police tried to stop them.

The annual meeting of the Trades Union Congress was in Bath that year. Amongst the delegates was **Fred Knee,** a Somerset man born in Frome, a key member of the London Trades Council and the Social Democratic Federation. He addressed a meeting at the disputed spot in Bath.

In his welcome to the TUC, the Mayor invited delegates to a garden party. Fred Knee was on his feet in a flash. "May I express my regret at being unable to accept this invitation. The Mayor has been responsible for the persecution of my local socialist comrades on account of their political opinions. This is one of the worst cases of persecution I have come

across, and in these circumstances it is impossible for me to attend the garden party."

Socialist meetings in the city were free from police interference from then on!

Congress Bell used at Bath in 1907

Open-air meetings

The first open meeting of the Marxist Bristol Social Democratic Federation was at 'Poyntz Pool', by St Jude's Church. A circle was formed with J Hunter-Watts in the centre. He spoke of "our message to the world, what it means to you and how it will relieve your poverty."

The next week local comrades took up the open-air approach at the Ropewalk, Bath Bridge, Bristol Bridge and the Midland Railway Yard. Annie Treasure brought a square of red silk as a flag to visualise "sure hope of the future".

The Plymouth Social Democratic Federation ran into similar restrictions in 1906 when they were prevented from meeting in Manor Street, Stonehouse. Several leaders were arrested when they refused to disperse but the ban was lifted after the Trades Council organised a big demonstration with some 5,000 people.

Fiery speeches at TUC

Jim O'Grady

In 1898 the TUC held its annual conference in Bristol. **Jason (Jim) O'Grady**, as chair of the host trades council had the honour of making the opening address.

The long, wide-ranging speech covered child labour, the need for an eight-hour-day, workmen's compensation acts, taxation of land values, nationalisation of railways; state ownership of royalties and much more.

According to **Sam Bryher's** account: "Jim was above all a socialist, and this ideal was ever in his thought and speech. The whole address was permeated by it.

"Never before had the collectivist idea of production and consumption been advocated from the presidential chair of a Trades Union Congress as the proper aim of trade union activity, and it was a point that raised much comment and discussion in the press of the country as well as labour circles."

Burnt minutes

The TUC's 1898 visit to Bristol was memorable because a large part of the Colston Hall conference centre burnt down half-way through the conference.

In a show of defiance and determination, the TUC General Council assembled in the burnt-out shell of the building. New rooms were quickly found and the conference was able to be completed as planned.

The Standing Orders Committee asked delegates to take the minutes as read "as they are burnt".

photo: TUC Library

Votes for women

The campaign to win votes for women had its champions across the South West. It was a long and hard battle to break down entrenched prejudices and vested interests. The men in power were not going to give up easily.

The votes for women movement was divided when the more militant suffragettes took direct action for the exclusive cause of female votes. They believed that the campaign for electoral reform had to be the sole priority and including wider social change would be a distraction.

The campaign won concessions and eventually full voting rights.

Agnes Beddow was the first president of the Suffrage Society in Bristol established in 1868 with a small office in Park Street.

Harriet McIlquham (1838-1910) was a campaigner for women's suffrage in Gloucestershire. She was a member of the Bristol and West of England Society for Women's Suffrage in 1877 and elected as a Poor Law Guardian for Boddington in Tewkesbury.

There was an attempt to annul her election because she was married but she proved she had rights due to her independent property. She travelled the country speaking and writing for women's rights.

In 1868 the Bristol and Clifton branch of the National Society for Women's Suffrage was established. It became the Bristol and West of England Society for Women's Suffrage. In 1880 its secretary was **Helen Blackburn** (1842-1903) who wrote widely on women's rights. Helping her was **Jeanette Wilkinson** who became active in the Society of Upholstresses and spoke as a delegate to the TUC.

Emily Spender (1841-1922) was the first secretary of the Bath Committee of the National Society for Women's Suffrage in 1871 and was a regular speaker at Suffragette meetings.

The Society organised a 'Grand Demonstration' at Colston Hall in November 1880 and in 1885 an Exhibition of Women's Industries was held. In 1898, the Bristol Society affiliated to the National Union of Women's Suffrage Societies (NUWSS) in the West of England Federation.

Frances Sterling (1869-1943) was the first female Poor Law Guardian to be elected in Falmouth in 1891. She gave up a painting career to work full time for the suffrage cause. She sat on the Executive of the NUWSS and in 1913 was Honorary Secretary.

Women get militant

There were divisions over tactics and the use of direct action. The Women's Social and Political Union (WSPU) led the more militant and high profile campaign.

In 1907 **Annie Kenny,** (1879-1930) formed the Bristol branch of WSPU and set up the West of England Society the following year. She lived in Gordon Road, Clifton where there is now a Blue Plaque to her memory.

Annie Kenny's former house in Gordon Road, Clifton, Bristol

Lady Emmeline Pethwick Lawrence (1867-1954) was born in Brandon Hill, Bristol and grew up in Weston-super-Mare. She became a suffragette speaker and pacifist writer. She edited *Votes for Women* and came up with the Suffragette colours of purple, white and green.

Elizabeth Sturge (1899-1944) and Helen Sturge (1858-1945) from Redland, Bristol, were pioneers for women's rights including education.

Elsie Howey and Vera Wentworth hid in the organ of Bristol's Colston Hall to shout down Augustine Birrell, cabinet minister. It took quite a while to discover the 'voices from the organ' in the complex instrument.

In 1909 Elsie Howey was as an unpaid organiser in Devon. She was frequently arrested and served one of the longest sentences given to a suffragette. The effects of force-feeding ruined her voice. Elsie's sister, Mary Howey, also became an organiser in the West Country.

Mary Howey and Annie Kenny launched the campaign in Cornwall in March 1909 with a large meeting in Penzance. This helped gather support and in June another large meeting was held in the town followed by others all over Cornwall.

Dorothy Pethick (1818-1970) was the younger sister of Emmeline. From 1908 she became an organiser for the WSPU and helped lead the Cornwall campaign. In 1909 she was arrested twice. In prison she refused to eat and was force-fed.

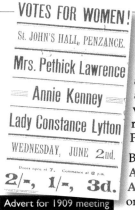

VOTES FOR WOMEN!

St. JOHN'S HALL, PENZANCE.

Mrs. Pethick Lawrence

Annie Kenney

Lady Constance Lytton

WEDNESDAY, JUNE 2nd.

Doors open at 7.   Commence at 8 p.m.

2/-, 1/-, 3d.

Advert for 1909 meeting

Dorothy was replaced in Cornwall by Mary Phillips. She was arrested in Exeter during a protest against a visiting minister. After release she was based in Plymouth.

Bristol Suffragettes Mrs Arnold Willcox and May Allen were sentenced to one month's imprisonment for breaking windows at the Treasury when Mr Asquith refused to receive Mrs Pankhurst. They refused to wear prison uniform, kicked a wardress in self-defence and broke the cell windows. As a consequence they had to serve eight days' close confinement in the punishment cells and went on hunger strike for three days.

Campaigners burned a Bristol timber yard, a mansion at Frenchay and another at Stoke Bishop.

On 15th November 1909, Winston Churchill came to Bristol to address a meeting in Colston Hall. He was met at Temple Meads Station by Theresa Garnett, a suffragette who lived in York Place, Clifton. She had already chained herself to a statue in the House of Commons as part of the campaign for votes for women. Theresa struck Winston Churchill, then the President of the Board of Trade, shouting "Take that in the name of the insulted women of England!"

Theresa was arrested for the attack but Churchill did not want to press charges so she was held for a month in Horfield Prison for disturbing the peace. During her sentence she went on hunger strike and was force-fed. She set fire to her prison cell in protest. After a period in solitary confinement she was found unconscious and ended her sentence in hospital.

Vera Wentworth, smashed a window at the Bristol Liberal Club. Jessie Lawes threw a stone from a tramcar at the Colston Hall and Mary (or May) Allen broke a window at the office of the Board of Trade in Baldwin Street. They were all sentenced to one month's imprisonment.

Ellen Wines Pitman received two months' imprisonment for breaking a window at the Post Office in Small Street.

Annie Williams (c1860-1943) from Cornwall gave up her job as head-mistress to work for the WSPU as organiser in Bristol. She was arrested three times, once on 29th June 1909 following an event at Canford Park in Dorset.

In 1909 a large meeting in Colston Hall, addressed by Christobel Pankhurst, demanded votes for women.

A few months later in the same hall, the National League for Opposing Woman Suffrage held a meeting with Lord Cromer and Sir Charles Hobhouse MP for Bristol East. Novelist, Mrs Humphrey Ward congratulated the anti-suffrage movement in Bristol upon its growth since her last visit in 1908. She wrote that only men could solve constitutional, legal, financial, military, and international problems. There was uproar when Dove Wilcox, a local suffragette, tried to ask a question and attempts to throw her out failed.

Mary Blathwayt of aristocratic background in Bath took up the suffragette cause. The family home at Eagle House in Bathford became a place where exhausted speakers could rest and activists recuperate after spells in prison and forced feeding. Suffragettes planted trees in 'Annie's Arboretum' named after Annie Kenney and relaxed in the 'Suffragette Field'.

In 1911 a by-election in West Somerset provided the suffragettes with a platform and an unlikely supporter in the Unionist (Conservative) candidate, Col. Dennis Boles, Baronet and Master of the local hunt. Emmeline Pankhurst spoke at Central Hall in Minehead pointing out how much the resort relied upon women workers. Annie Kenney tried to speak in Watchet but was shouted down by rival Liberals.

Born in Chile, **Juanita Maxwell Philips** (1880-1966) came to Honiton when she was 26. She soon got active in the cause of votes for women. She was jailed six times for her activities between 1908 and 1912. She later led the local war effort and became Mayor of Honiton eleven times.

By 1911 the Cornish campaign was split between the NUWSS and the WSPU. **Mrs Pascoe** was the Falmouth secretary of the more militant WSPU and in March 1912 she was arrested and spent a month in Holloway prison for smashing the windows of the Board of Education.

In June 1913 suffragettes were thrown out of a meeting in Trowbridge for heckling Walter Runciman MP and Commission of Woods in the Liberal Government. A day later 'Elmscross', an empty house in Bradford-on-Avon was set alight causing some £7,000 worth of damage.

Kitty Marion was one of the most destructive travelling activists. She endured 200 forced feedings in prison. She came to the West Country in 1913 to stay with **Olive Wharry** in Holdsworthy. Wharry was imprisoned eight times for various attacks. Marion is said to have set fire to 'Hollerday', the large empty house of the late Sir George Newnes near Lynton in Devon. On 6th August fires were lit at Dunkery Beacon just as crowds gathered for the local stag hunt. At the same time haystacks were burnt down at nearby Stringston.

At the end of October 1913, the pavilion at the University sports ground was seriously damaged by fire and suffragette literature was found at the scene. **Dorothy Evans** was believed to be the organiser. University students retaliated by attacking the headquarters of the WSPU in Queen's Road, burning the furniture outside in the road.

In November 1913 a large house known as 'Begbrook' at Frenchay burnt down. Support for violent actions was falling and the NUWSS became the larger body in much of the West Country.

Other mobile militants were **Gertrude Frances** who was arrested for a haystack fire at Inglesbatch near Bath and **Lilian Lenton** caught after an arson attack on 6th January 1914, on Alstone Lawn House in Cheltenham. A wing of St Paul's College was also attacked.

In the summer of 1913 the NUWSS organised a 'Pilgrimage' from Lands' End to London. Along the route their meetings attracted large crowds, including many hostile to the cause.

The march coincided with the WSPU arson attacks on pillar boxes that angered many people. Speakers were shouted down and in Falmouth some 2,000 people turned up and part of the crowd rushed the platform. The speakers escaped with the help of the police. Meetings in Truro, Bodmin and Looe were also very difficult for the 'pilgrims'.

The NUWSS was strong in Devon and was able to have paid organisers in Plymouth and then Exeter. In 1914 the Exeter Branch had 263 members.

But the WSPU attacks continued and in June a room in Lynton Town Hall was set on fire and there was a possible attack on the bowling club pavillion at Bideford.

Selina Cooper (1864-1946) was born in Callington, Cornwall. She was a suffragette and the first woman to represent the Independent Labour Party. She left Cornwall to move to the North of England after her father died of typhoid fever. She became active in the Cotton Workers' Union, Women's Co-operative Guild and local politics.

Cornwall attracted radical artists including some who supported the suffragette cause. **Barbara Leigh Smith Bodichon** (1827-1891) was a leading feminist and painter who bought the Parish Poor House in Penzance in 1875.

War changes

On the outbreak of war the militant but middle class suffragettes abandoned the campaign in favour of all-out support for the British

Government. The WSPU stopped publishing *The Suffragette* and began handing out white feathers to men who refused to join up. The WSPU faded from public attention and was dissolved in 1917.

The war saw thousands of women carry out jobs previously done by men. They proved their organisational and leadership skills. The NUWSS helped organise relief for women and children suffering as a result of the war and cared for refugees.

The establishment did everything it could to put women back into housework and servitude after the war. Life could never be the same, however, and the pressure for extended democracy became unstoppable.

Parliament agreed the Qualification of Women Act to give women over the age of thirty the vote providing they were householders, married to a householder or held a university degree.

Voting dilemma

Edna, Edith and Freda Stevens inherited a house from their father who had been Mayor of Swindon. All three registered to vote under the new law but a complaint was lodged (probably from the Tory agent). The tribunal ruled that only two of the sisters could vote and they had to decide which one lost out – Edith!

Votes at last

It was not until 1928 with Representation of the People Act that women were granted equal voting rights.

Women at work

In 1917 the Great Western Railway Company Board considered taking on women in the Swindon works. The loss of men to fight the war forced firms to recruit women. But the idea was formerly rejected by management due to the lack of toilet facilities. This was a common excuse used to keep women out of workplaces.

Despite the GWR policy, Fanny and Winnie Hyde are recorded as working there during World War I.

Emily Hobhouse

'That Bloody Woman'

Emily Hobhouse was born in 1886 in Liskeard, Cornwall. When her father died in 1895 she went to Minnesota, United States to help Cornish migrant mine workers.

In 1899, at the outbreak of the Second Boer War, she became involved with the South African Conciliation Committee. She saw first hand the horrors of the Boer concentration camps. She wrote a moving report of the suffering of women and children.

Back in England she received scathing criticism from the government and the media. She was described as 'That Bloody Woman'. But she succeeded in obtaining more help for the victims of the war.

A commission, under Millicent Fawcett, was established to investigate her claims. This corroborated her account of the shocking conditions and made numerous recommendations, for example improvements in diet and provision of proper medical facilities.

Hobhouse returned to Cape Town in October 1901, but was deported after five days. She went to France where she wrote the book *The Brunt of the War and Where it Fell*. Her experience made her a fierce opponent of World War I.

Hobhouse died in London in 1926 and her ashes lie in the National Women's Monument at Bloemfontein, South Africa.

DOCK, WHARF, RIVERSIDE AND GENERAL WORKERS UNION

BRISTOL CARTERS' BRANCH.

ERNEST BEVIN-FIRST PRESIDENT

OF Gt BRITAIN

AND IRELAND

THE GRIP OF BROTHERHOOD THE WORLD O'ER.

Ernest Bevin

Bristol Carters' Branch banner showing Ernest Bevin at the top.

Ernest Bevin (1881-1951) was one of the most influential trade unionists of the twentieth century. He was born into a large, poor family in Winsford in Somerset. He never knew his father. He became a farm labourer but after a fight with the farmer's son, he fled to Bristol. He lived in St Werburghs and did odd jobs before becoming a carter – delivering mineral water and pop.

Ernest became involved in local politics, joining the Bristol Socialist Society. In 1908 he was the Secretary of the Right to Work Committee. He led a silent demonstration of some 400 unemployed men into a service in Bristol Cathedral. The stunt shocked the City's establishment and the City Council agreed to a series of public works including the construction of the lake in Eastville Park – known for many years as 'Bevin's Lake'.

The work at Eastville Park engaged 300 men for 17 weeks. The wage bill was estimated at £4,000.

In 1910 a strike at Avonmouth spread to Bristol. The dockers were members of the Dock, Wharf, Riverside and General Workers' Union but the carters had no union. **Harry Orbell**, the dockers' organiser appealed to Bevin to help recruit the carters.

The Winsford house where Bevin was born

In August of that year, the Carters' Branch was formed with Ernest as Chairman. In 1911 he became a full-time officer.

One of his first achievements was to re-negotiate the bonus system for the carters that led them to overload the horses to such an extent that some died trying to climb Bristol's steep hills.

He became a national figure when he presented the case for a pay rise to a court of enquiry held under the Industrial Courts Act of 1919. With no legal training and little time to prepare he forcefully and imaginatively put the arguments to the court, closely watched by the media. He used plates of food to show how poor the offer was. News photos of the derisory quantities of food shocked the nation and helped him to win a national minimum wage for dockers of 16s a day for a 44-hour

photo: TUC Library

Ernie Bevin

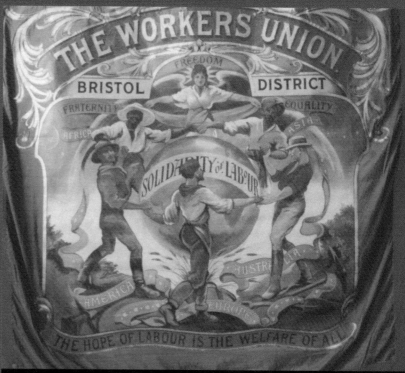

The Workers' Union, Bristol District Banner

week. The press dubbed him the 'Dockers' KC'.

Bevin was a tough, formidable organiser and he worked his way through the union to become General Secretary of the Workers' Union. He ruthlessly steered through a series of negotiations to merge fourteen unions into the Transport and General Workers' Union. He led the union during the General Strike in 1926, the depression of the 30s and the start of the war.

In 1940, the day after Winston Churchill became Prime Minister at the head of the National Government, Bevin was asked to become Minister of Labour. He agreed and a month later he was elected unopposed as MP for Wandsworth. He mobilised millions of people to the war effort and re-directed conscripts to work down the mines. Those chosen became known as 'Bevin Boys'.

In 1945, with the war over, Labour won a landslide victory and Bevin became Foreign Secretary. He led

Britain's negotiations with the Soviet Union and America. It was the start of the Cold War and a period of recognition that Britain was no longer the powerful force it once was in the world.

Bevin's sudden death in 1951 ended a remarkable career from Somerset farm worker to the top of world politics. Busts of Ernest Bevin are now displayed in Bristol and Somerset Councils.

Bill Morris, then general Secretary of the T&G, unveils a plaque to Ernest Bevin on his former house in St Werburghs

World War

The 1914-18 World War took a dreadful toll on working people across the country. The slaughter devastated families and communities and changed the way of life in the West Country.

Harry Patch (1898-2009) was the last First World War veteran before he died at the age of 111. Harry left his Combe Down home in Somerset to become a reluctant soldier with the Duke of Cornwall's Light infantry.

By the third battle of Ypres, Passchendale, Harry was a lance corporal and 'went over the top' as part of an offensive that cost some 70,000 lives. The horror that he witnessed traumatised him to such an extent that he could not talk about it until he turned 100-years-old. He recalled comforting a dying man ripped from shoulder to waist by shrapnel whose last word was "mother".

Harry and his comrades agreed to aim for the German legs to avoid killing them. On 22nd September 1917 he was badly wounded in the chest in an explosion that killed three of his mates. Harry came back to the West Country to recover during which time he met his first wife, Ada.

The memorial at Paddington Station to the 3,312 men and women of the Great Western Railway who gave their lives in the two world wars.

After the war he became a plumber in Bath. He later accused politicians who led countries to war as "organising nothing better than legalised mass murder."

As the old war veterans died, Harry became one of the diminishing few survivors who could recount first-hand experience of the trenches. With the help of Richard van Emden, he wrote his autobiography called *The Last Fighting Tommy*.

> " *The most important thing is: don't go to war, settle it over the table.* "
>
> Harry Patch

Harry's death in July 2009 and funeral at Wells Cathedral led to many tributes. Not even ceremonial weapons were allowed at the ceremony.

Stoke Canon collecting box

Stoke Canon Strike

In 1915 the village of Stoke Canon, just north of Exeter, was the centre of a bitter strike. Workers were in dispute over a pay claim and recognition of the National Union of Printing and Paper Workers. Charles Tremlett, Managing Director of the Stoke Canon Paper Mill, responded by evicting the workers from their tied houses.

With nowhere else to go, the union bought the families tents and they were forced to camp in a local field. The strikers won widespread support from around the area. The village schoolteachers took up the cause and funds were raised to support the families.

Tremlett could not recruit local labour to break the strike but eventually found Scottish workers who took jobs unaware of the situation.

The strikers, 19 men, 13 women and 6 boys, were supported by their union. Some found other jobs in munitions factories or joined the army.

Stoke Canon Paper Mill strikers camped in tents after their evictions in 1915

Refusing to kill

Some unions and trades councils came out against the call-up, especially at the start of the war. In June 1915, for example, Bristol and Plymouth Trades Councils passed resolutions against conscription.

The half-yearly report of Plymouth Trades Council in January 1915 said:

"Circumstances over which the millions of workers in Europe had no control whatever have involved them in all the horrors of a ghastly war. None of the workers will be one penny the richer or one bit the happier for the sacrifices they are called upon to make or the suffering they will have to endure. We find ourselves plunged into catastrophe without our knowledge or consent."

Politicised by their strike in 1913, the Cornish clay workers were reluctant to sign up to fight.

The conscientious objectors of the First World War laid the foundations of non-violent protest against war

The Independent Labour Party Branch in Dartmoor Prison in 1917

Following conscription in 1916 around 16,000 men registered as conscientious objectors. 4,500 were sent to do work such as farming, 7,000 were given non-combatant duties, but 6,000 were forced into the army and when they refused orders they were sent to prison.

Often ridiculed and taunted, these objectors were often brave pacifists and protesters against the war.

Dartmoor Prison was re-opened to house more than 1,000 conscientious objectors and renamed 'Princetown

Work Centre'. The Bishop of Exeter refused the use of the church in the prison.

Put to work in and out of the prison, the objectors cleared a rectangular patch on the moor surrounded by a seven-foot-high dry stone wall. It had no purpose and decades later was still known as 'Conchies Field'.

After the First World War, the No More War Movement was established to strive for revolutionary socialism but not to take part in any war.

Bodmin Badge Strike

In 1918 five nurses were victimised for wearing National Asylum Workers union badges. Nurse Hawken had organised 62 of the 70 staff into the union. The strikers held out until all were allowed back under the banner of 'All or None'. With lots of local support they won reinstatement and the right to keep the badges on.

In 1919, Exeter Asylum union rep, Phillip Glanville, was sacked and nurses went on strike in his defence. Despite local trade union support and the threat of a national strike the dispute ended in defeat.

Hammerman Poet

Alfred Williams (1877-1930) was a self-taught poet born in the village of South Marston in Wiltshire. He grew up in poverty after his father abandoned his wife and eight children. At fifteen Alfred entered Swindon railway works, where he worked in the stamping shop.

He published his first book of poems in 1909, *Songs in Wiltshire*. Nicknamed The Hammerman poet, his most famous work, *Life in a Railway Factory* (1915) was written at night after a gruelling day's work. He dared not publish the book while he worked for the Great Western Railway because the picture it painted of life at work would have earned him the sack. It was published after he was forced to leave the factory due to ill health.

Alfred Williams wrote thirteen books but died in poverty in 1930.

Bridport ropemakers

Bridport in Dorset became known as a centre for rope-making. The wide high street was built to allow the ropes to be stretched out and there remains a riposte for anyone caught leaving a door open: 'Were you born in Bridport', as the ropes would often be laid through the houses.

The work was labour intensive, much done on piece rates in homes. But unions got organised as this photo from Dundry's ropes in 1919 shows.

Strike at Dundry's ropemakers, Bridport, 1919
after the firm tried to keep emergency war wage levels

Bliss blacked

Edmund Shirey Bliss was the Gloucester Secretary of the Typographical Association in 1923 during the dispute over the first national agreement for printers.

Keen to see the union broken, Gloucester newspaper and jobbing printers, Chance and Bland, sacked Bliss. They declared that they "had nothing against his work." The TA members went on strike in support but after a month were forced back to work.

Blacklisted by local employers, Bliss established a co-operative called Gloucester Printers in Hopewell Street. The union, local Labour Party, Trades Council and co-op took out shares in the venture that proved a success and survived to the 1960s.

Shirley Bliss

image: Glos archives

Devon born union leader

Charles William Bowerman (1851-1947) was born in Honiton, Devon. He moved to London where he became a compositor and member of the London Society of Compositors in 1873. He became its General Secretary 1892-1906.

Bowerman joined the Fabian Society and, in 1897, he was elected to the Parliamentary Committee of the Trades Union Congress. In 1901, he was elected as a Progressive Party alderman on London County Council.

Bowerman was the President of the TUC in 1901 and Secretary of the Parliamentary Committee from 1911 until 1921, when he became the TUC's first General Secretary. He retired in 1923.

In 1906, Bowerman was elected Labour MP for Deptford, a post he held until 1931.

photo: TUC Library

Charles Bowerman

The General Strike

In May 1926 workers across Britain stopped work in support of the miners who faced cuts in pay and longer hours. The strike ended in defeat and division but it was a week when working people came together in strength and solidarity.

The dispute had been brewing for some time and when it came it set trade unions against the Conservative Government led by Prime Minister, Stanley Baldwin. Chancellor, Winston Churchill, took charge of the government's propaganda including acting as a zealous editor of the *British Gazette*. He sought to portray the strike as a revolutionary act that aimed to bring down democracy and impose communist rule. The TUC produced its own newspaper: *The British Worker*.

Despite strong support for the stoppage, fearing trade union divisions, the TUC called off the strike after nine days leaving the miners to fight on alone for another seven months. The defeat left trade unions badly weakened.

Bristol

On the first day of the strike 18,000 Bristol workers downed tools. Nine days later, just before the strike was called off, that number had doubled. Power station workers, builders, printers and engineers went on strike although the trams and local press managed to continue operations. Warships were moved into Avonmouth and City docks and sailors guarded the power station. A General Strike Committee was established by the Trades Council and special sub-committees were formed to deal with communications and publicity. A system of cyclist messengers carried information to all points of the city.

Devon

In Exeter some 3,500 workers answered the strike call. Railways came to a halt and only truncated editions of local newspapers appeared. The Devon County Show was postponed but buses continued to run.

After the strike was called off, Newton Abbot railway workers refused to return to work until local trade union and Labour Party

With Fleet Street printers on strike, the *Daily Mirror* came out printed one side only, on a duplicating machine

Strikers v Police in Plymouth

activist, **Mr WG Chinn** was re-instated. Workers marched through the town with banners "We Want Chinn" and they stayed out until the company gave way.

Exeter Trades Council continued business as usual during and after the strike. The first item of business of the meeting held on 10th May was not the progress of the strike but a letter from the town clerk on the long-running issue of street traders.

A football match was organised at Plymouth Home Park on Saturday 8th May between strikers and the police – the strikers won 2-1.

Gloucestershire
The presses of the newly formed co-operative printers were made available to volunteers from the Typographical Association to produce a daily newspaper. The *Gloucester Strike Bulletin* is a rare example of such a publication and gives a fascinating insight into the strike from the union side. Such publications were discouraged by the TUC who wished all communications to go through the official *British Worker*.

In the first edition of the *Gloucester Strike Bulletin*, the workers of Gloucester are congratulated for "their fine stand against the tyranny of low wages and long hours down the mines." The case was made for the nationalisation of the coal industry.

As the strike developed, the *Bulletin* reported on growing support around the region. The docks came to a standstill and the unions issued permits to let essential foodstuffs

Standing firm: reports from strike committees around the West Country

pass. Electricity was cut to allow hospitals and homes to have power but not industry. Railway workers were almost all out as were engineers, wood workers, printers and builders. Postal workers said that "they were serving the workers best at the moment by remaining at their posts."

The third edition had become "In conjunction with Cheltenham" where the Trades Council had formed a Council of Action, backed by 2,000 organised workers.

On the railways the reports were: "Lydney, Cinderford, Newnham, Exeter, Taunton, Totnes, Penzance and Bristol all out except a few clerks at Exeter."

A mass meeting at the Skating Rink, India Road, Gloucester received a rousing speech from **Albert Purcell**, the MP for the Forest of Dean. Gloucester Trades Council and Labour Party Chairman **Jack Hieatt** gave a "fine fighting speech." He described how he had just returned from "a gigantic mass meeting in Swindon, he said that never in his life had he seen anything to equal the spirit of solidarity which had been displayed there."

Ralph Anstis in his book *Blood on Coal*, describes the strike in the Forest of Dean: "The effects of the rail strike were soon noticeable. At Awre station milk churns were left uncollected and Symonds Yat, Upper Lydbrook, Coleford, Parkend, Whitecroft, Bullo Pill and Blakeney stations were closed with the staff out in support of the miners. In Lydney six hundred tinplate workers ceased work."

Two editions of *Gloucester Strike Bulletin* on the last day reflect the sense of shock that the strike had been called off

On Sunday 9th May the North Street Picture House in Cheltenham was filled to capacity to hear strike reports ending with the Cheltenham Labour Male Voice Choir render some "rousing glees in a splendid manner".

Stroud was reported to have held "Fine meetings," with "Position satisfactory and orderly." Cheltenham had only two trams running and in Tewkesbury the strike was still going strong.

The *Bulletins* reported on the Strike Fund, football matches between the areas, concerts, a call for pickets

Gloucester Strike Bulletin
In Conjunction with Cheltenham.

STOP PRESS
END OF STRIKE
Nothing Official Yet.

OUR MOTTO MUST BE
All out together
All IN together

Cheltenham News

STRIKE STILL ON.
Employers want you to crawl back on their conditions.
Show what you think of them by standing out.
Capitalists Creating Chaos

to guard the allotments of trade unionists for fear of looting and other national news.

The seventh and final edition first appears with the headline "END OF STRIKE" and "Our motto must be all out together, all in together". But by the end of the day a second version was quickly produced saying "STRIKE STILL ON. Employers want you to crawl back on their conditions. Show them what you think by staying out."

Unions fought against victimisation as the strike collapsed and discipline was maintained. The all-male Typographical Association, stayed on strike when one employer refused to take back women bindery-hands. All were allowed back to work.

Somerset
At the start of the dispute a mass meeting was held in the YMCA Hall, Taunton. With 400 packed inside around a similar number unable to get in, the meeting heard from **Jas Young** for the railway workers. A joint strike committee was formed. The following day the strike was on, bringing to a halt the railways, the movement of coal, livestock, bricks and tiles.

By the third day of the strike about 1,000 brick and tile workers walked out, prompted by the sacking of strikers, although some confusion remained over the scale of the stoppage in the building trade.

A mass meeting held at Jarvis's Field in Taunton received a report on the situation in Bridgwater from **Jimmy Boltz** of the T&G. About 1,000 workers joined the strike at Highbridge especially from the large locomotive works. There was a report of a consignment of cheese needing to use a cross-channel steamer to get from Highbridge to Weston.

Swindon

Between 5,000 and 6,000 people gathered in Swindon Park to hear telegrams read out from all the unions calling on members to stop work. **Jack Hieatt**, T&G and Gloucester Trades Council Chairman spoke in solidarity along with **Councillor WH Robins** of the Railway Clerks.

Support for the strike held firm. On 10th May the Swindon Engineers met in the Mechanics Institute. The minutes record that "All members of the DC present. It was one of the finest meetings ever held, the hall being packed to excess and the members very enthusiastic."

The next day, when the strike was called off they assumed they had won and were shocked to learn of the terms. Another mass meeting in the park resolved not to return to work without a guarantee that all strikers would be re-instated. Employers tried to impose conditions for re-engagement and so the strike continued. On 13th May there was a riot when the Mayor ordered the trams to start running. Two left the depot for Old Town and Rodbourne. At the town centre thousands met them. Women were reported as having aprons full of stones. Fearful of the consequences, the Mayor ordered the trams back to the depot. Two days later a settlement was reached for a full return to work.

After the Strike

The failure of the General Strike was a disaster for trade unionism and working people. The government used the outcome to introduce savage new anti-union legislation.

The Trade Disputes and Trade Union Act of 1927 outlawed sympathy strikes and confined strikes to the trade or industry involved. It opened up unions to civil damages and limited the right to picket. It attacked the political use of union funds and banned civil servants from joining unions with political objects. Membership slumped to below five million for the first time since 1916.

Union funds had been drained by the dispute leaving them ill-equipped to fight back. Unemployment soared and employers took advantage of union weakness. Unions did not recover until after 1946 when the laws were relaxed.

The miners fight on

The South West had its collieries in Somerset and the Forest of Dean. The miners received a lot of support from their local communities. In east Bristol, the community pulled together to support the local miners. Public collections, co-op food vouchers and family support kept the miners fed. Eventually the miners were forced back to work.

Miners' Leader from Somerset

Arthur James Cook (1885-1931) was the son of a soldier born in the Somerset village of Wookey in 1885. In the early 1900s Cook left to be a miner in South Wales. By 1919 he was miners' agent (a union official) in the Rhondda.

Cook was a brilliant, erratic and emotional speaker . In 1924 he was elected General Secretary of the Miners' Federation at the age of 39. He played a key role in the 1926 miners' srike. He became the best known miners' leader. He died in 1931 aged just 47.

photo:TUC Library

MINERS OF SOMERSET!

WHILE YOU STRIKE THE PITS LOSE MONEY.

In May they could have paid the old wages for 7 hours.

Later on they could pay the old wages for 8 hours.

Now they can only offer 35½% for 8 hours.

If the Strike continues they will not be able to pay 35½%.

WHAT ARE YOU WAITING FOR?

Longer Strike MEANS Lower Wages !

The fight for jobs

Throughout the 1920s and 1930s the plight of the unemployed was a central issue for the labour movement. How to represent the unemployed roused fierce debates within unions and the Labour Party and ultimately split the minority Labour Government.

The TUC tried to get trades councils to support the unemployed and in 1921 the Bristol Unemployed Association was organised by **Teddy Parker**, Secretary of Bristol Trades Council.

The National Unemployed Workers' Movement was set up in 1921 to draw attention to the plight of unemployed workers and to fight the Means Test – where workers had to prove their hardship. It organised the unemployed on a national basis and the central element of its activities was a series of hunger marches.

The first national hunger march in 1922 generated media scare stories that it was a "Red Plot" funded from "Bolshevik gold". The march was supported by the TUC and joint activities were organised such as 'Unemployed Sunday' a national protest on 7th January 1923.

In September 1923 the TUC met in Plymouth and endorsed statements of joint work with the NUWM. Another national demonstration was held and the TUC held a special Congress on unemployment.

In 1927 unemployed South Wales miners marched to London. On 9th November they entered Bristol with every marcher wearing a miner's lamp.

The miners joined the Bath Remembrance Parade before moving on through Chippenham to Swindon. They were met by AJ Cook and Labour leaders from Swindon.

Wal Hannington, leader of the NUWM, said: "Thousands of Swindon workers gathered in the streets. Railwaymen in working clothes, carrying red flags, marched at the head of the army. Crowds lined the streets with tear-dimmed eyes as the marchers passed."

They were fed and put up in the public baths where a great meeting was held. 3,000 filled the hall with many more unable to get in.

The government was under pressure to cut spending and a committee including Margaret Bondfield from the TUC General Council recommended cuts in benefit levels. This brought protests across the labour movement. The suggested reduction to 8s led Bondfield to be nicknamed 'eight-bob-a-week Maggie'.

The NUWM was seen by many as a Communist Party front and its attacks on the TUC led to bitter divisions. By the time the second national hunger march was organised in January 1929 tensions were growing between the NUWM, the TUC and the Labour Party. A contingent left Plymouth on 8th February.

In May 1929 Labour formed a minority government with registered unemployment at over 2.5 million and rising. The NUWM march in 1930 set off despite opposition from Labour and TUC leaders.

The decision to cut unemployment benefit split the cabinet and in 1931 Ramsay MacDonald joined with the Tories and Liberals to form a new National Government.

In September 1931 the NUWM organised a march to the TUC Congress in Clifton, Bristol. It led to

Unemployed workers march from South Wales to Bristol

Bristol riots as police charge the out-of-work protesters

serious clashes with the police and many local workers turned out to support the protest.

In 1932 the NUWM organised more marches across the country including a number in Bristol. 'Struggle or Starve' was the theme.

Power not Pancakes

On Shrove Tuesday 1932 the police charged the march in Old Market Street, Bristol and two weeks later there was an even larger confrontation. The marches and pickets on the Poor Law Administrators led to the postponement of the benefit cuts.

But the NUWM's rise was short-lived. The leaders were arrested and by 1933 the Bristol branch was all but finished. Another march left the West Country in 1934.

Cornwall and Devon February 1934 March to London

Plymouth 7th; Ivybridge 7th; Totnes 8th; Newton Abbot 9th; Exeter 10th (rest here 11th); Honiton 12th; Chard 13th; Yeovil 14th; Shaftesbury 15th; Salisbury 16th; London 25th.

Walter Ayles

Born in London in 1879, Walter Ayles was one of five children of railway porter Percy Walter Ayles and his wife Elizabeth.

Aged thirteen he worked in a cardboard-box factory and then apprenticed at London and South-Western Railway engineering works. After a lockout in 1897 he went to Birmingham and became district secretary of the Amalgamated Society of Engineers.

In 1904 he joined the Independent Labour Party and was elected to the Birmingham Board of Guardians, Aston.

In 1910 Ayles moved to Bristol as ILP branch full-time Secretary. In 1912 he was elected to Bristol City Council for Easton, a seat he held until 1922.

His 1913 pamphlet *Bristol's Next Step* and 1923 ILP booklet *What a Socialist Town Council would do* helped spread his name. He was elected to ILP National Council 1912-1927 and chaired Bristol Labour Party for nine years.

A Methodist and Congregationalist preacher for twenty years, he later joined the Society of Friends (Quakers) and was an active teetotaller. An effective speaker in the West of England, Ayles' election meetings at Bristol North were described as occasions of almost religious fervour.

He was a firm pacifist and conscientious objector when the war

Walter Ayles

broke out. He became Secretary of the No More War Movement. He was imprisoned for refusing national service and as a consequence could not stand for Parliament in 1918.

He wrote several books and pamphlets including *Militarism unmasked, Burn your gunboats: the case for complete disarmament, The hell of unemployment: the only way out* and *Why I worked for peace during the Great War: complete and uncompromising reply.*

Ayles was elected MP for Bristol North 1923-1924 and 1929-1931. He lost in 1935 and he moved to win Southall in 1945. He was elected Labour MP for Hayes and Harlington in 1950. He died in 1953.

Plymouth born mutiny

In 1931 the Royal Navy faced a mass mutiny that had its inspiration in Devonport, Plymouth.

There were strikes in Plymouth port in January 1931 when both watches on HMS *Lucia* refused orders after being denied Sunday leave. This was a time of heightened trade union activity and political discussion on and off the ships.

The *Rodney*, the *Adventure*, the *Norfolk* and the *Hood* left Devonport on 7th September 1931. The usual waving crowds of wives and children had gathered on Plymouth Hoe and at Rusty Anchor. But the mood at home was one of anxiety as the men were facing the threat of drastic pay cuts. Ramsay MacDonald's National Government had agreed a pay cut that would reduce wages to 1925 levels – for the 'lower decks' that meant one shilling taken from their four shillings a day.

On 11th September, the ships were berthed at Invergordon on the Cromarty Firth in Scotland. The pay cuts were front-page news. A meeting of 600 sailors voted unanimously to strike.

24-year-old **Len Wincott** who sailed from Plymouth emerged as one of the leaders. He was an Able Seaman on the *Norfolk*.

The Admiralty's attempts at conciliation failed to impress the agitated crews. On 15th September the crew of the battleship *Rodney* refused orders. Ten ships were affected by the mutiny. As each ship's company stopped work they gathered on deck and cheered – passing the message down the line. Sailors used a system of whistles as signals for the action. As a consequence whistling on board Navy ships is banned.

Many of the sailors sang the *Red Flag* as the mutiny spread. Even the marines backed the striking seamen.

It was an unprecedented show of defiance and solidarity, half the Atlantic fleet – some 12,000 seamen

– mutinied. The rebellion excited headlines around the world. The pound plummeted on foreign exchanges. Within 24 hours the Admiralty capitulated and agreed to restore part of the wage cut. The ships were ordered to return home.

The government said it wanted no reprisals but Len Wincott and 396 ratings were discharged from the service.

In 1932, the Atlantic Fleet was renamed the Home Fleet, to purge the memory of the mutiny.

Len Wincott's involvement in the mutiny would shape a life full of contradictions. He worked in the Soviet Union in a factory, as a translator, an actor, and was drafted into the Red Army during the Second World War where he survived the siege of Leningrad. After the war, he appeared in Soviet films, ironically, playing the classical Englishman.

But he fell foul of Stalin's Soviet regime, and he was accused of spying for the British. He spent nearly twelve years in a labour camp from 1944.

The one-time mutineer was invited to the British embassy in Moscow each year to celebrate the Queen's birthday.

Wincott returned to Plymouth for the launch of his book, the *Invergordon Mutineer*. He died in the Soviet Union in 1983. His ashes were scattered over Plymouth Sound from a Royal Naval tender.

In the end, the Navy afforded him every respect.

Thanks to Neil Young and his article in the *Western Morning News* October 2007

HMS Norfolk

Dorset poets

Poets Sylvia Townsend Warner (1893-1978) and life-time partner Valentine Ackland (1906-1969) shocked conventional attitudes at the time when they lived together in Dorset villages of Chaldon and Frome Vauchurch.

The lesbian couple joined the Communist Party in 1935 and campaigned for the Spanish Republic. They volunteered for the Red Cross during the Civil War in Spain. Sylvia Warner spoke at Left Book Club meetings in Dorchester and wrote articles for the *Left Review* on the hidden poverty in rural England. She published seven novels, four volumes of poetry, a volume of essays, and eight volumes of short stories.

Valentine Ackland published her

Sylvia Townsend Warner | Valentine Ackland

first poems in *Modern Anthology* in 1923. Although she married when she was nineteen she was not happy and divorced six months later.

Dressing like a man, she moved to Chaldon in Dorset where she was able to live more freely and it was there that she met Sylvia Townsend Warner. After the Second World War, Valentine recovered from alcoholism and ended a long-term love affair that had threatened her relationship with Sylvia.

Frome Vauchurch

Dorchester

Weymouth • Chaldon

thanks to www.townsendwarner.com

Radical artists

Born in Bath in 1890, Doris Hatt studied Art there before progressing to the Royal College and the Vienna Conservatoire of Art. In the 1920s she worked in Paris where she befriended Picasso, Braque and others, She developed a radical style with a strong sense of colour and boldness of composition.

In 1932, Doris designed a remarkable

modernist house in the seaside town of Clevedon, Somerset. She caused a scandal by living there with her lesbian partner and artist Margery Mack Smith. The Communist couple, attempted to sell the *Daily Worker* to locals. They must have helped Bert Searl get elected as Communist councillor for Clevedon in the 1950s

Doris Hatt continued to paint until her death in 1969. Margery born in Bristol in 1890 died in 1975, aged 84.

Nancy Astor

Born in America, **Nancy Astor** moved to England in 1904. In 1906, she married the wealthy politician Waldorf Astor. He became the Conservative MP for Plymouth Sutton in 1910 but had to give up his seat when he inherited his father's title of Viscount Astor.

Nancy stood in his place and won the election in November 1919, beating the Liberal, Isaac Foot, the father of Michael Foot.

She became the first woman MP to take her seat in the House of Commons. Winston Churchill compared her arrival with someone intruding into his bathroom.

She was MP for Plymouth Sutton for 26 years and played a heroic part during the bombing of the city. Although a Conservative, she was a fervent fighter for women's causes and equal rights.

> " *I knew what kept me going – I was an ardent feminist.* Nancy Astor 1956 "

SUTTON DIVISION.

Parliamentary Bye-Election, 1919.

To the Electors of the Sutton Division of Plymouth.

Nancy Astor **election leaflet**

Shop work to cabinet

Margaret Bondfield (1873-1953) was the first woman cabinet minister in Britain. Born in Chard, Somerset, the eleventh child of Anne Taylor and William Bondfield, she was a textile worker with left-wing views. She began an apprenticeship at the age of fourteen in a draper's shop in Brighton and soon got involved in the union.

In 1896 the Women's Industrial Council commissioned her to investigate the pay and conditions of shop workers. In 1898 she was elected assistant secretary of the Shop Assistants' Union and in 1908 became secretary of the Women's Labour League. She was President of the TUC General Council in 1923.

In 1923 Margaret Bondfield was elected Labour MP for Northampton but lost her seat a year later. She won again in 1926, in a by-election in Wallsend. She was appointed Minister of Labour by Ramsay MacDonald in 1929. This was the first time that a woman had been made a Cabinet Minister.

She supported cuts in unemployment benefit to eight shillings a week, earning her the nickname 'eight-bob Maggie' and protests from labour activists.

After she lost her seat in the 1931 general election she became chair of the Women's Group on Public Welfare.

She also wrote a number of books including: *Socialism for Shop Assistants* (1909), *Why Labour Fights* (1941) and *A Life's Work* (1949).

Margaret Bondfield

Living-in

Conditions for shop workers were hard. Low pay was compounded by arrangements for living-in with workers sometimes forced to sleep under the counter.

Margaret Bondfield was herself a live-in assistant and campaigned for better conditions. Her pamphlet *Socialism for Shop Assistants* highlighted the degradation of the system: "The utter absence of privacy at any time night and day is far too common."

Food was often miserable with bread and margarine a staple diet.

In the "oversexed atmosphere", abuse of young shop women was common.

Margaret Bondfield took up the cause through her union activities but she also argued for a socialist alternative where men and women would be engaged in a service to the community and would acquire a new dignity and purpose in life.

The Right Hon.
MARGARET BONDFIELD
CH., LLD., JP., 1873 - 1953
THE FIRST WOMAN CABINET MINISTER
1929 - 1931
WAS BORN IN THIS TOWN
Shop Worker, Christian, Socialist, Trades Unionist, she devoted her life to improving the lot of the downtrodden.
PRESENTED TO THE TOWN OF CHARD ON THE 760th ANNIVERSARY OF ITS FIRST CHARTER BY U.S.D.A.W. AND THE LABOUR PARTY
Unveiled by the Rt. Hon. Barbara Castle M.E.P. On the 20th September 1985

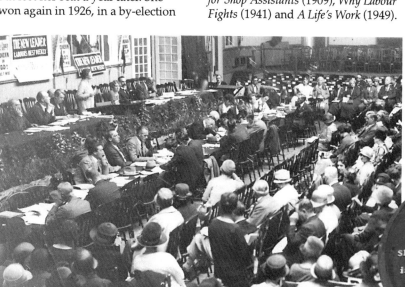
Margaret Bondfield speaks to the TUC Women's Conference in Bournemouth in 1926

photo: TUC Library

Henry Fawcett

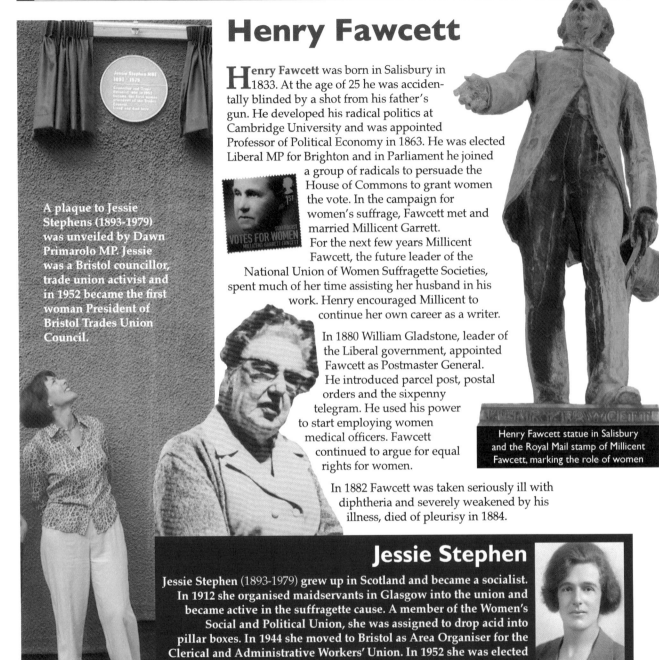

Henry Fawcett was born in Salisbury in 1833. At the age of 25 he was accidentally blinded by a shot from his father's gun. He developed his radical politics at Cambridge University and was appointed Professor of Political Economy in 1863. He was elected Liberal MP for Brighton and in Parliament he joined a group of radicals to persuade the House of Commons to grant women the vote. In the campaign for women's suffrage, Fawcett met and married Millicent Garrett. For the next few years Millicent Fawcett, the future leader of the National Union of Women Suffragette Societies, spent much of her time assisting her husband in his work. Henry encouraged Millicent to continue her own career as a writer.

In 1880 William Gladstone, leader of the Liberal government, appointed Fawcett as Postmaster General. He introduced parcel post, postal orders and the sixpenny telegram. He used his power to start employing women medical officers. Fawcett continued to argue for equal rights for women.

In 1882 Fawcett was taken seriously ill with diphtheria and severely weakened by his illness, died of pleurisy in 1884.

A plaque to Jessie Stephens (1893-1979) was unveiled by Dawn Primarolo MP. Jessie was a Bristol councillor, trade union activist and in 1952 became the first woman President of Bristol Trades Union Council.

Henry Fawcett statue in Salisbury and the Royal Mail stamp of Millicent Fawcett, marking the role of women

Jessie Stephen

Jessie Stephen (1893-1979) grew up in Scotland and became a socialist. In 1912 she organised maidservants in Glasgow into the union and became active in the suffragette cause. A member of the Women's Social and Political Union, she was assigned to drop acid into pillar boxes. In 1944 she moved to Bristol as Area Organiser for the Clerical and Administrative Workers' Union. In 1952 she was elected President of the Bristol Trades Council and to the City Council.

Jessie was awarded an MBE in 1977 and died in 1979.

The fight for pensions

Before 1908, working people who needed help in old age had to rely on charity or parish relief. Otherwise they ended up in the local workhouse where life was deliberately brutal.

In 1901 baby boys were expected to live for 45 years and girls 49 years. Few who reached the end of their working lives had a pension. In 1891 England had 1.3 million paupers including some 419,000 over the age of 60.

In 1898 trade unions, socialists, progressive Liberals, co-operative societies and church groups began a nationwide campaign for an old-age-pension. In 1899 the Hannah Hall in Bristol was the venue for a major conference to demand a state pension.

The TUC Congress held in Bath in 1907 passed a landmark motion demanding an old age pension. Margaret Bondfield from Chard represented the Union of Shop Assistants on the National Pensions Committee Executive.

After a decade of campaigning, the Liberal government passed the Old Age Pensions Act in 1908. The first state pension of five shillings a week became payable at the beginning of 1909 and there was a rush at the post offices on the morning of the first day. Although set very low, it became the foundation of the State Pension.

Some 4,000 people in Bristol qualified as being aged over 70 and in receipt of an annual income of less than £21.1.0 per annum.

Excluded were those not of 'good character', 'lunatics' and those guilty of 'habitual failure to work'. Initially, most of the recipients were women.

Pensioner Campaigns

At the TUC conference in 1978, a Campaign for Pensioners was agreed and Jack Jones, who had just retired as General Secretary of the Transport and General Workers Union, proposed that a National Pensioners' Convention be arranged.

On the 14 June 1979 the first National Pensioners' Convention was held in Westminster; attended by 2,500 older people, who adopted a *Declaration of Intent*: "This Convention declares that every pensioner has the right to choice, dignity, independence and security as an integral and valued member of society".

In 1986, the steering committee agreed to encourage the development of regional and local pensioners' groups. West Country NPC groups were formed and the organisation became an independent and separate entity – run by pensioners for pensioners.

Jack Jones campaigning for pensioners at the 2000 Tolpuddle Rally

First female doctor

Elizabeth Blackwell was born on 3rd February 1821, near Bristol. The family emigrated to America in 1832 where Elizabeth tried to enter the field of medicine. After many rejections she tried Geneva Medical College in New York.

The administration consulted the students who, believing it to be a practical joke, endorsed her admission. On finding out that her interest was serious they tried to make life difficult and even kept her from medical demonstrations.

Blackwell won many over with her determination and talent. In 1849 she graduated to become the first woman doctor. She went on to become a leading public health activist.

Dr Elizabeth Blackwell at work

The Labour Party

The Labour Party grew across the South West and with mounting trade union support challenged the Liberals to represent working class interests. It was West Country miners that elected the first Labour MP in the region.

The first Labour MP in the South West was **Fred Gould,** elected for Frome, Somerset in 1923 and again in 1929. The constituency included Keynsham and south east Bristol along with the mining areas of north Somerset. Meetings were normally held in Radstock.

Fred Gould MP

photo: National Portrait Gallery

In 1931 some 17 per cent of workers in the area were employed in the mines but it was also a stronghold for the National Union of Boot and Shoe Operatives of which Fred Gould was the secretary of their Midsomer Norton branch. As MP he became parliamentary private secretary to a minister at the Board of Trade. Having lost the seat in 1931 his union moved him to fight Leicester East where there were more footwear workers although he was unsuccessful.

With Fred Gould and his union's money gone, Frome Labour selected **RWG 'Kim' Mackay,** as candidate. He was a wealthy Australian solicitor promoted by Sir Stafford Cripps MP for the neighbouring Bristol seat. Mackay was a very effective organiser and built the Frome party. He was narrowly defeated in 1935 and in 1942 fought Llandaff and Barry by-election as an Independent Labour Party candidate in violation of the wartime electoral truce. He was expelled from the Labour Party and became the national organiser for the Common Wealth party. He later rejoined Labour and was elected MP for Hull. Without his support the Frome Party was less effective.

Walter Farthing was elected in Labour's landslide in 1945 but failed to make his mark and the seat fell to the Tories at the next election.

Fred Gould's son, **Sir Ronald Gould** (1904-1986) became active in the National Union of Teachers and was elected President in 1943.

Vernon Bartlett

In November 1938 Bridgwater played a crucial role on the world stage in the fight against fascism when a by-election campaign on the issue of the Munich Agreement was fought there.

Vernon Bartlett (1894-1983) born in Westbury, Wiltshire, shocked the political establishment when he won a by-election to become the MP for Bridgwater in 1938 standing on an anti-fascist programme. He was the Popular Front candidate opposed to appeasement and held the seat for twelve years.

With the Compliments of Mr. Vernon Bartlett

Vote for BARTLETT

In 1942 Vernon Bartlett helped Richard Acland, JB Priestley and others establish the socialist Common Wealth Party. At the 1945 election, he kept his Bridgwater seat, standing as an independent.

In 1950 he joined the Labour Party and retired from parliament.

Bournemouth Fabians

Founded in 1884, the Fabian Society was part of the coalition that formed the Labour Party. Fabians promoted research and campaigned for the welfare state, independence for British colonies and democratic socialism.

Bournemouth was one of the first towns to have a Fabian Society and the most famous early members – **Beatrice and Sidney Webb** – became associated with the south coast resort.

Beatrice attended school in Bournemouth and in 1886 her father settled in a house near the Royal Bath Hotel. She was in Bournemouth when her letter on unemployment was printed in the *Pall Mall Gazette* and seen by Joseph Chamberlain, a leading Liberal. She had an infatuation with the ageing widower and it stirred her political writings.

During work on co-operative history, Beatrice met Sidney Webb. In 1890 she noted in her diary: "At last I am a socialist." Sidney came to Bournemouth to recover from scarlet fever and in 1891 they were married.

Sidney Webb wrote *Clause IV* of the new Labour Party constitution calling

Beatrice and Sidney Webb

for collective ownership of the means of production, distribution and exchange.

In 1910 Beatrice spoke in Bournemouth on her *Minority Report on the Poor Law Commission*. Organised by the Poole and Bournemouth branch of the National Committee for the Prevention of Destitution, the meeting heard the Fabian case for public spending to relieve poverty. Beatrice appealed to those living comfortable lives in the town to help.

The Bournemouth Fabians continued to promote their policies and attract radical speakers. For a while the left-leaning paper *Tribune* was printed on the *Bournemouth Times* presses and the Fabian Society formed the Bournemouth Civic Society to protect the town's heritage.

Radical Dick

Beatrice Webb (1858-1943) was the granddaughter of radical MP Richard Potter. Richard Potter was returned as Liberal MP for Wigan in 1832, following the Reform Act. He later unsuccessfully contested Gloucester. His political views earned him the nickname 'Radical Dick'. Richard Potter's son, also called Richard, was Chairman of the Great Western Railway.

Beatrice Webb

Workers in power

In April 1890 the Agent for the Bristol Miners' Association, Mr W Whitefield, wrote to all 3,000 members suggesting that they pay 3d a quarter to send three or four Labour MPs to Parliament. By 1906 the miners joined the Labour Representation Committee.

During this period various national Labour leaders came to the Somerset coal area including George Lansbury, Kier Hardie and Arthur Henderson. On 20th August 1915 the Radstock and District Labour Representation Committee was formed to get candidates elected on all local and national bodies. In 1917 the Radstock Independent Labour Party complained at being barred from Victoria Hall due to the war.

On 16th January 1918 inaugural meeting of the Radstock Trades and Labour Council was held at the Miners' Office.

In service and forgotten

Photo: Planet News/Science & Society Picture Library

Red Kate Spurrell

Kate Spurrell was a teacher in Plymouth and in the 1920s was accused of preaching communism. She was active in support of the General Strike, speaking at rallies and raising funds. She stood for Labour in Totnes in 1929 and in 1935 for the Independent Labour Party in Camborne. She was friendly with Jimmy Maxton the radical leader of the ILP.

Spurrell and Lady Nancy Astor were fierce political opponents in Plymouth and always mutually critical in public. Spurrell asked Lady Astor, then Mayoress, for help in evacuating children. Help was given generously and a lasting friendship formed.

In 1942 she officially opened the Nursery Centre at Dartington Hall.

Throughout the nineteenth century and up to the First World War, domestic service was the largest employment for women.

Girls of ten to twelve – sometimes younger – would leave home to join a strange household. The hours were long and the pay poor. Life beyond work was spent between dark basements and attic bedrooms.

By the 1920s, domestic service declined as women found work in factories and offices. Female trade union membership rose sharply. 357,000 women were members in 1914 and more than a million by 1918 a rise of 160 per cent. Pay, however, was only half that of men's.

A correspondent to the *Daily Mail* complained in 1923: "It is almost impossible to get a domestic servant in this town and it is high time this dole business ceased. The streets are full of girls dressed to death, who frankly say that as long as they are paid to do nothing they will continue as they are."

Domestic service had fallen to eight per cent of women workers by 1931. The shortage of candidates became known as the 'servant problem'.

Child of the Forest
Winifred Foley wrote of her life in her popular book, *A Child in the Forest*. She was born in 1914 in the Forest of Dean. When

her fourteenth birthday came it was her time to leave. "For girls, going into service was our only future. My childhood was dead – now I was the skivvy."

Winifred describes how she ceased to be a person once in her maid's cap and apron. "I would become a menial, a nobody, mindful of my place, on the bottom shelf."

When working for an old lady in the Cotswolds for five shillings a week, hours: 6.30am to 11pm. The daughters took pleasure in abusing the young maid. Winifred ran away and worked for a Cheltenham family who "were trying to keep up an appearance beyond their means" and she nearly starved.

For Winifred like so many other servants, marriage and a family was her escape.

Women's lot
In 1859, the Bristol Female Mission Society was established by women for women. It was said to have 'rescued' about 1,200 women from prostitution and trained them in domestic service.

A girl marrying at 19-years-old in 1871 would expect to have at least seven children over 25 years. One out of four would die in the process.

Today, women in Britain have less than two children on average.

Winifred Foley, a child of the Forest and domestic servant

Stafford Cripps

Sir Stafford Cripps (1889-1952) was born in London to an aristocratic family. In 1931 he was appointed Solicitor General and got with it a knighthood.

His strong socialist views included the nationalisation of the means of production and distribution. He was elected MP for Bristol East and was one of the founders of the Socialist League that argued for a united front to defeat the rising threat of fascism. He was the main force behind a Unity Campaign that brought the Socialist League, the Independent Labour Party and the Communist Party together to fight the far-right. When the Socialist League disbanded its newspaper, *Tribune* carried on.

Stafford was expelled from the Labour Party in 1939 for his views on a Popular Front with the Communist Party. Winston Churchill appointed him as ambassador to the Soviet Union in the wartime coalition. He championed the alliance with the Soviet Union to defeat Hitler.

In 1945 he rejoined the Labour Party and was given the job of President of the Board of Trade and in 1947 became Chancellor at a time of deep economic crisis. He increased taxes and supported the nationalisation of strategic industries such as coal and steel. His harsh tax policies were not popular, especially amongst the middle classes. By 1950 his poor health broke down and he was forced to resign. He died two years later.

Vote for Cripps!

GENERAL ELECTION *Election Address*

painting by Arthur Boughley, National Archives

Stafford Cripps

photo Dave Chapple

Kingsley Hall

56 Old Market Street, Bristol was an important meeting room for the labour movement in Bristol and by the 1930s housed the offices of Bristol Trades Union Council. Built in 1706 it was used in the late 1800s by East Bristol Conservatives. In the 20th Century it became Bristol headquarters of the Independent Labour Party who renamed it in honour of the Christian Socialist Charles Kingsley.

Jennie Lee fights for Bristol

Lord Apsley, the MP for Bristol Central, was killed on 17 December 1942 whilst serving with the Arab Legion in Malta. This triggered a by-election. The Coalition parties agreed not to contest by-elections but Jennie Lee, Aneurin Bevan's wife, stood as Independent Labour, John McNair stood for the Independent Labour Party and F Dunn as Independent. The Conservative candidate was Violet Bathurst, Lady Apsley, widow of the late MP.

Jennie Lee's banners called her "The Peoples Champion" and demanded: "We want Beveridge and Jenny Lee". But with the left vote split, the result was a Conservative victory.

Spanish International Brigades

In the 1930s workers from the West Country gave up their jobs to go to Spain to fight to defend democracy.

In April 1931 the new Republican Government in Spain began implementing social reforms. They were strongly opposed by the landowners, Catholic church and traditional elements within the army.

In the 1933 elections Spain swung to the right and the new government reversed many of the changes. Parties of the left united in the Popular Front and won the 1936 elections.

After violent street battles between left and right in 1936, Nationalist army officers led by General Franco staged a coup to overthrow the Republican Government. They were aided by fascist Italy and Nazi Germany which supplied money, weapons and troops. Britain refused to intervene.

International Brigades
Some 30,000 foreign volunteers, including many from Britain, went to fight in the International Brigades for the Republic.

They knew that democracy was under threat and that if the fascists won in Spain then the rest of Europe would be at risk.

The course of the war
The International Brigades successfully defended Madrid in November 1936. But in 1937 Franco's forces seized Malaga and the Basque region.

The town of Guernica was destroyed by bombing. Picasso captured the horror of the war in his painting of the scene.

In 1938 Republicans recaptured Teruel but then lost it to the Nationalists after a fierce battle. Nationalists broke through to the sea, cutting the Republican forces in half.

The battle at the River Ebro exhausted the Republican forces and in 1939 the Nationalists overwhelmed what was left of them. The International Brigades were sent home.

In the aftermath, tens of thousands of Republican men and women were executed or imprisoned. Many were forced into exile.

Franco remained in power until his death in 1975 after which Spain successfully made the transition to a modern European democracy.

West Country Brigaders

West Country trade unionists who joined the call to Spain and died for the cause are remembered on plaques at the Tolpuddle Martyrs' Museum and in Castle Park, Bristol. Research was done by **Dave Yeomans**.

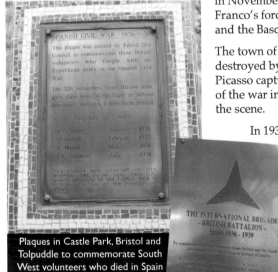

Plaques in Castle Park, Bristol and Tolpuddle to commemorate South West volunteers who died in Spain

Food for Spain leaflet from Bill Nicholas in Bristol

The Spanish International Brigade stall at the
Tolpuddle Martyrs' Festival in 2008

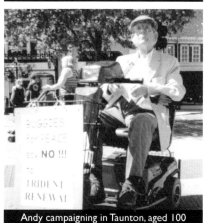

Howard Andrews in Spain
during the Civil War

Andy campaigning in Taunton, aged 100

Andy back in Spain for the 75th anniversary

Brigaders with West Country links include **Penny Fyvel**, who retired to Bournemouth, was a nurse in Spain and wrote a book about her life.

Known in Spain by her maiden name of Phelps, she worked in makeshift frontline hospitals in conditions of great hardship and danger. She suffered serious injuries in a bombing raid that put an end to her service in Spain.

Many more in the West Country, like **Bill Nicholas** from Bristol – organised collections and rallied support for the republican fighters.

Howard Andrews (known as Andy) was a hospital worker for the Brigades. He helped fight the fascists in the East End of London and recognised the importance of the battle in Spain.

He settled in Taunton after the war and died in 2008 at the age of 101.

The International Brigade Memorial Trust was formed in 2002: "To educate the public in the history of the men and women who fought in the International Brigades and in the medical and other support services in the Spanish Civil War."

Dartmoor Riot

Prison violence may not be worthy of celebration but the mutiny that occurred in Dartmoor Prison in 1932 forced the authorities to re-think harsh penal policies.

It was a short-lived affair on 24th January 1932 with some 250 convicts wrecking property and burning buildings. It was sparked by an incident when a prisoner was knocked unconcious by a guard. There were other issues such as poor food.

With the prison under their control, the inmates took to eating, smoking, music and dancing. Police and army units arrived from Plymouth to quell the riot. 32 rioters were charged and 'loyal' prisoners were rewarded with early release.

Rosebud protest

In 1935 proposals were drawn up to demolish the cramped fishing cottages in Newlyn and build a new estate to be called Gwavas. Many people were upset that the houses where generations of families were born and raised would vanish, and that the heart of the village would be torn out.

Photo: Charles Hoyland, amateur photographer experimenting with colour photography.

The Rosebud in London

The site and design of the new estate was not liked: at the top of the steep hill, it would be isolated and hard to reach for the elderly and infirm.

The colony of Newlyn School artists backed the villagers who wanted to save the houses and a local issue became a national one.

A petition was gathered and a Newlyn fishing boat, sailed to Westminster to deliver it straight to Parliament. On Monday 21st October 1937 the *Rosebud* arrived in London to great attention from the press.

The petition was delivered amidst a fanfare of publicity and the government responded by saving some of the houses.

Newlyn's saved houses

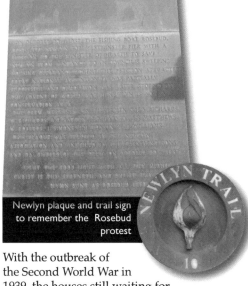

Newlyn plaque and trail sign to remember the Rosebud protest

With the outbreak of the Second World War in 1939, the houses still waiting for demolition were pressed into use as emergency accommodation. These houses were modernised and survive to this day.

Remnant of the Rosebud

Bodmin Moor

Truro

Penzance

Newlyn

West at war

War memorial depicting Exeter in 1942

War devastated working class communities in the West Country. The lives lost are remembered by the hundreds of war memorials in towns and villages across the region.

People recognised the danger of fascism spreading across Europe. Men of military age were conscripted to fight, many did not return.

War came to the South West in the form of German bombing raids aimed at the key military targets such as Bristol and Plymouth.

Bath
Bath's civilian population was subjected to a fierce onslaught during three nights in April 1942. The Luftwaffe attack, in retaliation for RAF raids on the Baltic cities, destroyed many of the city's buildings with incendiary bombs. They returned to machine gun the unprotected streets. 417 people lost their lives and a further 425 were injured.

Plymouth
The first bombs to be dropped on Plymouth fell just before midday on Saturday 6th July 1940.

In late March, 1941 German bombers devastated Plymouth. In just seven nights the centres of Plymouth and Devonport were laid to ruin. Many of the 292 civilians killed during the raids were buried in mass graves at Efford Cemetery. As the city tried to recover, more raids came in April, killing 72 in one night.

The 590th bombing raid on Plymouth took place on Sunday 30th April 1944. The main target of the attack was the water-front where eighteen people were killed.

Bristol
With the docks and aircraft manufacturing, Bristol was a key target for German bombers. On 24th November 1940 Bristol experienced its first Blitz. The raid lasted six hours and destroyed much of the old city, including the main shopping area, now Castle Park. Bombs were also dropped on Bedminster, Knowle, St. George and Clifton. 207 were killed.

Coventry had been badly bombed and the government feared the loss of morale from more press coverage of devastated cities. So it was reported that raids had hit 'a town in the west'.

Just two weeks later Bristol was bombed again. In two raids 256 people were killed. On 3rd January 1941 the targets were the docks and Temple Meads railway station. One raid lasted nearly twelve hours killing another 149 people. During the raid a massive 4,000lb bomb fell unexploded on Knowle. Nicknamed Satan, the bomb was made safe and was included in the 1945 London victory parade.

On 16th March 1941 came another heavy raid. On this day 162 bombers attacked Avonmouth, Whitehall, Easton, Eastville, St. Paul's and Fishponds. When the raid ended 257 people had died and 391 people had been injured.

Working class communities suffered most from the onslaught.

Exercise Tiger

746 men died off the south Devon shore in training for the Normandy Landings. In 1944 a series of blunders proved disastrous for the troops rehearsing for the invasion.

General Eisenhower felt that the men needed to experience real battle conditions. So when the landing craft came ashore at Slapton they were met with live firing. 308 died from 'friendly fire'.

The training took troops from Torbay and Plymouth to land ashore at Slapton. Of the two ships appointed to protect the exercise, one stayed in Plymouth for repairs and the other was badly positioned to avoid the surprise German E-boat attack.

The fast German torpedo boats proved devastating. The US and British forces were on different radio frequencies due to a typing error and

Slapton plaque to US dead

in the confusion more were killed by 'friendly fire'. Many men drowned in the cold sea waiting to be rescued, not used to the ill-fitting life-belts and struggling under the weight of heavy combat packs.

Survivors were sworn to secrecy and the death toll only announced after the actual D-Day landings.

Local resident **Ken Small** has campaigned to uncover the truth and commemorate the lives lost. He had a Sherman tank raised from the sea bed

and, along with a plaque, stands in memory of the Americans killed.

Politics and war

The war politicised a generation of working class voters. The determination never to return to poverty and unemployment grew. The need for central planning of transport and essential industries convinced people of the value of nationalisation. People from different class backgrounds were thrown together in the heat of battle and many came out believing that socialism offered a more equal and fair society.

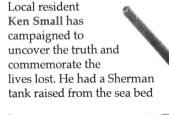

Sherman tank as memorial to those killed off Slapton

Remains of Tyneham village in Dorset

Tyneham sacrifice

Tyneham is a ghost village near Worbarrow Bay in south Dorset. The village, and surrounding countryside, were commandeered just before Christmas 1943 by the War Office for use as firing ranges for training troops in the run-up to the D-Day landings. The last of the 252 villagers evicted left a notice on the church door:

"Please treat the church and houses with care; we have given up our homes where many of us lived for generations to help win the war to keep men free. We shall return one day and thank you for treating the village kindly."

No-one has been allowed to return to live there and the area remains a military training area. Some of those born in the village campaigned to return or at least have access to the village. **John Gould** was born in Tyneham in 1912, as a Labour Party member, he wrote to Harold Wilson, Prime Minister appealing for help.

In 1975, after a local campaign, the Ministry of Defence began opening the village and footpaths across the ranges at weekends and throughout August. The church and school house have been preserved as museums.

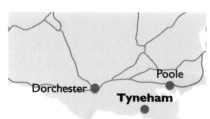

John Gould was born at TYNEHAM 60 YEARS AGO HE WANTS TO COME HOME

John Gould protests in 1972

Richard Acland and the Common Wealth Party

An aristocrat like **Sir Richard Thomas Dyke Acland,** (1906-1990) seems an unlikely candidate for a mention in this book. Born in Broadclyst, Devon he was a barrister and architect. He stood unsuccessfully as a Liberal candidate for Torquay in 1929, and for Barnstaple in 1931, finally winning the North Devon seat in 1935.

His politics shifted dramatically to the left and in 1942 he broke with the war coalition government to lead the socialist Common Wealth Party.

The Party advocated public ownership of land as well as wider common ownership. He gave away his Devon family estate of 19,000 acres (8,097 hectares) to the National Trust.

Acland's published works include *Unser Kampf* (1940), *The Forward March* (1941), *What it will be like* (1942) and *How it can be done* (1943).

The Common Wealth Party won three stunning by-elections only to be wiped out at the polls in 1945. Acland himself fought the London seat of Putney where he came a poor third.

By 1946 the Common Wealth Party had split but those involved went on to form the Industrial Common Ownership Movement. The Party had believed in regional devolution and members became active in the environmental movement.

Richard Acland joined the Labour Party and was elected as the MP for Gravesend in 1947. He resigned in 1955 over Labour's support for the Conservative Government's nuclear policy and helped form the Campaign for Nuclear Disarmament in 1957.

He continued to write on education and world peace until his death at Broadclyst, Devon, in 1990.

WHAT'S BEHIND THIS?

1945 Common Wealth election leaflet with a fake hoarding of Conservative anti-Common Wealth posters, 'What's Behind This?', is answered by a Zec cartoon from the *Daily Mirror* on the reverse – "it's big business and state control that's behind it".

A statue of thanks from Gaetano Celestra, Italian Prisoner of War, Somerset, 1945

Italian prisoners

During the war Italian prisoners were held in a camp at Penleigh near Wells in Somerset. Prisoner Gaetano Celestra was a stone mason and in appreciation of the kind way the prisoners were treated he built a statue based upon the legend of Romulus and Remus, the founders of Rome. It stands alongside the A39 at Pen Hill.

Sir Richard Acland

Photo: National Portrait Gallery

Union men

James Thomas was born in Newport in 1874 and brought up by his grand-mother who took in washing from the crews on the ships in the docks.

At twelve he began work as an errand boy. In 1892 he became a railway fireman in a local colliery. Jimmy joined the Associated Society of Railway Servants Union and became an activist.

He became a full-time officer for the union and moved to Swindon, then a centre for the railways. He became a popular figure amongst the local workforce and was elected as a councillor for the town.

He moved to Derby where he was elected Labour MP in 1910. Thomas retained his links to the union and helped organise the rail strike of 1911. He helped form the National Union of Railwaymen and was elected General Secretary in 1917.

Thomas led the national strike of 1919. The rail unions complained the government was exploiting a war time agreement to cut pay due to falling inflation. As General Secretary, Thomas promised that it would be a 'model strike' without violence, although there were reports of incidents and the Riot Act was read

Jimmy Thomas

in Glasgow. The government backed down after one of the most successful strikes organised by the rail unions.

After the 1924 General Election Thomas became Secretary of State for the Colonies. In the 1926 General Strike the mine workers' union accused him of betrayal for failing to show them enough support.

The charge of treachery grew when he joined Ramsey MacDonald's National Government that imposed cuts in unemployment pay. The Labour Party expelled him.

Jimmy Thomas retained his government position until 1936 when he was accused of leaking Budget secrets in return for £15,000 from a stock-broker friend. He claimed the cash was an advance for a proposed autobiography but the story seemed implausible and he was forced to resign.

Throughout his turbulent career he enjoyed the loyalty of the Swindon rail workers and when he died in 1948 his body was brought back to the town for his funeral. Workers lined the streets of Swindon to honour him.

His son Leslie Thomas became the Conservative MP for Canterbury.

Herbert Bullock

Herbert Bullock (1885-1967) was a trace horse driver for the glue factory in Bedminster. He lived at 3 Hedwick Avenue, St George, Bristol. He became active in the National Union of General and Municipal Workers (now GMB) and in 1926 became an officer for the union working out of an office in Kingsley Hall in Bristol. In 1935 he was a National Industrial Officer. He was elected onto the TUC General Council in 1937 and demonstrated his interest in adult education and youth welfare. In 1950 he became President of the TUC just before he retired.

Herbert Bullock sitting with Vincent Tewson, TUC General Secretary at the 1950 Trades Union Congress

photo: TUC Library

West Country Foots

Isaac Foot

Isaac Foot was born in Plymouth in 1880, the son of a carpenter. In 1904 he stood for election to Plymouth Borough Council as a representative for Charles Ward but was unsuccessful, as he was again in 1906 as the Liberal candidate for Compton Ward. Third time lucky, he was elected in 1907 to represent Greenbank Ward.

Isaac tried several times to become a local MP before winning in Bodmin in 1921. This was the first of a series of elections and he had to fight the same seat in 1923 and 1924, when he was again defeated. He won in 1929 and served until 1935, when he transferred his campaign to St Ives and then, in 1945, to Tavistock.

He was appointed Minister for Mines in 1931-32 and was made a Privy Councillor in 1937. He held numerous other positions, including in the Methodist Church and temperance movement.

Isaac Foot died at his home in Callington, Cornwall, in 1960.

Isaac Foot

Fred Cole, T&G Organiser, shows Michael Foot around Tolpuddle

He had five sons and two daughters including: Sir Hugh Foot, former Governor of Jamaica, and Governor of Cyprus; Mr Dingle Foot, QC, Liberal MP for Dundee and Labour MP for Ipswich; and Michael Foot.

Michael Foot

Michael Foot was the first Labour MP for Plymouth Devonport in 1945 – a seat he held for ten years. After that he was elected MP for Ebbw Vale in South Wales.

He was a leading figure in the Campaign for Nuclear Disarmament and an influential political speaker and parliamentarian. He wrote widely and published biographies on many politicians of left and right.

Michael Foot became the Labour Leader during the Thatcher Government. Although the party went on to suffer one of its worst defeats in 1983, he remained one of the most respected politicians of the twentieth century.

In 2003 Foot, aged 90 and a passionate supporter of Plymouth Argyle Football Club, was registered as a player and given the shirt number, 90. This made him the oldest registered player in the history of football. He died in 2010.

The New Hope for Britain
Labour's Manifesto 1983

THINK POSITIVE THINK LABOUR.

60p

1983 Labour Manifesto: dubbed by the Party's right-wing as "the longest suicide note in history".

1945 Labour Landslide

After the horrors of the war and memories of the 1930s depression, people wanted a new vision for society.

The 1945 General Election saw Labour sweep to power on a radical programme and nationalisation, the NHS and welfare reform. The South West returned the following Labour MPs:

Bristol Central
Stan Awbery
Bristol East
Stafford Cripps
Bristol North
Will Coldrick
Bristol South
William Wilkins
Forest of Dean
Morgan Price
Frome
Walter Farthing
Gloucester
Moss Turner-Samuels
Penryn and Falmouth
EM King
Plymouth Devonport
Michael Foot
Plymouth Drake
Herbery Moses Medland
Plymouth Sutton
Lucy Middleton
Stroud
Ben Parkin
Swindon
Thomas Reid
Taunton
Victor Collins
Thornbury
Bert Alpass

Cotswold Red Baron

Wogan Phillips (1902-1993) was the son of a ship owner. He became Lord Milford, the Second Baron of Milford and the only communist in the House of Lords.

After Oxford University studying art, he sympathised strongly with the miners' cause during the General Strike of 1926. He joined the Communist Party in 1937, much to the disgust of his staunch Conservative father who responded by disinheriting him.

Phillips went to Spain at the outbreak of the Spanish Civil War and joined the Medical Aid to Spain as an ambulance driver. He was later wounded but helped evacuate Republican political refugees.

Wogan spent the war working as an agricultural labourer in Gloucestershire and later he became a farmer in the Cotswolds and Chair of Cheltenham branch of the National Union of Agricultural Workers. He was editor of the *Country Standard,* the Communist Party's rural and countryside journal.

Phillips regularly stood as a Communist candidate in local elections, being elected for Cirencester Urban District Council in 1946 but lost at the onset of the Cold War.

Red Baron
In 1963, on the death of his father, he became a Lord. In possibly the most original of maiden speeches, he called for the abolition of the un-elected Lords.

In 1950 Hymie Fagan described communist General Election meetings in Tewkesbury (*News & Views* March 1950) . "The meetings in this constituency were carried through in the teeth of the most violent hostility from the reactionaries. In this part of Gloucestershire there are large numbers of fascist 'displaced' persons – retired Army officers, landowners, wealthy farmers, landed gentry – as well as a large colony of Moseley fascists.

"These followed our comrades round from meeting to meeting, howling, shouting, threatening physical violence. They threw potatoes, tomatoes, eggs, and even a turkey. The bird was thrown from a car which, loaded with fascists, attempted to force the car of the candidate, Wogan Philipps, into a ditch."

"Yet every meeting was carried through to the end. Not only that, but the comrades also sold 1,250 *Socialist Roads* and 800 *Election Specials,* mostly door-to-door. Ten thousand leaflets were distributed and twelve quire of *Daily Workers* sold on the three weekends prior to polling day."

Phillips died in 1993 leaving his third wife and son.

Co-operative Movement

There were earlier examples of small co-operative societies but it was in 1844 when the Rochdale Pioneers established a consumer co-op that the co-operative movement really took off. Ordinary working people, especially trade unionists and socialists, organised themselves to set up shops that shared the profits in what became known as the 'divi'.

In the mid-1800s food was expensive and often adulterated. Most basic commodities were targets to be bulked out with cheap ingredients. Milk was often watered down with chalk added. Bread had alum mixed in, flour had white lead, sugar had ground glass. Tea, beer, jam, cider, chocolate and other foods were likely to be abused.

Working people needed a source of food they could afford and trust.

Edward Vansillant Neale (1810-92) Christian Socialist and leading co-operator was born in Bath. Neale lost a lot of money in failed co-operative ventures but in 1851 he founded the Central Co-operative

George Barefoot first secretary of the Gloucester Co-operative Society

Agency, a wholesale depot that was a forerunner of the Co-operative Wholesale Society.

In 1852 he founded the Co-operative League a forum for co-operative ideas and was keen to bring organisation to the Co-operative Movement. In 1873 he became General Secretary of the Co-operative Union, a post he held until 1891.

Swindon Co-op

The Swindon Co-operative Society was founded in 1850 with a small bread shop. In 1862 the New Swindon Industrial Co-operative Society was formed and in 1880 a third society was formed called the Kingshill Co-operative Society.

Gloucester Co-op

The Gloucester Co-operative and Industrial Society was formed in 1860 by a group of railway workers. The first meeting was to be in a house near Barton Gates but so many turned up an alternative venue was needed. **Joseph Clay**, the Secretary of the local branch of the Amalgamated Society of Engineers, arranged for a room at the Hope Inn to be used.

The minutes of the first meeting record the election of **William Pollard**, a bookbinder as President and **George Barefoot**, coppersmith, as Secretary.

Subscriptions had reached £19 16s

The first Gloucester co-op is opened in Prince Street in 1860

7d, reported **Benjamin Brook**, a fitter, and Treasurer. His wife hid the money in the chimney. A shop and bakehouse was quickly opened in Princes Street.

The Society gave funds to help the free public library. An Educational Committee was formed and the first Annual Tea held in 1863.

Stroud Road, Gloucester Co-op opened in 1876

Photos: Gloucester Co-operative and Industrial Society Ltd, Jubilee History

114 High Street, Tewkesbury
opened in 1886

By 1910 the Society had 18 shops, a
bakery and a depot in Gloucester.
Between 1887 and 1900 it also had a
dairy farm of 100 acres at Saintbridge.
The Gloucester Society helped set
up co-ops across the county such as
Cheltenham and Tewkesbury.

238 High Street, Cheltenham co-op opened
1880

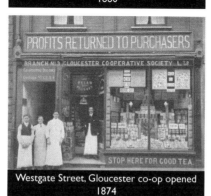

Westgate Street, Gloucester co-op opened
1874

Co-op ideas spread

Radstock Co-operative Society began
in 1868. The first successful co-op in

the Forest of Dean was founded in
1874 in Cinderford.

In 1879 the Annual Co-operative
Congress with 131 delegates was held
in Gloucester. In 1904 the Women's
Guild Congress was held in the city.
The agenda included Labour repre-
sentation and women's suffrage.

Bristol Co-operative Movement

The Bristol Co-operative Movement
had a difficult start. The first co-op
was formed in 1840 by **Felix Simeon**
and **Richard Daniel** with a store
in Broad Weir, "for the purpose of
more justly distributing wholesale
provisions to the producers of real
wealth." In 1859 the Bristol Industrial
Co-operative Society was launched
with a shop at 2 Whitsun Street but
this was dissolved in 1861. **James
Pleace,** a carpenter and joiner led a
more successful co-op. He left for
Australia and the Society had grown
to have a number of shops but failed
in 1871.

In 1881 the Bedminster Industrial
Co-operative Society was formed and
its first shop was opened in 1882 at 88
West Street, Bedminster. The Bristol
and District Co-operative Society was
started in 1884 by a group of trade
unionists including shoe-maker John
Wall, in a shop in Houlton Street, St.
Paul's.

The store opened two nights a week
for its first six months. Average
weekly trading was £10 and at the
end of the first quarter £130 had
been taken and a 'divi' of 1s 6d was
handed out.

Relations with local trade unions
were not easy. On 5th February 1891
a co-op delegation met the Trades
Council to win support. The next

Gloucester Women's Co-operative Guild in 1910
established in 1891. Back row: Ms Wanklyn, Chamberlain, Skevington, S Bye, Hayes, Twigg, Hale;
front row: Kerley, Trigg, Critchley, Waite, Prosser and J Bye

First successful co-op shop, 88 West Street, Bedminster

that the Bedminster Co-op was working its men more than fifteen hours a day, and had dismissed union men to pay non-unionists 21s a week. The Co-op claimed that the charges were inaccurate and misleading and answered each allegation in detail. A delegation from the Trades Council met the Society but there were more complaints over pay in the boot department.

Relations improved when **John Curle,** Secretary of the Trades Council stood and was elected as President of the Co-operative Society and other trade unionists joined the committee.

Stores opened in St George's Road, Hotwells, Lawrence Hill, and Lower Ashley Road.

In 1893 the Co-operative Congress met in the Hall of the YMCA, St James' Square, Bristol. Tom Mann and Ben Tillett took part. The Co-op started a dairy in 1921 in Ducie Road. By 1918, the Bristol Society was strong enough to acquire land in Castle Street for new central premises which opened as a department store in 1930.

By 1940, the Bristol Society's annual sales exceeded £3 million. By then the Co-op provided tailoring, chiropody, hairdressing, removals, travel, milk, bread and funeral services. The Society also provided a strong programme of social and educational activities.

Plymouth Co-op

It was Christmas Day, 1859 when **John Slade, John Shovel** and **Charles Goodanew** met to set about forming the Plymouth Mutual Co-operative Society. The first formal meeting was held in the tiny back room of Goodanew's shop.

Plymouth had a growing population and sanitation was poor. Charles had already lost four of his nine children and the new co-operative concept of providing quality food at fair prices fitted his determination to improve local living standards.

The first shop opened in Catte Street on 2nd February 1860. By September the Co-operative Society moved to

month the Co-op declined to promote the Women's Trade Union Society. The Baker's Union delegate alleged

Bristol Co-operative Society premises in Redcliffe Way

Souvenir to mark the opening of the new Central Co-operative Buildings in Plymouth in 1894

bigger premises in Kinterbury Street and within a year 100 members had joined. By 1864 the shop moved again to Cornwall Street complete with library and education department.

By 1880 the annual turnover was nearly £100,000 with 5,000 members

getting a 'divi' of 2s 4d. The Society had become a major trader in the area.

In June 1886, Plymouth hosted the annual Co-operative Congress. A second lifeboat built with donations from co-op stores was launched to be stationed at Illfracombe.

The Congress came to Plymouth again in 1910 with 1,600 delegates. By then the local Society had grown with 106 stores, 1,147 staff and 37,184 members.

Co-operative growth

In 1880 there were nine societies in Devon: Barnstaple, Bideford, Buckfastleigh, Devonport Coal, Exeter, Newton Abbot, North Tawton, Plymouth and Tiverton. Cornwall had ten societies.

The Co-operative became part of the lifeblood of society. It established an extensive infrastructure of farms and wholesale suppliers. Co-ops served almost every occasion from retail to funerals, from baking to banking.

Former flour mills of the Bristol Co-operative Wholesale Society at Avonmouth

Almost every town and village had a co-operative store but some struggled without enough trade. Enthusiasm and co-operative principles were not enough and some failed through lack of management skills.

By the 1960s the growing supermarkets forced many small stores to close or merge.

Co-ops today

The Co-operative Movement remains a large and diverse family of stores and societies. It has led the way on selling Fairtrade products and adopting ethical and environmental standards.

Many rural communities in the West Country have re-discovered co-operative ideas to maintain village stores. Farmers have combined in large co-operative ventures and co-ops form an important part of our health and educational sectors.

In 1903 Plymouth Co-operative Society introduced a horse-drawn green-grocery service, shown here in St Michael Avenue, Keyham

Greener Together
the co-operative way

Solidarity with seamen

The Canadian Seamen's Union (CSU) was established in 1936 to improve archaic working conditions and wages for seamen in the Great Lakes.

Using a 'red scare' in 1949, shipping companies imported US gangster, Hal Banks of the Seafarers' International Union (SIU), to violently break the CSU. The SIU, a quasi-company union, was stripped of its union status and disaffiliated by the Trades and Labour Congress in 1950.

On 14th May 1949 the ship *Montreal City*, with a scab SIU crew, arrived at Avonmouth. Dockers refused to unload the ship and on 16th May employers' threats brought out Avonmouth dockers on a lightning strike. Employers then refused to take back the dockers until they handled the ship. The strike became a lockout.

On 22nd May, 600 Bristol dockers came out in solidarity with Avonmouth. Three days later lock-gate men and tugmen in Avonmouth also came out in support.

Troops used
On 27th May, the government sent troops to unload a banana ship in Avonmouth. Crane drivers refused to work alongside troops.

A scab ship was diverted from Avonmouth to Liverpool. Merseyside dockers refused to handle her and 45 were suspended. 1,000 Liverpool dockers joined the strike. On 30th May, 1,400 more dockers in Liverpool came out. Avonmouth men instructed their 'lock-out Committee' to seek support from other ports.

On 2nd June, troops began unloading all ships in Avonmouth. About 11,000 dockers had now joined the strike. On 6th June, seamen on the *Trojan Star* refused to sail out of Avonmouth because the lock-gates were manned by troops. Other seamen joined in.

On 14th June, Avonmouth dockers returned to work, but in London employers refused to hire labour for newly arrived ships unless the scab Canadian ships *Argomont* and *Beaverbrae* were unloaded.

By 5th July, more than 8,000 London dockers were on strike. On 7th July, troops moved into London docks to unload ships. Drivers of meat haulage and fruit and vegetable firms refused to carry goods unloaded by troops.

State of Emergency
On 8th July, the government announced a State of Emergency on 11th July. This ensured water-men, lightermen, tugmen and bargemen also joined in. More than 10,000 dockers were now on strike.

On 12th July the government sent more strike-breaking troops into the docks. Another 3,000 dockers came out. The Executive of the Lightermen's Union told members not to work alongside troops. An Emergency Committee was set up to run the docks.

More than 15,000 men went on strike. They returned to work on 22nd July when the Canadian Seamen's Union, having obtained concessions, announced that they were terminating their dispute.

Solidarity relief on Transport House, Bristol

The NHS is born

Bristol was one of the first cities outside London to have an infirmary to care for the poor. The Board of Trustees, that found donors for the hospital wanted "a place of refuge in sickness and in wounds for their fellow creatures."

The conditions were poor and the wards cramped and it was re-built between 1782 and 1814.

The Plymouth Medical Society was established in 1794 by **Robert Remmett** and **Dr Charles Yonge**. By 1798 the Plymouth Public Dispensary was opened in Woolster Street. Supported by voluntary subscriptions, the objective of the Society was to relieve the suffering of the industrious poor who were unable to pay the cost of health care.

In 1809 the dispensary moved to better premises in Catherine Street with the help of a £1,000 legacy after the death of Charles Yonge.

It was in 1840 that **Daniel Gooch**, the 21-year-old Locomotive Superin-

GWR Medical Fund facilities ran from the Milton Road Baths

East Reach House, Taunton
Opened in 1812 as a nurse training hospital

tendent at the railway works, wrote to Isambard Kingdom Brunel to suggest Swindon as the site for his railway works. In 1847 he established a health scheme for the workforce.

Subscriptions were deducted from wages in return for basic health care. By 1871 Gooch had risen to chair the firm and with a £1,000 donation established the GWR Medical Fund Hospital in Milton Road, Swindon.

Members were entitled to cradle-to-grave care. Sick railway workers had access to a dispensary, dentist, ophthalmic clinic, ear, nose and throat service, physiotherapy, swimming baths and chiropody.

"There it was, a complete health service", said Aneurin Bevan, "all we had to do was expand it to embrace the whole country." He urged sceptics of the proposed NHS to visit the town to see how the scheme worked.

Former GWR Medical Fund Hospital

West Country health union leaders

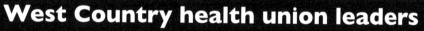

Born at Weston-Super-Mare, **Clifford Comer** became a mental nurse at Wells hospital in 1918. He became branch secretary of the National Asylum Workers Union and Mental Health and Institutional Workers Union.

He was elected to Somerset County Council for Labour. In 1932 Comer was appointed the union's first national organiser and in 1938 he moved to London. He became Assistant General Secretary of the Confederation of Health Service Employees (COHSE) in 1947 and a year later was elected

General Secretary. He retired unexpectedly in 1953. He died in 1978, aged 83 in Weston-Super-Mare.

Claude Bartlett joined the Asylum Workers Union in 1919 and was President of the Ivybridge Branch in Devon for 35 years. He became President of COHSE in 1946 joined the TUC General Council two years later. In 1959 he was elected President of the TUC, an achievement for a lay member.

Clifford Comer

Claude Bartlett

Council housing

Providing 'homes fit for heroes' after the end of the First World War proved an impetus for council house building.

In Gloucester the first 280 homes were constructed between Linden Road and Tuffley Avenue under the First Assisted Scheme. Work started in October 1919 and was completed by September 1922.

Thousands of families were homeless after Second World War and in 1946 some took matters into their own hands and squatted in the empty military camps. White City, in Bristol, was occupied after **Henry Hennessy,** a Labour Alderman offered to help homeless families move into the site in August 1946. Hundreds of people took over the huts. The council was forced to adopt the camp until new homes could be provided.

New council house in Finlay Road, Gloucester in 1933

Fred Phillips

Bridgwater has a reputation as a radical town. Before council re-organisation in 1974 it was called a 'Red Borough'.

For a period the Town Council was led by Fred Phillips, a refugee and veteran of the German anti-Nazi underground. The Labour council pushed through an ambitious programme of modernisation, house-building and provision of public amenities often in defiance of Conservative governments.

Travelling the county on a scooter, Fred's enthusiasm helped boost Labour Party membership.

The 1945 Labour Government built on a large scale but housing standards were kept. The incoming Conservative Government of 1951 responded with the high rise council estates that became a blight in later years.

Time for a Change
A new Council of Labour in Bradford-on-Avon, Wiltshire, drew up *A Policy for the People* for local elections in 1946. Housing was the central issue: "Unsatisfactory houses which are a disgrace to the town but which are defended by the preservationists (who care not to live in them)." The election booklet declared "There must be a clean break with the inglorious past and a bold advance into the future."

Harold Turner wrote a detailed report into the state of houses in the town and was one of three Council of Labour candidates to be elected.

Plymouth reconstruction
The Blitz devastated Plymouth and after the war a radical *Plan for Plymouth* reconstructed the centre and provided many new homes.

The Whitleigh Estate was started in 1949 to house 7,400 people. The first tenants moved in to 602 Budeshead Road on 14th August 1950 for a weekly rental of 25s 6d. In the 1950s some 2,524 houses and flats were built. Plymouth's 10,000th post-war council house was a Cornish-style house in Kirkwall Road at Crownhill opened on 22nd June 1954.

Post-war Plan for Plymouth

Devon workers get militant

Devon is not known for its militancy yet for about ten years in the 60s and 70s the county witnessed a wave of strikes.

Skilled workers and members of the small Association of Engineering and Shipbuilding Draughtsmen went on strike at Centrax in Newton Abbot, Devon around 1959.

In 1964 there was a thirteen-week long strike at Tecalemit organised by the small National Society of Metal Mechanics. The first ever strike at the naval dockyards in Devonport, Plymouth took place in 1968.

In 1969 to 1970 there was a long dispute at Centrax. At times there were violent scenes on the picket-lines but effective 'blacking' by unions led to a settlement through the then Department of Employment and Productivity.

Ottermill Switchgear
During this period another dispute

The derelict Ottermill Switchgear factory

took place at Ottermill Switchgear. The electrical manufacturing business was sited in the old Otter Mill in Ottery St Mary. The strike produced a poem to the boss.

Ottery St Mary Strike Song

Ottery Clementine
In a fact'ry, in a village,
We were slaving day and night,
Worked so hard for only peanuts
Now you'll find us out on strike.

Dr Hardy*, Dr Hardy,
We are ready for a fight;
However hard you try to stop us,
We are goin' to win this strike.

Like all the firms that are in the district
You have robbed us of our right
To provide well for our fam'lies
That is why we're out on strike.

We've been cheated and degraded
Now at last we've seen the light
We must put an end to serfdom
That is why we're out on strike.

If you're wond'ring how we're doin'
Well the money's very tight
But unless we reach starvation
We are goin' to win this strike.

Tell all the workers in the country,
Tell them brothers of our plight
And that we at Ottr'y Switchgear
With their help, will win this strike.

*Dr Hardy was the Managing Director

Draghtsmen and Allied Technicians' Association march in Newton Abbot in 1961

Centrax strikers: Association of Engineering and Shipbuilding Draughtsmen on the picket-line

BETTER PAY—
EN WE'LL STAY!

T.U.C. leader
in Dorset

Mr Vic Feather, general secretary of the Trades Union Congress, speaking in Dorset yesterday at the annual Tolpuddle rally

Vic Feather gets a rough ride at Tolpuddle in 1970

Fine Tubes Strike

In 1968 James T Barclay, a management consultant, was brought in to run US-owned, Fine Tubes in Plymouth, a specialist engineering firm. Hostile to the unions, he immediately set about antagonising the workforce.

He tried to harass and victimise the senior steward, **Dick Williams,** by moving him to lower paid work and generally frustrate the unions at every turn. In a row over pay and productivity, the mood of the workforce became more militant and on 15th June 1970, the refusal by Barclay to meet the stewards led to a walk-out that turned into Britain's longest strike, lasting three years.

169 workers out of 190 went on strike. This was in the middle of the General Election and three days into the strike Ted Health led the new Conservative Government into office promising new employment laws.

Picket rotas were organised and company responded by declaring all the strikers dismissed.

A Plymouth promotion for American investment was met with protests demanding fair play and at the Tolpuddle Martyrs' Rally in July 1970 the strikers joined others from Ottermill Switchgear and Centrax to heckle Vic Feather, TUC General Secretary. This marked the tension between rank-and-file activists and trade union officialdom that ran throughout the dispute – a feature of industrial relations in the 1970s.

The strikers sought to win 'blacking' action from unions in firms that handled the tubes. Although they gained a lot of moral support, the campaign had limited success.

The strike dragged on through the winter. Spirits were lifted by the election of **Herman Welch,** Secretary of the Strike Committee, to the Plymouth Council. He stood as the Labour candidate against a Tory who fought a dirty campaign against the 'militant striker'.

300 people came to picket on 30th July 1971 and the unions tried their best to maintain the momentum of the dispute. In February 1972, the Conservative's Industrial Relations Act came into force making it illegal to take action against a third-party not involved in the dispute. The 'blacking' campaign was outlawed.

After two years the remaining 43 strikers met and agreed to fight on. They were still winning support from around the country. Coventry Rolls Royce workers, British Aircraft workers, South Wales miners, Avonmouth dockers and many others declared their solidarity. A national conference was held in Birmingham but general secretaries stayed away and although the event raised over £1,000, much of the promised support failed to materialise.

On 19th March 1973 some 700 people from as far away as Scotland rallied outside the Plymouth factory. Afterwards they retired to a mass meeting in the ABC Cinema. But the rally had little impact on Fine Tubes and the last 31 strikers voted to end the dispute on its third anniversary. The longest strike in British history had been beaten and the period of Devon militancy was over.

David Owen, the then Plymouth MP, explained to Parliament that: "throughout the country people are involved in sympathy action with the Fine Tube strikers and this is probably the most classic case of factory workers being involved in sympathy action with their fellow trade unionists up and down the country."

Fine Tubes, Plymouth, site of the three-year strike 1970-1973

Ken Gill

Communist **Ken Gill** (1927- 2009) from Wiltshire became a leading figure in the turbulent industrial relations of the 1970s.

He was General Secretary of the Technical, Administrative and Supervisory Section (TASS), from 1974 to 1988, when it merged with ASTMS to form the Manufacturing, Science and Finance Union.

Ken Gill was born in Melksham, and gained radical political views through poverty in his childhood. During the war his family took in a communist cobbler as a lodger who convinced the young Gill of the cause of socialism. He became the local Labour Party agent for Chippenham.

In 1949, at the end of his apprenticeship as a draughtsman, he moved to London. As a young communist at the height of the Cold War, he travelled to East Germany for the 1951 World Youth Festival and was arrested on his way there by the US military police.

In 1962 he was elected a regional officer for the Draughtsmen and Allied Technicians' Association. His new Liverpool base and willingness to lead workers in a series of battles helped get him elected as Deputy General Secretary and then to the top of TASS.

Ken Gill became a high profile trade union figure. He was on the TUC General Council for eighteen years and formed a left-wing group that pushed for radical policies in the face of economic down-turns and political crisis. He led union opposition to Barbara Castle's Industrial Relations' Bill, *In Place of Strife* and to wage restraint under Labour and Tory governments.

Ken Gill became the first communist TUC President in 1974. He campaigned on equality and international issues, especially anti-apartheid and solidarity with Cuba.

Union strife

In the 1970s, the growing trade union movement had to defend itself from a range of legal attacks. West Country unions were engaged in the demonstrations against the Industrial Relations Bill and in support of the Shrewsbury building workers jailed for conspiracy following a national strike of 1972.

The *Pentonville Five* were dock shop stewards jailed in July 1972 for contempt of court. Following their arrest, a wave of strikes swept the country. The TUC held a massive rally outside the prison and called for an official national strike.

The unions won when the Official Solicitor drew on ancient powers to release the five shop stewards.

Free Des Warren – one of the Shrewsbury building workers – protest at Tolpuddle

Ladies' Mile

With her husband wounded in the First World War and two children to look after, Victoria Hughes (1897-1978) took a job as lavatory attendant at the toilets near the Clifton suspension bridge. When she moved to look after the nearby loos on Ladies' Mile, she realised that many of her customers weren't the well-to-do ladies of Clifton and the Downs but local prostitutes in need of help and support. Victoria showed them compassion and would offer tea and advice. In 1977, at the age of 80 she shocked the local community by publishing her account of her long service in *Ladies' Mile* and has since been honoured with a Blue Plaque.

Ladies' Mile Victoria's book that shocked Clifton

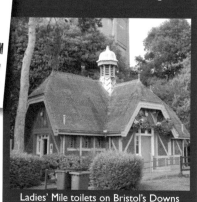

Ladies' Mile toilets on Bristol's Downs

Killed for gay kiss

George Brinham of the Amalgamated Society of Woodworkers was secretary of the Torquay Labour Party, 1937 to 1946. He was elected to the National Executive and was Labour Chair in 1960. He was in charge of the Young Socialists. The left *Labour Review* attacked his appointment due to his "addiction to homosexuality".

On 17th November 1962 he met Laurence Thomas Somer at Charing Cross in London. Somer was a sixteen-year-old cellarman who had run away from home. After meeting they had a coffee, a drive and went to Brinham's flat for a couple of brown ales. They went to the cinema to see a cartoon show and the pub, after which they went back to his flat.

Somer later told the *News of the World*: "He'd made this pass at me see. He put his arms around me and said give me a kiss. It made me feel sick." Somer grabbed a heavy cut-glass decanter and smashed it over Brinham's head, again and again.

Somer stole a car and went home to the Midlands where his mother reported him to the police. Brinham's body was found the following week.

Somer was acquitted of murder and manslaughter after the judge said: "this man had attempted to make homosexual advances . . . as clear a provocation as it is possible to have."

Bob Cant in *Radical Records, thirty years of Lesbian and Gay History* remarked: "It would not have been unreasonable, even in 1963, to expect that somebody might have stood up and said that it was a hell of a price to pay for trying to steal a kiss."

The fight against racism

> The South West has not escaped the scourge of racism. Its population is overwhelmingly white British but fear of strangers and prejudice against 'outsiders' is not far beneath the surface.

Black GIs

When the US joined the Second World War some three million service men and women were stationed in Britain many in the West Country. Ten per cent were African Americans in segregated units including those around Bristol and Gloucestershire.

They were welcomed as part of the war effort, often they were the first black people locals had ever seen. Many made friendships and relationships that forged long-lasting ties between black and white, US and Britain. But there were outbreaks of racism and resentment. In 1944 a number of minor clashes led to a more significant confrontation with some 400 black soldiers fighting police in Bristol city centre. A black soldier was killed as some 120 military police fought to calm the riot.

Bus Boycott

In the 1960s workers from the West Indies came to Bristol. The Bristol Omnibus Company refused to employ black workers. Ian Patey, the general manager, told the local paper: "The advent of coloured crews would mean a general falling off of white staff. You won't get a white man admit it but which of them will join a service where they find themselves working under a coloured foreman?"

Paul Stephenson, then aged 23, launched a campaign to boycott the buses until the policy changed. The protest won support from Tony Benn and Harold Wilson, Leader of the Labour Opposition. who went on to introduce the first Race Relations Act.

Paul Stephenson suffered abuse and threats in the course of the boycott but he held firm. Ron Nethercott, the Regional Secretary of the Transport and General Workers Union, condemned the boycott and abused Paul Stephenson. Paul reacted by successfully suing him for libel.

As the boycott gathered pace, the parent company ordered the bar be lifted and **Raghbir Singh** became the first non-white bus conductor in Bristol. The campaign galvanised the black community in the city.

South West Racism

In 1982 a black student working for a management degree arrived at a hotel in Cornwall to begin a placement arranged by his college. The management was shocked to find that the trainee was black and the next day he was asked to leave as his colour "might affect the trade." He complained to the Industrial Tribunal and became the first successful case under the Race Relations Act in the South West.

Keep them in Birmingham

In 1992 **Eric Jay** wrote a seminal report for the Commission for Racial Equality about racism in the South West. Called *Keep them in Birmingham,* it presented a disturbing picture of prejudice and discrimination. In particular it challenged the complacency of public authorities and the attitude that 'there is no problem here'.

The report catalogued incidents of discrimination such as the black chambermaid sacked because her employer did not want to risk alienating customers and the hair-dressing salon who refused to have black trainees "because our clients don't like it." The report listed violent attacks, harassment and general bigotry towards black and minority ethnic people.

Eric Jay's shocking findings forced councils to re-think although he described the actions needed as "A long haul".

Justice for Marlon Thomas

18-year-old Marlon Thomas was attacked by racist thugs in the Bob Wilson fairground on the Bristol Downs in 1994. Marlon suffered horrific injuries and was left severely disabled. There was a massive campaign to see justice done for Marlon and his family. Supporters demanded that the police recognise the racist nature of the attack.

Respect

In the 1990 there were a series of events and activities to celebrate the growing diversity of the region and to help tackle racism. 1994 saw the first Festival Against Racism in Bristol. This later grew into the Respect Festival which at its height attracted some 15,000 people to Eastville Park.

Similar events continued in Exeter and Plymouth and they encouraged people to get involved in the fight against racism and gave a platform for communities to share their culture and heritage.

St Paul's Riots

Sparked by a police drugs raid on the Black and White Café in St Paul's, on 2nd April 1980, the riot was the first in a series of violent events in large cities across the country.

St Paul's suffered from poor housing, high unemployment and a lack of public services. The education system had failed to respond to the changing needs of the area. The M32 motorway had cut the area off from neighbouring Easton. The local community,

St Paul's riot

especially young black people complained about police harassment.

The tensions were made worse by rising racism and the activities of the far-right National Front. The mix was explosive and when the police conducted an aggressive raid on the café the community fought back.

The riot continued for many hours and caused much damage to a branch of Lloyds Bank and a post office. Fire engines and police cars were damaged.

Bristol Trades Union Council held an enquiry into the origins of the 'eruption'. The report called *Slumbering Volcano?* found resentment against heavy-handed policing but listed many practical recommendations around the key issues raised such as poor quality of local housing, education, unemployment, transport and community relations.

James Peters

James Peters was a great South West figure and the first black man to play rugby for England. He was a 'strict teetotaller'. He made 35 appearances for Bristol before moving to Plymouth in 1902, where he worked on the docks.

James was an outstanding flyhalf for Plymouth and Devon. Between 1906 and 1908 he won five caps for England. *The Sportsman* commented: "For a first international the dusky Plymouth man did many good things, especially in passing."

Equal pay

Princess Campbell

Princess Campbell came to the UK from the Caribbean in the 1950s and trained as a nurse to become Bristol's first black sister. She worked at Glenside Hospital.

She remembers that when she started the black nurses got the worst jobs and the worst shifts. She went on to complete many years of distinguished service.

She then went on to open a number of multi-cultural sheltered housing provisions and founded the United Housing Association.

The long campaign for equal pay between men and women has seen battles take place in the West Country.

Speech therapists
Dr Pamela Mary Enderby was a speech therapist employed by the Frenchay Health Authority in north Bristol. In 1986, with the help of her trade union, she began a legal claim for equal pay for work of equal value.

Speech therapists were predominantly women and at that time she was paid £10,106, well below other comparable professionals such as a principal pharmacist who got £12,527 and a "Grade III principal pharmacist" was paid £14,106. They were predominantly men.

This launched the most lengthy and comprehensive equal pay claim ever. The case involved 26 court appearances (including the European Court of Justice), 2,000 applicants and sixteen test cases.

The case proved a success for women workers but was a powerful example of the long and drawn out process which can be involved in Equal Pay cases. The case started in 1986 and it took just over ten years to bring it to its final conclusion.

The resulting compensation cost the government some £30 million.

The Enderby case led to the Labour government instituting a review of pay and grading scales throughout the health service in the form of the 'Agenda for Change'.

Gloucestershire nursery nurses
In September 1997, four women won a landmark victory in achieving equal pay for work of equal value.

The nursery nurses were employed by Gloucestershire County Council and with the help of their union, Unison, they claimed that their salaries were in breach of the Sex Discrimination Act. They argued that their jobs entailed similar work and qualifications to male technicians who were paid up to 25% more.

When the industrial tribunal found in the women's favour it proved another milestone in the fight for equal pay.

Fight goes on
The struggle to get equal and fair treatment for women workers is a thread that has run through trade union life and continues.

The GMB union won a particular campaign at ABB Containers in Stroud. Unions at Avon Rubber in Wiltshire worked to change the system that meant that women were discriminated against because 'heavier work' got a higher rate. In an NHS laundry women were banned from heavy jobs and promotion was based on a system that disadvantaged women. Unison in South Somerset won compensation for members after winning an equal pay claim.

Equality South West
Equality campaigners across the South West have supported the formation of Equality South West. The body brings together equality networks and promotes equality across the West Country.

Anti-Apartheid campaign

When the National Party took power in South Africa in 1948 people across the world watched with horror at the introduction of racist segregation between whites, coloureds and blacks. The African National Congress led the fight against apartheid but the fight spread around the world.

In 1959 the call was made in London for a boycott of South African goods. Activists in the West Country took up the cause. Bristol was the centre of the organisation for the Anti-Apartheid Movement. It spread awareness, helped exiles and raised funds. The boycott grew to include sport.

Each June a sponsored walk was held across the Mendips that became known as the Soweto Walk.

Ron Press (1929-2009) was born into a trade unionist family in South Africa. He joined the South African Communist Party and in 1956 became General Secretary of the Textile Workers Union. When he was first arrested he was represented by Nelson Mandela. He led strikes of Indian workers, was banned from gathering and was tried for high treason.

In 1962 his wife became ill and the couple came to Bristol. He became Secretary of the Anti-Apartheid Movement and later was made a life member of Bristol Trades Union Council.

Jo Emery devoted twenty years to fighting apartheid in Bristol. In 1961 she went to South Africa to undertake community development, particularly among women.

She helped people survive the oppressive apartheid regime, and took part in actions against the government. Jo was a member of Black Sash, a prohibited women's resistance movement. Her many African friends gave her the name Thandi, which means "one who gives and receives love".

Bristol card to Nelson Mandela

After the Soweto uprising and massacre of 1976, she was forced to return to Bristol. On learning of Jo's death in 2007, Archbishop Desmond Tutu said: "It was because of persons such as she that we are free today. Thank you Thandi."

Nelson Mandela was released in 1991, having spent 27 years in prison. On 10th May 1994, Mandela was sworn in as president of South Africa, after the ANC won an overwhelming victory in the elections.

Secret Somerset Talks

Mells Park near Frome in Somerset was the secret location for early negotiations between the South African apartheid regime and the resistance movement led by the African National Congress.

The talks were arranged in the late 1980s by Michael Young, a director of the Consolidated Gold mining company. Thabo Mbeki, then a member of the African National Congress and future President of South Africa, met Willie Esterhuyse, who represented PW Botha's white regime.

Apartheid protest on a May Day March in Bristol in the 1950s

Peace campaigns

Fear of nuclear war led many local campaigns to demand: 'ban the bomb'.

On 13th January 1981 Bristol City Council joined other local authorities in declaring the city to be a 'nuclear free zone'. The largely symbolic resolution was designed to add to the growing campaign against nuclear weapons.

In 1984, in response to new Civil Defence Regulations, Bristol Council published a frank account of what would happen to the city should a nuclear bomb land.

The Campaign for Nuclear Disarmament had local groups across the South West.

1981 saw the first Glastonbury CND Festival, which attracted more than 18,000 people and made £20,000 profit. As the event grew the cash raised soared.

BRISTOL & THE BOMB

Bristol City Council published its frightening account of what a nuclear strike on the city would do.

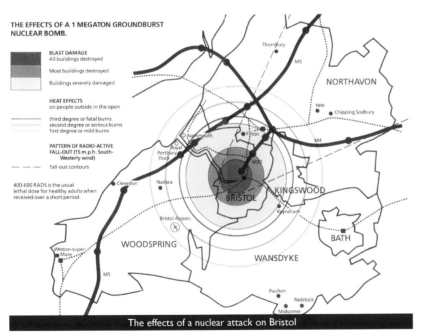

THE EFFECTS OF A 1 MEGATON GROUNDBURST NUCLEAR BOMB.

BLAST DAMAGE
All buildings destroyed

Most buildings destroyed

Buildings severely damaged

HEAT EFFECTS
on people outside in the open

third degree or fatal burns
second degree or serious burns
first degree or mild burns

PATTERN OF RADIO-ACTIVE FALL-OUT (15 m.p.h. South-Westerly wind)

fall-out contours

400-600 RADS is the usual lethal dose for healthy adults when received over a short period.

The effects of a nuclear attack on Bristol

Trowbridge Communists

Idris and Phyllis Rose were passionate socialists and members of the Communist Party in Trowbridge.

Idris, a painter and decorator, stood for the local District Council seventeen times and in May 1969 both he and his wife were elected. They served on the Council until local government re-organisation in 1974.

Idris felt strongly about council housing that he regarded not only as a social service but a means to re-distribute wealth and reduce inequality.

Another communist councillor was Bert Sally Searle elected in Clevedon.

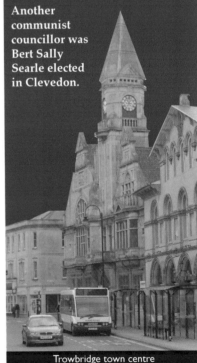

Trowbridge town centre

Trade union rights

On 25th January 1984, the Conservative Foreign Secretary, announced that trade unions would be banned from the Government Communication Headquarters (GCHQ). The trade union movement was outraged. The community of Cheltenham, where thousands of people depended upon the base for work, was shocked.

The decision marked the start of one of the most intensive campaigns ever mounted by the trade union movement. The TUC called a Day of Action on 28th February. Hundreds of thousands joined in the protest at this denial of basic rights.

The ban demonstrated the prejudice against trade unionism held by the Thatcher Government. It was condemned around the world and each January, on the anniversary of the ban, thousands marched through the Cotswold town to demand the restoration of union rights. Cheltenham voters let the Tories know what they thought at the next General Election when the safe Tory seat returned Nigel Jones for the Liberal-Democrats.

Fourteen trade union members inside GCHQ refused to be bullied into giving up their rights. They rejected the £1,000 bribe and continued to defy the ban and were sacked. Led by their chair, **Mike Grindley**, they took their fight to the courts, the International Labour Organisation and campaign meetings around the world.

The civil service unions stood by their members financially and made sure that the protest gathered momentum. Soon after the 1997 General Election Robin Cook, the new Labour Foreign Secretary honoured their pledge to restore trade union rights. The sacked workers were offered their jobs back and compensation. A victory rally was held and many celebrated as the members went back to work.

The sacked trade unionists who stood against the might of the Thatcher Government until their reinstatement in 1997:

Bill Bickham, Allan Chambers, John Cook, Mike Grindley, Brian Johnson, Clive Lloyd, Gareth Morris, Gerry O'Hagan, Alan Rowland, Robin Smith, Harry Underwood, Dee Goddard, Graham Hughes and Roy Taylor

Long Bristol print dispute

On 26 April 1993, 121 print workers were sacked from Arrowsmiths in Winterstoke Road, Bristol. The workers were refusing to work overtime as part of their pay claim for a rise of £6.50 a week. There had been a legal ballot with a massive 98-14 majority in favour of the overtime ban. But such was the legal position at the time, that any action of this sort made workers liable to dismissal.

The lock-out was the start of one of the West Country's longest and most bitter disputes. Big demonstrations were held in Bristol and the workers won support from across the country as well as local MPs.

Even though the workers had been sacked, they were denied unemployment benefits until a legal challenge over-turned the decision. When the sacked workers' jobs were advertised in the local job centre, members of the civil service union, the CPSA, refused to handle them and were themselves sacked.

After eighteen months the union helped find alternative work for most of the members and when the factory was put up for sale, the union called off the dispute.

Victoria Arrowsmith-Brown, Managing Director, and the company had paid a high price for the sackings. Key contracts had been lost and customers stayed away from the picket lines. The company struggled on for a while as a shadow of its former self.

The dispute highlighted the lack of legal rights for workers at that time. It exposed how workers could be sacked even after a legal ballot for an overtime ban.

Unions used the Arrowsmith example to convince the Labour Party to include legal reforms when elected. As a result workers involved in legal industrial action are protected from dismissal for the first few weeks.

End of the line for print firm pickets in 18-month fight

WESTERN DAILY PRESS, THURSDAY, OCTOBER 20, 1994 — 15

Battle is over: Discarded banners litter the scene of the bitter dispute

DISCARDED protest banners and old coffee cups were all that was left yesterday of one of the West's most bitter industrial disputes.

I would do it again, says sacked worker

By Rachel Carlyle

because the pickets felt at risk from violence.

Of the 121 who were sacked, at least 60 now have other jobs and 16 people are collecting pensions. The others are still looking for work.

delivered food and coffee to the pickets, as well as offering moral ...

Tramping to Internet

When craft printers found themselves without work some would 'tramp' from town to town in search of employment. The system was encouraged by the early union societies to relieve unemployment and prevent employers from cutting pay.

A 'Tramping Relief' system was developed under which members could report to the local secretary. A *Relief Map* gave mileage allowances to be paid and overnight expenses. Advice would be given on available work and those vacancies to avoid if the employer refused to pay the rate or recognise the Society.

So effective was the system that non-society workers would try to forge cards. This led, in 1830, to the formation of the first national union to oversee the scheme.

This tradition was maintaintained through the payment of Unemployment Benefit and job search assistance.

Co-operative training

In the 1990s printing faced technological changes and cut backs. In Gloucestershire unemployed print workers formed a unique co-operative training and employment service. Members could learn the very latest technology, get news on vacancies and help with CVs and job applications.

The Graphical Employment and Training Group was very successful, helping hundreds back into work.

The fight for work

Under the Conservative Government of Margaret Thatcher, unemployment across the country rose sharply. The South West was not immune and many jobs were shed as companies closed down or laid-off workers.

By 1983 there were around 250,000 people out of work, including a quarter of all those under 25 years old. The TUC supported a *People's March for Jobs* that set off from Land's End towards London on 11th May. Twenty unemployed marchers were selected to represent the South West.

As they marched through the region they generated press coverage that helped highlight the plight of those looking for work.

In Gloucestershire, trade unionists led an initiative called *Gloucestershire Campaign for Jobs and Recovery*. It brought together a range of partners and concerned individuals to organise against unemployment and

The South West March for Jobs

to develop ideas to develop the local economy. A large meeting of unemployed people was held in Gloucester Cathedral and protest marches were held against cuts in public services.

TUC Unemployed Workers' centres were established across the South West to provide advice and support.

The March sets off from Lands End

The People's Marchers

Bath	**Richard**
Gail Griffith	Debanme
Terry	Chris Small
Wooltorton	**Cheltenham**
Richard Baker	Frank Herrity
	Penzance
Bristol	Dave Lawson
Veronica Ralph	**Plymouth**
Paul Williams	Kevin Jones
Steve Coward	Margaret
Mick Connor	Midgley
Sally Cable	**St Austell**
Ian Denison	Chris Dudley
Paul Dielhern	Karl Tahair
Robert Phelan	Robert Trahair
Camborne	

Tony Benn

Tony Benn is one of the foremost parliamentarians of the twentieth century. He served as Labour MP for Bristol South East from 1950 to 1983 and was the longest serving Labour MP.

Following his World War II service as a pilot in the Royal Air Force, Tony Benn worked for the BBC before being elected to follow Stafford Cripps as Labour MP for Bristol South East in 1950. Benn became the youngest MP, or 'Baby of the House'.

Bust of Tony Benn in the Council House, Bristol by sculptor Ian Walters

Tony Benn speaking in Tolpuddle in 2006

When his father, Viscount Stansgate, died in 1960, Benn became a peer and was prevented from sitting as MP. He fought to retain his seat in a by-election and although disqualified the people of Bristol South-East still re-elected him. The government accepted the need for a change in the law and passed the Peerage Act allowing renunciation of peerages.

Tony Benn held several ministerial posts including Postmaster General, Minister for Technology, Aviation and Power, Secretary of State for Industry, Minister for Posts and Telecommunications and Secretary of State for Energy.

As a minister he made key decisions about industry in Bristol, campaigning for the Concorde development programme and agreeing a major subsidy for Rolls Royce to produce the RB 211 jet engine.

After Labour lost power in 1979, Tony

Benn became a leading figure on the left of the Party and was narrowly defeated as Deputy Leader. The right-wing press attacked him at every turn. He has always refused to engage in personal attacks even on his fiercest political opponents.

In 2001 he stood down as MP "to devote more time to politics". He kept diaries throughout his life and used them to write numerous books.

Tony Benn with his son, Hilary in Tolpuddle in 2004

PRIVATE EYE

It may be hard to believe that this is

THE MOST DANGEROUS MAN IN BRITAIN

and indeed simply as a man the charge is ludicrous. But an Minister of Technology, Mr Wedgwood Benn is one of the m   spicuous (cont. on back page)

Popular speaker

As a public speaker, Tony Benn, is in huge demand. The South West TUC invited him to speak at Tolpuddle for the first time in 2000. He has been a regular ever since. He remains a key political agitator and commentator.

Dangerous: the media stirred up a campaign of hysteria against Tony Benn

Dennis Potter

Dennis Potter was born in 1935 at Brick House on Joyford Hill, in the village of Berry Hill, in the Forest of Dean, Gloucestershire.

The son of a miner, Dennis won a scholarship to New College Oxford to read Philosophy, Politics and Economics. He took an active role in the Union and the Labour Club.

His early writing showed his radical political views in *Does Class Matter* for the BBC and his first book, *The Glittering Coffin*, a polemic on the state of British nationhood and culture. He wrote, and appeared in *Between Two Rivers* on the changing nature of the Dean.

His satirical sketches were featured on *That Was The Week That Was*. He also wrote for the workers' newspaper, *The Daily Herald.*

Dennis stood unsuccessfully as Labour candidate in 1964 but he had grown so disillusioned by party politics that he claimed not even to have voted for himself.

He suffered increasingly from the scourge of psoriatic arthropathy. Potter settled down in 1964 in Ross-on-Wye. In 1977 *Brimstone and Treacle* was banned by the BBC but his masterpiece: *Pennies from Heaven* established Dennis Potter as a household name.

In 1978 *The Singing Detective* was broadcast but it wasn't until 1987 that the BBC eventually broadcast *Brimstone and Treacle*. In 1993 *Lipstick On Your Collar* was shown.

Dennis Potter died on 7th June 1994 of cancer of the pancreas, a growth which he referred to as 'Rupert', after the media tycoon, Rupert Murdoch.

In his interview with Melvyn Bragg in 1994, Potter described growing up in the Forest of Dean: "It is a strange and beautiful place, with a people who were as warm as anywhere else. We were, at that time, both a brave and a steadfast people and we shared an aim, a condition, a political aspiration if you like, which was shown immediately in the 1945 general election."

Prolific Playwright

Between 1965 and 1976 Dennis Potter's plays on TV included: *The Confidence Course; Alice Stand Up, Nigel Barton; Vote, Vote, Vote for Nigel Barton. ; Emergency Ward 9; Where the Buffalo Roam ; Message for Posterity ; The Bonegrinder; Shaggy Dog; A Beast with Two Backs ; Moonlight on the Highway; Son of Man ; Lay Down Your Arms; Angels Are So Few ; Paper Roses; Traitor; Casanova (six-part serial) ; Follow The Yellow Brick Road; Only Make Believe; A Tragedy of Two Ambitions; Joe's Ark; Schmoedipus; Late Call; Double Dare and Where Adam Stood*

Gay Rights

The Campaign for Homosexual Equality (CHE) had a number of branches across the West Country, including the first one established in 1970 in Bristol.

CHE and the Gay Liberation front pressed for law reforms in the long-running fight for rights for lesbian, gay, bisexual and transgender people.

In 1971 the Bath Gay Awareness Group was formed. This became Gay West that has been serving the South West's gay community since 1982.

Ben Bradshaw was openly gay when he fought the marginal seat of Exeter for Labour at the 1997 general election. The Conservative candidate, Adrian Rogers led a right-wing family values pressure group.

The campaign was vitriolic and bitter with allegations of homophobia and sin. Bradshaw won with a majority of 11,705 to become the second openly gay man elected to Parliament.

Ben Bradshaw speaking at the Tolpuddle Martyrs' Festival in 2010

photo Clint Randall

Smash the Poll Tax

The Community Charge was introduced in 1989 by the government of Margaret Thatcher. It was a fixed tax per adult resident regardless of income and ability to pay.

The 'Poll Tax' generated a storm of protest that forced the government into a retreat and led to Thatcher's downfall.

The Community Charge, quickly dubbed the Poll Tax, was deeply unpopular. It shifted the tax burden from rich to poor. There were mass protests, called by the All-Britain Anti-Poll Tax Federation to which the vast majority of local Anti-Poll Tax Unions were affiliated.

The campaign for mass non-payment rapidly gathered support even though non-payers faced prosecution. In some areas, 30 per cent of former ratepayers defaulted.

Danny Burns was secretary of the Avon Federation of Anti-Poll Tax Unions and helped co-ordinate the campaign in the South West. In his book *The Poll Tax Rebellion* he describes how the tactics in Bristol succeeded in changing non-payment from a passive individual act to an active collective one.

Groups such as that behind the *Militant* helped lead the opposition and the number of people refusing to pay the tax increased and protests escalated.

The cost of collecting the tax rose steeply while the returns from it fell. The unrest culminated in a number of Poll Tax riots. The most serious was the protest at Trafalgar Square, London, on 31st March 1990 with some 200,000 protesters. People felt shocked by the violent scenes as police and protesters battled through the streets of the capital.

Popular opinion was firmly against the tax and Tory MPs were in panic over the political consequences.

This unrest helped bring down Margaret Thatcher in 1990. Her successor, John Major, replaced the Poll Tax with the Council Tax, similar to the former rating system.

Battle of the Beanfield

On 1st June 1985 several hundred new age travellers headed for Stonehenge in Wiltshire to set up camp in time for a festival before the summer solstice. English Heritage had been granted an exclusion zone by the High Court and the police were determined to confront the convoy.

A roadblock was established near Shipton Bellinger about seven miles from Stonehenge. The convoy of up to 140 vehicles carrying about 600 people became trapped in a field. The media had whipped up hostility to the travellers. Emboldened by public opinion and using tactics learned in the miners' strike, some 1,300 police officers attacked the vehicles, smashing windows and beating people in what became known as the 'battle of the beanfield'.

537 people were arrested and seven healthy dogs belonging to the travellers were put down by the police. All those arrested were charged with obstruction of the police and the highway, but most of the charges were dismissed in the courts.

Six years later the police were found guilty of wrongful arrest, assault and criminal damage.

Road rebels

The rise in road traffic had led to increased demand for more roads that in turn led to even more cars and congestion. Cars and super-markets were taking priority over people and the countryside.

Protests against ever more road-building were focussed on the West Country.

Save the Stroud Trees

In the summer of 1989, a line of trees in Strafford Park, Stroud was to be felled to widen the road for a Tesco supermarket. The Save the Trees campaign was formed to rescue the leafy avenue. The year-long protest culminated in a tree-top sit-in that became national news.

Ron Birch, co-ordinated the campaign that gathered more than 10,000 petition signatures. A large protest march and rally helped sustain the tree climbers. Save the Trees won their campaign and traffic calming measures were installed instead – a new feature in those days.

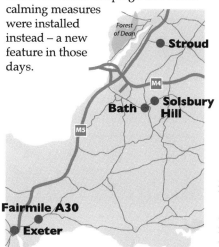

Solsbury Hill

In 1994 environmental protestors set up camp and took to the tree-tops in a bid to stop work on the Batheaston to Swainswick by-pass at Bath. The road cut through the Bronze Age beauty spot at Solsbury Hill. Although the work was completed, the camp was one of the first direct action protests against road building.

Swampy

Daniel Hooper, known as Swampy, is the environmental protester who became the centre of the campaign to stop the widening of the A30 Exeter to Honiton road.

Swampy fighting the building of the new A30 in Devon

He became a nationally known figure after spending a week in a complex series of tunnels dug in the path of the road in Fairmile, Devon, resisting attempts at eviction by police. Several people took part in the protest, but Swampy was the last one evicted.

Although the new road was opened in 1999 the protest had highlighted the arguments against road building.

The direct action delayed construction and pushed up costs.

In 1997, the new Labour Government slashed the road building programme. The argument against more and more roads had been won.

SURFERS AGAINST SEWAGE

In 1990 a group of surfers in Cornwall set up a local group to stop sewage pollution into the sea. They were literally 'sick of getting sick' through repeated ear, nose, throat and gastric infections after going in the sea.

Led by founding member Chris Hines, Surfers Against Sewage used imaginative and hard-hitting demonstrations to gain publicity. Gas-masked 'hit squads' forced South West Water to clean up the beaches.

Stop the War

The war against Iraq generated massive opposition including across the West Country.

The US Airforce used the Fairford Airbase in Gloucestershire for its long range bombers and so became a place of protest. A peace camp was set up at Fairford on 17th February 2003.

On 13th May 2005 protesters set up a peace camp on Drake's Island, just off Plymouth.

Dying for work

Thousands of West Country workers have died as a result of their work. Most are largely forgotten casualties of hazardous working conditions and employers who placed little value on safety. The campaign to make work safer has been long and is far from over today.

Each year on Workers' Memorial Day, 28th April, trade unionists commemorate them and re-double their efforts to make work safe.

The West Country has had its fair share of dangerous jobs. The sea has taken many lives along with the hazards of agriculture, quarrying, transport and mining. Exposure to asbestos is still taking its toll amongst those connected with ship building and construction in particular.

Severn disaster

On the fog-bound night of 25th October 1960 two tanker ships collided and hit the Severn Railway Bridge, near Purton. Five men were killed and the bridge was wrecked beyond repair.

The wreck of one of the ships sunk in 1960

Forest of Dean miners

Coal dominated the economy of the Forest of Dean for many generations. In 1945 half the male working population were employed in mining. The pits closed in the 1960s although a few free miners keep digging.

One tragedy happened in 1902 at the Union Pit. Four miners were killed including brothers **Thomas and Amos James**. Three colliers survived the five days it took to dig down to the men but the brothers were found dead in a final embrace. A sculpture carved from Forest stone and set amidst the trees near Cannop stands in their memory.

The James Brothers, Forest of Dean miners killed in the Union Pit in 1902

Memorial to Forest of Dean miners in Cinderford

Cinderford town centre designed as a miners' lamp

Coal truck memorial in Littledean

Wreaths are laid in 2006 at the New Fancy memorial to miners killed in the Forest of Dean

Radstock remembers its mining past

Wells Way Pit disaster

Somerset coalfields had one of the best safety records with the miners well organised. But it was still dangerous work.

In 1839 twelve men and boys were killed in Wells Way Colliery near Radstock. The rope lowering the miners into the pit was cut – apparently deliberately, although no-one was found responsible.

Miners' Memorial in St. John's churchyard Midsomer Norton commemorating the Wells Way Colliery disaster of 1839 and an embroidery on display in Radstock Museum

Norton Pit Disaster

In 1908 an explosion at the colliery at Norton Hill, Midsomer Norton, left ten dead. Those killed included **Gilbert Jones**, aged 25, who had been married only five weeks, **Ernest Jones** and his sixteen year-old brother **Stanley**. The youngest victim, **Harry Sage**, a fourteen-year-old powder boy, had just left school.

The precarious engine house of the Botallack tin mine

Levant disaster

31 lives were lost on 19th October 1919 at the Levant Mine when a rod broke in the shaft plunging the workers to their deaths.

Levant mine ruins

Cornish mining

Cornwall's tin mines were perched on top of the rugged cliffs with the tunnels reaching under the sea for the valuable tin.

Botallack Pit
On 18th April 1863 eight men and one boy were killed in a hoisting accident in the mine's diagonal shaft.

Delabole Slate
On 21 April 1869, a crack appeared in the ground at Delabole slate quarry. Within minutes a rock fall killed fifteen people.

Wheal Owles
On 10th January 1893 at Wheal Owles, St Just twenty workers were drowned when the mine flooded.

The roll call of those who lost their lives in the Wheal Owles disaster of 1893

East Wheel Rose
In May 1854, after torrential rain over Newlyn, floodwater swept into the East Wheel Rose lead mine drowning 39 men and boys in Cornwall's worst pit disaster. A story is told of a timber-man, **Samuel Bastion**, who went down into the mine to lie across a manhole, diverting the flow of water and saving eighteen lives.

Beaminster Tunnel memorial

Just before the Beaminster Tunnel in Dorset there is a small stone with a white cross. This is a memorial to William Aplin, a labourer, who was killed by falling earth just three days before the road was opened in June 1832. During construction the tunnel provided 50 much-needed jobs.

Stone in memory of labourer killed during construction of Beaminster Tunnel

GREATER LOVE HATH
NO MAN THAN THIS,
THAT A MAN LAY DOWN HIS LIFE
FOR HIS FRIENDS

Memorial outside Avon Fire Service in Bristol

Box Tunnel

Brunel led the building of the longest railway tunnel in the world in 1836. Towards its completion some 4,000 workers, mostly Irish navvies, and 300 horses were engaged. It opened in 1841 having killed around 100 workers during construction.

THIS PLAQUE COMMEMORATES
WORKERS MEMORIAL DAY
28th APRIL 1997
"Remember the dead
Fight for the living"

UNISON

Wreaths laid in 2006 at the Workers' Memorial plaque in Castle Park, Bristol

Memorials at Unison's office in Taunton

Rebels and riots today

The South West is now often viewed as a reasonably prosperous place. A lovely place to live, visit or retire to. The region's economy has done well and standards of living for most people has been pretty good. Parts of Dorset have the highest life expectancy rates in the country, house prices in some areas rival central London and education levels are above average.

There are pockets of deprivation, however. Rural charm can hide deep poverty faced by some families. The average performance of the region masks some stark divisions. For example, youth participation in higher education is around 80 per cent of the population of Bristol West compared to ten per cent in neighbouring Bristol South. Cornwall has the lowest wages in the UK but some of the highest house prices.

In the 1997 General Election the region elected 22 Conservative MPs, 15 for Labour and 14 for the Liberal Democrats. In 2010 Labour was reduced to just four seats.

But since the election, demonstrations against public spending cuts and

Protest rally in the Forest of Dean

government policies have marched through every West Country town, city and even forest. Communities have been shocked by news of library and youth centre closures. Campaigns have been launched to save lollipop crossing patrols, coastguard stations and care homes.

Hardest Hit rally in Bristol

The spirit of past rebellions was rekindled when plans to privatise the country's forests was disclosed. The Forest of Dean was the starting point for the massive protest against the idea. A huge rally met amidst the trees around Speech House on 3rd January 2010. An effigy of Big Ben was burned to the cheers of around 3,000 people despite falling snow.

The protest spread and in the face of overwhelming opposition the government backed down – perhaps to come back with other ways to fragment the public forest estate.

In Bristol rebellion has taken different forms of action. **Banksy** has poked fun at authority with clever art. His anti-establishment paintings have proved highly popular.

street art by Banksy photo Andy Moss

Banksy art in Bristol

Bristol Rebel City – Avon Gorge graffiti highlights how some would like to see Bristol

When Tesco opened a new store in Stokes Croft near the centre of Bristol it sparked a furious reaction. Feeling powerless in the planning process to protect the area's vibrant mix of local shops from the powerful supermarket corporation, people organised a boycott and street occupation. The protest turned to riot and the stores windows were smashed.

Riot cause
Given rising inequality and desperation some people will feel so excluded from mainstream society they will turn to violence.

Stokes Croft and 'Riot Tescos'

Other forms of protest are being used and tested including social media campaigns. UKUncut has used direct action to press for tax justice in the face of avoidance on a massive scale by big corporations. The Occupy movement swept across the world with its opposition to corporate greed and inequality.

Trade unionists faced with pay and pension cuts have taken industrial action and brought out thousands in demonstrations and rallies across the South West. The Day of Action on 30th November 2010 over public sector pensions saw the largest stoppage since the 1926 General Strike.

More protests are bound to occur as austerity takes hold. These will be modern rebellions with new grass roots' leaders. The battles that have been fought by every generation will be waged again.

This involved can call upon the lessons of history and the experience of previous generations who have stood up to be counted.

Pensions Justice – 30th November 2012 saw one of the largest demonstrations ever in Bristol

Marching across the West Country
Taunton is just one of many

APPENDIX

Swing Rebellion in the West

1830

8 November
Maddington, Wilts wheat rick fire
Wandorough, Wilts straw rick fire

15 November
Knook, Wilts arson against farmer

17-22 November
Marlborough, Wilts arson

18 November
Collingbourne, Wilts arson against farmer
Ludgershall, Wilts arson against farmer
Wadswick, Wilts arson against farmer

19 November
Oare, Wilts arson against farmers
Wilcot, Wilts riot

20 November
Stanton St. Bernard, Wilts arson of threshing machines

21 November
All Cannings, Wilts arson against farmer
Amesbury, Wilts arson against farmer
Everley, Wilts arson against farmer
Hippenscombe, Wilts arson against farmer
Horton, Wilts threatening 'Swing' letter to farmer over threshing machine
Salisbury, Wilts threatening 'Swing' letter to farmer
Stanton St. Bernard, Wilts arson against farmer
Winterslow, Wilts arson against farmer

22 November
Bere Regis, Dorset wage meeting and riot against farmers
Everley, Wilts arson against farmer
Allington, Wilts arson against farmer
Buttermere, Wilts arson against farmer
Chilton Foliat, Wilts demands for food or money
Collingbourne K, Wilts demands for food or money
Downton, Wilts destruction of threshing machine
Enford, Wilts destruction of two threshing machines
Figheldean, Wilts demands for food or money
Fowey, Cornwall food riot against dealers
Froxfield, Wilts destruction of two threshing machines
Gt. Bedwyn, Wilts two demands for food or money, destruction of three threshing machines
Hippenscombe, Wilts destruction of two threshing machines
Idmiston, Wilts destruction of threshing machine
Mildenhall, Wilts destruction of threshing machine
Netheravon, Wilts destruction of two threshing machines
Newton Toney, Wilts destruction of threshing machine
Ramsbury, Wilts three riots, demands for food or money, destruction of five threshing machines
Salisbury, Wilts riot
Tidcombe, Wilts destruction of threshing machine
West Dean, Wilts destruction of threshing machine
Whiteparish, Wilts destruction of threshing machine

Wilcot, Wilts destruction of threshing machine

23 November
Alton Barnes, Wilts riot, demands for food or money, destruction of threshing machine
Alton Priors, Wilts destruction of threshing machine
Aldbourne, Wilts riot, five demands for food or money, destruction of eight threshing machines
Burbage, Wilts four demands for food or money, destruction of two threshing machines
Chirton, Wilts demands for food or money, destruction of two threshing machines
Collingbourne, Wilts demands for food or money
Cranborne, Dorset demands for food or money
Dowton, Wilts destruction of threshing machine
Easton, Wilts demands for food or money, destruction of three threshing machines
Ham, Wilts riot, two demands for food or money, destruction of threshing machine
Hannington, Wilts demands for food or money, destruction of threshing machine
Liddington, Wilts demands for food or money, destruction of threshing machine
Milton, Wilts riot, two demands for food or money, destruction of two threshing machines
Netheravon, Wilts riot
Odstock, Wilts demands for food or money
Ogbourne St A, Wilts two riots, two farm machines destroyed
Pewsey, Wilts six farm machines destroyed

Ramsbury, Wilts demands for food or money
Severake, Wilts demands for food or money
Shalbourne, Wilts riot, two demands for food or money, five farm machines destroyed
Standlynch, Wilts demands for food or money
Wanborough, Wilts eight demands for food or money, two farm machines destroyed
West Harnham destruction of equipment at paper maker costing £18.7.0
Whiteparish, Wilts two demands for food or money
Wilton, Wilts farm machine destroyed
Woodborough, Wilts farm machine destroyed
Wootton Rivers, Wilts three demands for food or money

24 November
Alderbury, Wilts riot, demands for food or money, destruction of threshing machine
Barford St Martin, Wilts demands for food or money, destruction of machinery at silk mamanufacturer, costing £185.15.0
Bishops Cannings, Wilts demands for food or money
Boveridge, Dorset demands for food or money from gentleman
Broad Chalk, Wilts riot, three demands for food or money, destruction of threshing machine
Burcombe, Wilts destruction of threshing machine
Coombe Bissett, Wilts two demands for food or money, destruction of threshing machine
Cricklade, Wilts destruction of

threshing machine
Draycott Foliat, Wilts destruction of threshing machine
Dinton, Wilts demands for food or money
Ebbesbourne, Wilts demands for food or money
Firfield, Wilts destruction of threshing machine
Fugglestone St Peter, Wilts demands for food or money, farm machine destroyed
Handley, Dorset demands for food or money, destruction of threshing machine and other farm equipment
Hannington, Wilts riot, two demands for food or money, destruction of threshing machine
Highworth, Wilts six counts of theft
Westbourne Stoke, Wilts destruction of threshing machine
West Grimstead, Wilts destruction of threshing machine
Wilton, Wilts farm machine destroyed
Wroughton, Wilts riot

25 November
Boyton, Wilts destruction of threshing machine
Cricklade, Wilts riot, destruction of three threshing machines incitement to break
Fonthill Giff, Wilts riot
Fonthill Bishop, Wilts destruction of threshing machine
Hinsford, Dorset arson against farmer
Laton, Wilts destruction of threshing machine
Lyneham, Wilts destruction of two threshing machines
Piddletown, Dorset arson

Stanton, Wilts demands for food or money
Stanton Fitzwarren, Wilts destruction of threshing machine
Tisbury, Wilts riot against MP, destruction of threshing machine £353.2.5
Tollard Royal, Wilts demands for food or money, destruction of three threshing machines

26 November
Bere Regis, Dorset riot
Cricklade, Wilts riot
Beverstone, Glos riot, theft, destruction of threshing machines costing £40+ and £20
nr Exeter, Devon threatening 'Swing' letters to farmers
Fairford, Glos destruction of threshing machine, farm machines destroyed, £300 damage claimed
Horsley, Glos destruction of threshing machine £10
Long Newton, Wilts destruction of two threshing machines
S Brewham, Somerset riot and threat to threshing machine
Tetbury, Glos riot
Tisbury, Wilts destruction of two threshing machines
Woland, Dorset destruction of threshing machine

27 November
Broughton Gifford, Wilts arson against overseer
Buckland Newton, Dorset demands for food or money, destruction of threshing machine
Coln St Aldwyn, Glos destruction of threshing machine, farm machine destroyed
Eastleach Martin, Glos destruction of threshing machine
Eastleach Turville, Glos destruction of threshing machine

Mappowder, Dorset demands for food or money costing £1
Pulham, Dorset wage meeting and riot, demands for food or money from farmers
Quimmington, Glos destruction of threshing machine
Taunton, Somerset radical poster, demonstration

28 November
Eastleach Turville, Glos destruction of threshing machine
Moreton-in-Marsh, Glos arson
Rockley, Wilts destruction of threshing machine by fire

29 November
Bibury, Glos destruction of threshing machine
Castle Hill, Dorset destruction of threshing machine
Coln Rogers, Glos destruction of threshing machine
East Stour, Dorset demands for food or money, destruction of threshing machine
Lulworth, Dorset wage meeting riot
Poulton, Glos riot
Preston, Dorset arson against farmer
Southrop, Glos riot
Stour Provost, Dorset riot, destruction of threshing machine
Winfrith, Dorset wage meeting and riot
Wingfield, Wilts destruction of two threshing machines
Winsley, Wilts destruction of threshing machine
Wool, Dorset wage meeting and riot

30 November
Banwell, Somerset poorhouse riot, demands for food or money, theft of overseer's tobacco worth 2/6
Banwell, Somerset riot, police lock-up destroyed

Cann, Dorset destruction of threshing machine
Shaftsbury, Dorset riot to get police to release prisoners

1 December
Bere Regis, Dorset arson against JP
Draycott, Somerset threatening 'Swing' letter to parson
Henstridge, Somerset destruction of two threshing machines costing £10 each
Ilton, Somerset wage meeting and riot against farmer
Lytchell, Dorset destruction of threshing machine
nr Sherbourne, Dorset destruction of threshing machine
Stalbridge, Dorset riot
Tut Hill, Dorset riot

2 December
Dumbleton, Glos arson against farmer

7 December
Ilfracombe, Devon four threatening 'Swing' letters
Deerhurst, Glos arson

8 December
Pardon Hill, Glos arson costing £150

10 December
Swimbridge, Devon meeting/riot against tithes and parson

11 December
Castle Hill, Devon wage meeting, riot against farmers and parsons

12 December
Buckhorn Weston, Dorset arson against farmer
Canford Magna, Dorset arson against farmer

15 December
Abbotskerswell, Devon arson and destruction of threshing machine

Sandford, Devon arson against farmer

18 December
Callington, Cornwall wage meeting and riot against farmers and gentry
Launceston, Cornwall wage meeting and riot against farmers and gentry

20 December
Moreton-in-Marsh, Glos wage meeting and riot against overseer

22 December
Cockington, Devon arson
Highweek, Devon arson and destruction of threshing machine

20-25 December
Morval, Cornwall threatening 'Swing' letter to farmer over threshing machine
St Neot's, Cornwall threatening 'Swing' letter to parson over tithe

28 December
Newton Abbott, Devon destruction of threshing machine by fire

29 December
Kilmington, Wilts incitement to riot

31 December
Stonehouse, Devon arson against brewers

1831

8 January
Aust, Glos arson costing £120
Langton, Dorset arson against JP costing over £500

8-12 January
nr Blanford, Dorset 3-8 fires

10 January
Upton Lovell, Dorset arson against parson costing £400

11 January
Bromsberrow, Glos
Potterne, Wilts arson
West Lavington, Wilts arson against publican

mid January
Ilminster, Somerset threatening parson, landlords
Langport, Somerset arson

22 January
near Bath, Somerset arson
Amesbury, Wilts arson

25 January
Modintonham, Cornwall arson

15 February
Penzance, Cornwall food riots against dealers

22 February
Helston, Cornwall food riots against dealers

8-11 June
Forest of Dean, Glos enclosure riots

28 August
Broad Chalk, Wilts arson

1-27 October
Tiverton, Devon strike, hosiers, reform meeting

22 October
Yeovil, Somerset

29 October
Bristol reform meeting

From *Captain Swing* by Eric Hobsbawm and George Rudé Phoenix Press 1969 and *Wiltshire Machine Breakers* 1993 and *Gloucestershire Machine Breakers* by Jill Chambers 2002

References and sources

People, riots and rebellion
Allan, DGC *The Rising in the West 1628-1631* Economic History Society 1952

Anstis, Ralph *Warren James and the Dean Forest Riots* 1986

Backwith, Dave and Ball, Roger *Bread or Batons? Unemployed workers' struggles in 1930s Bristol* Bristol Radical History Group 2012

Ball, Roger *The 'Bristol Riot' and its 'Other': St Paul's and Southmead in April 1980* The Regional Historian University of the West of England Autumn 2010

Bristol Trades Union Council *Slumbering Volcano? Report of an enquiry into the origins of the eruption in St Paul's Bristol on 2nd April 1980.*

Burns, Danny *The Poll Tax Rebellion* AK Press

Chambers, Jill *Wiltshire Machine Breakers* 1993

Chambers, Jill *Gloucestershire Machine Breakers* 2002

Clark, Peter *The Lefties' Guide to Britain* Politico's, London 2005

Cobbett, William *Rural Rides* Penguin Books, first published 1830

Cole, GDH and Raymond Postgate *The Common People 1746-1938* Methuen & Co, London 1938

Draper, Jo *Regency Riot and Reform* Dovecote Press, Dorset 2000

Ereira, Alan *The People's England* Routledge and Kegan Paul, London 1981

Fletcher, Anthony and Stevenson, John *Order and Disorder in Early Modern England* Cambridge University Press

Hobsbawm, E and Rude, G *Captain Swing* Phoenix Press 1969

Jones, Philip D *The Bristol Bridge Riot and it Antecedents: 18th Century perception of the crowd* The Journal of British Studies

Malcomson, Robert *A set of Ungovernable People: the Kingswood Colliers in the Eighteenth Century* Kingswood History Series, Kingswood Borough Council 1986

Mills, Steve *A Barbarous and Ungovernable People A short history of the miners of Kingswood Forest.* Bristol Radical History Group 2009

Morton, AL *A People's History of England* Left Book Club 1938

Mudd, David *Cornwall in Uproar* Bossiney Books, Bodmin 1983

Poole, Steve *'A lasting and salutary warning': incendiarism, rural order and England's last scene of crime execution* UWE, Bristol

Poole, Steve *The Stogursey Rising of 1801* UWE, Bristol

Poole, Steve and Spicer, Andrew edited *Captain Swing Reconsidered* Southern History Society 2010

Randall, Adrian *Before the Luddites* Cambridge University Press 1991

Sharp, Buchanan *In Contempt of all Authority, Rural artisans and riot in the West of England, 1586-1660* Breviary Stuff Publications, London 2010

Stevenson, John *Popular Disturbances in England 1700-1870* Longman London 1979

Suchacki, Jan *The Chard Lace Riots, a social, economic and historical account of the mill strikes and town disturbances of 1842, Chard* 2000

Thomas, Susan *The Bristol Riots* Bristol Branch of the Historical Association 1995

Thompson, EP *The Making of the English Working Class* Penguin Books, first published 1963

Todd, Margo *Reformation to Revolution* Routledge

Walker, Michael *Country Standard* various issues

Wells, Roger *Wretched Faces – Famine in wartime England 1793-1801* Breviary Stuff Publications 2011

West Country
Bettey, JH *Rural life in Wessex 1500-1900* Moonraker Press, Wiltshire 1977

Wreford, H, Clinch, R and Williams, M *Secret West Country* Bossiney Books, Bodmin 1986

Swindon: Social life, A History of the County of Wiltshire: Volume 9 1970 www.british-history.ac.uk

www.Bridgwatersomerset.info

Bristol
Bild, Ian *Bristol's Other History* Bristol Broadsides 1983

Hughes, Victoria *Ladies Mile* Abson Books, Bristol 1977

Paul Townsend has compiled a comprehensive account of Bristol's history and lots of great photos see: www.gertlushonline.co.uk

Cornwall
Dalton, Alan *Turn Left at Land's End* Red Boots, London 1987

Kent, Alan M *The Literature of Cornwall* Redcliffe Press 2000

Perry, Ronald and Thurlow, Charles *Extraordinary Earths* Cornish Hillside Publications, St Austell 2010

Stevens, GA *Do You Know Cornwall?* Tor Mark Press, Truro

Tregida, Garry *Representing the Duchy, Francis Acland and Cornish Politics 1910-1922* Cornish Studies

Devon
Colyton Parish History Society *Colyton Parish through the ages* 2001

Dell, Simon *Bicentenary of Dartmoor Prison* The Dartmoor Company 2009

Goodall, Felicity *Lost Devon* Birlinn, Edinburgh 2007

Dorset
Draper, Jo *Dorset, the complete guide* Dovecote Press, Dorset 1986

Gloucestershire
Graham, Alistair *The Forest and Wye* Clarion April/May 2009

Smith, B and Ralph, E *A History of Bristol and Gloucestershire* Darwen Finlayson, Beaconsfield, 1972

Somerset
Hayward, LC *From Portreeve to Mayor, the growth of Yeovil 1750-1854* Castle Cary Press 1987

Brian Smedley bridgwaterinternational. piczo.com

Wiltshire
Rundle, Penelope *Salisbury, the City and its charters*

Radical Religion
Bernstein, Eduard *Cromwell and Communism Quakers in the Seventeenth Century* Extract on www.marxists. org 2007

Biggs, Barry J *The Wesleys and the early Dorset Methodists* Woosorrel Publications 1987

Political reform
Hovell, Mark *The Chartist Movement* Manchester University Press 1918

Wooldridge, Chris *A brief history of Chartism and the Lowbands and Snig's End Estates* Ford House Press, Newent 1997

Labour and Left politics
Chapple, Dave *Idris and Phyllis Rose: Trowbridge Communist Councillors* 2009

Howe, John *Liberals, Lib-Labs and Independent Labour in North Gloucestershire 1890-1914* College of St Paul and St Mary in Cheltenham

Thorpe, Andrew *'One of the most backward areas of the country': the Labour Party's Grass Roots in South West of England 1918-45*

Thorpe, Andrew *Frome Divisional Labour Party, 1919-1949, North Somerset Constituency Labour Party 1949-1983* Microform Academic Publishers 1998

Winter, Barry *The ILP past and present* Independent Labour Publications, Leeds 1993

Civil War
Bernstein, Edward *Cromwell and Communism, Quakers in the Seventeenth Century*

Lewis, David *Levellers All* WEA Levellers' Day Committee

Newman, PR *Atlas of the English Civil War* Routledge, London 1998

Whiting, JRS *Gloucester Besieged* Gloucester City Museum 1975

Vine, Mark *The Crabchurch Conspiracy, Weymouth 1645* Friary Press 2004

Trade unionism and workers' rights
Atkinson, Brian *Trade Unions in Bristol* Historical Association 1982

Bristol Broadsides *Placards and Pin Money* 1986

Carpenter, Mick *Working for Health, the history of COHSE* Lawrence and Wishart, London 1988

Chapple, Dave *Bridgwater 1924-1927: Class Conflict in a Somerset Town* Somerset Socialist Library 2006

Denton, Charles *Trades Councils, Lessons of History and Future Prospects* 1996

France, Hywel and Smith, David *The Fed* Lawrence and Wishart, London 1980

Gordon, Alex and Mathers, Andy *Settling Accounts, a life lived through Bristol's labour movement.* Edited transcript of interviews with Bill Nicholas, Bristol Trades Union Council and South West TUC 2008

Grindley, Mike and Waller, Jill *A Fair Day's Pay for a Fair Day's Work* Cheltenham Local History Society 2010

Groves, Reg *Sharpen the Sickle! The History of the Farm Workers' Union* Porcupine Press, London 1959

Hayes Peoples' History a site dedicated to the Hayes Labour Movement and more: http://ourhistoryhayes.blogspot.com/

Horn, Pamela *Joseph Arch* Roundwood Press, Kineton 1971

Kirkby, Andrew *Exeter Trades Council 1890-1990, In the Cause of Liberty* Sparkler Books 1990

Large, David and Whitfield, Robert *Bristol Trades Council 1873-1973* Historical Association 1973

Organ, David M *The life and times of David Richard Organ* Apex Publishing, Cheltenham 2011

Owen, Brendon *One from the Plough. The Life and Times of George Mitchell* Gazebo Press, Montecute 2001

Porter, JH *Devon and the General Strike, 1926* International Review of Social History Vol 23 1978 Cambridge Journals

Ravensdale, J.R. *The 1913 China Clay strike and the Workers' Union* Exeter Papers in Economic History No.6, 1972

Richardson, Mike *Trade Unionism and industrial conflict in Bristol* Bristol Business School, University of the West of England 2000

Sables, Gerald *A Souvenir of John Gregory*

Scarth, Bob *We'll all be union men. The story of Joseph Arch and his Union* Industrial Pioneer Publications, Coventry 1998

Scotland, Nigel *Agricultural Trade Unionism in Gloucestershire 1872-1950* Cheltenham and Gloucester College of Higher Education

Symonds, Julian *The General Strike* Readers Union, The Cresset Press, London 1959

Wicks, Martin *The First Hundred Years: Swindon Trades Union Council Centenary 1891-1991* 1991

Tolpuddle Martyrs
Brooks, Harry (Introduction by JH Thomas MP) *Six Heroes in Chains* J Looker, Poole 1929

Brown, Alan *Tolpuddle Boy, transported to hell and back* Hodder Children's Books, London 2002

Douglas, Bill *Comrades* (book from the film) Faber and Faber London 1987

Firth, Marjorie and Hopkinson, Arthur (Foreword by Walter Elliot MP) *The Tolpuddle Martyrs* Marton Hokinson, London 1934

Howell, George *Labour Legislation, Labour Movements, Labour Leaders* T Fisher Unwin, London 1902

Humphries, Barbara *The Tolpuddle Martyrs, victims of the rich man's law* Militant, London 1976

Hutt, Allen *Class against Class Tolpuddle and Today, a historical comment on the TUC Tolpuddle Centenary campaign* Martin Lawrence Ltd, London 1934

Lean, Garth *Brave Men Choose* Blandford Press, London 1961

Lowther, Elsie *The day of small things, the story of the Tolpuddle Martyrs* Epworth Press, London 1940

Lambert, RS *The Dorchester Labourers* a play in two parts (adapted from the wireless version by Williams, WE broadcast on 19th April 1934) Workers' Education Association, London 1934

Lezard, Tim and Costley, Nigel *My Tolpuddle* Trades Union Congress 2008

Loveless, George *The Church shown up* (a letter to Rev Henry Walter) Central Dorchester Committee, London 1838

Loveless, George *The Victims of Whiggery* Central Dorchester Committee, London 1839

Loveless, John; Brine, John; Standfield, Thomas and Standfield, John, four of the Tolpuddle Martyrs *The Horrors of Transportation* Central Dorchester Committee, London 1838

Malleson, Miles and Brooks, Harry *Six men of Dorset, the Tolpuddle play* Trades Union Congress 1934

Marlow, Joyce *The Tolpuddle Martyrs* History Book Club, London 1971

Norman, Andrew *The story of George Loveless and the Tolpuddle Martyrs* Halsgrove Devon 2008

Padden, Graham *Tolpuddle, an historical account through the eyes of George Loveless* Trades Union Congress 1984

Selley, Ernest *Village Trade Union in Two Centuries* George Allen and Unwin, London 1919

Sorensen, Reginald *Tolpuddle or 'Who's Afeared', an historical play* TC Foley, London 1928

Rattenbury, Owen (Foreword by Arthur Henderson MP) *Flame of Freedom, a romantic story of the Tolpuddle Martyrs* Epworth Press, London 1931

Roebuck, John A MP, *The Dorchester Labourers. On the qualification clause of the Corporation Bill* John Longley, London Steam Press of C & W Reynell, c1835

Thomas, Lloyd *God is our guide. The Tolpuddle Martyrs and their Methodist Roots* 2007

Thompson, EV *The Tolpuddle Woman* BCA London 1994

Trades Union Congress *The Martyrs of Tolpuddle* Trades Union Congress, London 1934

Trades Union Congress *The story of the Dorchester Labourers, a guide to the Old Crown Court, Dorchester and the village of Tolpuddle*

Trades Union Congress, London 1957 reprinted as *The story of the Tolpuddle Martyrs*

Walker, W Maitland *An impartial appreciation of the Tolpuddle Martyrs* Dorset Natural Historical and Archaeological Society 1934

Wirdnam, Audrey *Pidela, an account of the village of Tolpuddle from early times 1989*

Women's rights
Bearman, CJ *An Examination of Suffrage Violence* English Historical Review Vol CXX No.486, Oxford University Press

Bradley, Katherine *Friends and visitors: History of the women's suffrage movement in Cornwall 1870-1914* Hypatia Trust, Penzance 2000

Clarke, Jennifer *Exploring the West Country, A Woman's Guide* Virago Press, London 1987

Crawford, Elizabeth *The Women's Suffrage Movement, A Refeference Guide 1866-1928*, Routledge, London

Matherson, Rosa *The Fair Sex, Women and the Great Western Railway* Tepus Publishing, Stroud 2007

Our Famous Women Worthington Publishers, Chicago, US 1884

Race and slavery
Bristol Museums, Galleries and Archives *Slave Trade Trail around Central Bristol* 1998

Dresser, Madge and Fleming, Peter *Black and White on the Buses - the 1963 Colour Bar Dispute in Bristol* Bristol Broadsides (Co-op) 1986

Dresser, Madge and Fleming, Peter *Bristol ethnic minorities and the city 1000-2001* Phillimore, West Sussex 2007

Gray, Todd *Devon and the Salve Trade* The Mint Press, Exeter 2007

Hart, Richard *The Abolition of Slavery* Community Education Trust 1989, re-published by Caribbean Labour Solidarity 2007

Johnson, Thomas L *Twenty-Eight Years a Slave, or The Story of My Life in Three Continents* W Mate and Sons, Bournemouth, 1909 see: www.docsouth.unc.edu University of North Carolina Library

MacKeith, Lucy *Local Black History, a beginning in Devon* Archives and Museum of Black Heritage, London 2003

Parker, Adjoa Louisa *Dorset's Hidden Histories* Development Education in Dorset 2007

Walmsley, Philip *Stroud versus Slavery* Stroud Local History Society 2003

Wynn, Neil *A Race War, Black American GIs in Bristol and Gloucestershire during World War II* Bristol Radical History Group pamphlet 2008

Co-operative
Graham, Alistair *The Forest Pioneers, the story of the co-operative movement in the Forest of Dean* 2002

Jackson, Edward *Industrial Co-operation in Bristol* Co-operative Wholesale Society, Manchester 1911

King, Roy *The Poor Fabricators: an introduction to the history of trade unions in Kingswood* Kingswood History Series, Kingswood Borough Council 1986

Purnell, Francis and Williams, Henry *Jubilee History of the Gloucester Co-operative and Industrial Society Limited* 1910

Robinson, Chris *150 years of the Co-operative in Plymouth* Pen and Ink Publishing 2009

Stafford, Eric *Brick upon Brick 1944-1994* The first 50 years of the South West Co-operative Housing Society 1994

Wyler, Steve *A history of community asset ownership* Development Trusts Association, 2009

Smuggling
Carter, Captain Harry *The Autobiography of a Cornish Smuggler, 1749-1809* D Bradford Barton, Truro, first published 1894, reprinted 1971

Chapple, Roy F *Old Smuggling Days in East Devon* Axe Valley Heritage Association 2003

David, Kevin *We come for our own and we shall have it, Smuggling in Poole and Dorset* Bristol Radical History Group 2008

Department for Transport, Environment and the Regions: *Marine Accident Report 3/98, Report of the Inspector's Inquiry into the Grounding of the Feeder Container Ship MV CITA off Newfoundland Point, Isles of Scilly on 26 March 1997* HMSO 1998

Hippisley, Antony D *Smuggling in the West Country 1700-1850* Coxe Tabb House 1984

Lark, R and McBride, D *The Cita, Scillies own 'Whisky Galore' wreck* Cornwall 1997

Platt, Richard *Smugglers' Britain*

www.smuggling.co.uk

Others
Bristol City Council *Bristol and the Bomb* 1984

Buckley, Allen *Cornish Bal Maidens* Tor Mark 2010

Burnett, John *A Social History of Housing 1815-1970* David and Charles, Devon 1978

Byrne, Eugene *Stolen Paradise: Civilian squatters in military camps in and around postwar Bristol* in The Regional Historian Issue 23 University of the West of England Summer 2011

Evans, Dave *Dennis Potter* www.yorksj.ac.uk/potter/biog.htm

Foley, Winifred *A child in the Forest* Thornhill Press Cheltenham 1974

Fyvel, Penelope *English Penny* Arthur H Stockwell, Devon 1992

Gilchrist, Alison *The well-connected community* The Policy Press 2009

Gwynn, Robin D *Huguenot Heritage* Routledge

Hannington, Wal *Unemployed Struggles 1919-1936* Lawrence and Wishart London 1936

National Pensioners Convention *The battle for the old age pension* 2008

Pye, Denis *Fellowship is Life, the story of the Clarion Cycling Club* Clarion Publishing 1995

Walker, Aidan; Parfitt, Sue and Self, David *Obituary to Jo Emery* Wednesday April 4, 2007 The Guardian

A comprehensive account of local workhouses is at www.workhouses.org.uk

Index

Other Breviary Stuff books

Ralph Anstis, *Warren James and the Dean Forest Riots, The Disturbances of 1831*

£14.00 • 242pp paperback • 191x235mm
ISBN 978-0-9564827-7-8

The full story of the riots in the Forest of Dean in 1831, and how they were suppressed, is told here for the first time. Dominating the story is the enigmatic character of Warren James, the self-educated free miner who led the foresters in their attempt to stave off their increasing poverty and unemployment, and to protect their traditional way life from the threats of advancing industrial change.

John E. Archer, *By a Flash and a Scare, Arson, Animal Maiming, and Poaching in East Anglia 1815-1870*

£12.00 • 208pp paperback • 191x235mm
ISBN 978-0-9564827-1-6

By a Flash and a Scare, illuminates the darker side of rural life in the nineteenth century. Flashpoints such as the Swing riots, Tolpuddle, and the New Poor Law riots have long attracted the attention of historians, but here John E. Archer focuses on the persistent war waged in the countryside during the 1800s, analysing the prevailing climate of unrest, discontent, and desperation.

Bob Bushaway, *By Rite, Custom, Ceremony and Community in England 1700-1880*

£14.00 • 206pp paperback • 191x235mm
ISBN 978-0-9564827-6-1

Bringing together a wealth of research, this book explores the view that rural folk practices were a mechanism of social cohesion, and social disruption.

Through them the interdependence of the rural working-class and the gentry was affirmed, and infringements of the rights of the poor resisted, sometimes aggressively.

Malcolm Chase, *The People's Farm, English Radical Agrarianism 1775-1840*

£12.00 • 212pp paperback • 152x229mm
ISBN 978-0-9564827-5-4

This book traces the development of agrarian ideas from the 1770s through to Chartism, and seeks to explain why, in an era of industrialization and urban growth, land remained one of the major issues in popular politics. Malcolm Chase considers the relationship between land consciousness and early socialism; attempts to create alternative communities; and contemporary perceptions of nature and the environment. *The People's Farm* also provides the most extensive study to date of Thomas Spence, and his followers the Spenceans.

Malcolm Chase, *Early Trade Unionism, Fraternity, Skill and the Politics of Labour*

paperback • 191x235mm
ISBN 978-0-9570005-1-3

Once the heartland of British labour history, trade unionism has been marginalised in much recent scholarship. In a critical survey from the earliest times to the nineteenth century, this book argues for its reinstatement. Trade unionism is shown to be both intrinsically important and to provide a window onto the broader historical landscape; the evolution of trade union principles and practices is traced from the seventeenth century to mid-Victorian times.

Barry Reay, *The Last Rising of the Agricultural Labourers, Rural Life and Protest in Nineteenth-Century England*

£12.00 • 192pp paperback • 191x235mm
ISBN 978-0-9564827-2-3

The Hernhill Rising of 1838 was the last battle fought on English soil, the last revolt against the New Poor Law, and England's last millenarian rising. The bloody Battle of Bosenden Wood, fought in a corner of rural Kent, was the culmination of a revolt led by the self-styled Sir William Courtenay. It was also, despite the greater fame of the 1830 Swing Riots, the last rising of the agricultural labourers.

Buchanan Sharp, *In Contempt of All Authority, Rural Artisans and Riot in the West of England, 1586-1660*

£12.00 • 204pp paperback • 191x235mm
ISBN 978-0-9564827-0-9

Two of the most common types of popular disorders in late Tudor and early Stuart England were the food riots and the anti-enclosure riots in royal forests. Of particular interest are the forest riots known collectively as the Western Rising of 1626-1632, and the lesser known disorders in the Western forests which took place during the English Civil War. The central aims of this volume are to establish the social status of the people who engaged in those riots and to determine the social and economic conditions which produced the disorders.

Dorothy Thompson, *The Chartists, Popular Politics in the Industrial Revolution*

paperback, 191x235mm
ISBN 978-0-9570005-3-7

The Chartists is a major contribution to our understanding not just of Chartism but of the whole experience of working-class people in mid-nineteenth century Britain. The book looks at who the Chartists were, what they hoped for from the political power they strove to gain, and why so many of them felt driven toward the use of physical force. It also studies the reactions of the middle and upper classes and the ways in which the two sides – radical and establishment – influenced each other's positions.

E. P. Thompson, *Whigs and Hunters, The Origin of the Black Act*

paperback • 191x235mm
ISBN 978-0-9570005-2-0

With *Whigs and Hunters,* the author of *The Making of the English Working Class,* E. P. Thompson plunged into the murky waters of the early eighteenth century to chart the violently conflicting currents that boiled beneath the apparent calm of the time. The subject is the Black Act, a law of unprecedented savagery passed by Parliament in 1723 to deal with "wicked and evil-disposed men going armed in disguise". These men were pillaging the royal forest of deer, conducting a running battle against the forest officers with blackmail, threats and violence.

David Walsh, *Making Angels in Marble, The Conservatives, the Early Industrial Working Class and Attempts at Political Incorporation*

£15.00 • 268pp paperback • 191x235mm
ISBN 978-0-9570005-0-6

A BREVIARY STUFF PAPERBACK ORIGINAL

In the first elections called under the terms of the 1832 Reform Act the Tory party appeared doomed. They had recorded their worst set of results in living memory and were organizationally in disarray as well, importantly, seemingly completely out of touch with the current political mood. During the intense pressure brought to bear by the supporters of political reform was the use of "pressure from without" and in this tactic the industrial working class were highly visible. Calls for political reform had been growing since the 1760s and given fresh impetus with the revolutions in America and France respectively. The old Tory party had been resistant to all but the most glaring corruption and abuse under the pre-Reform system, not least to the idea of extending the electoral franchise to the "wineish multitude", as Edmund Burke notoriously described the working class. Yet within five years

after the passing of reform the Conservatives – the natural heirs to the old Tory party – were attempting to politically incorporate sections of the working class into their ranks. This book examines how this process of making these "Angels in Marble" to use Disraeli's phrase from a later era, took shape in the 1830s. It focuses on how a section of the industrial working class became the target of organizational inclusion into Peelite Conservatism and ultimately into the British party political system.

Roger Wells, *Insurrection, The British Experience 1795-1803*

£17.50 • 364pp paperback • 191x235mm
ISBN 978-0-9564827-3-0

On the 16 November 1802 a posse of Bow Street Runners raided the Oakley Arms, a working class pub in Lambeth, on the orders of the Home Office. Over thirty men were arrested, among them, and the only one of any social rank, Colonel Edward Marcus Despard. Despard and twelve of his associates were subsequently tried for high treason before a Special Commission, and Despard and six others were executed on 21 February 1803. It was alleged that they had planned to kill the King, seize London and overturn the government and constitution.

Roger Wells, *Wretched Faces, Famine in Wartime England 1793-1801*

£18.00 • 412pp paperback • 191x235mm
ISBN 978-0-9564827-4-7

The history of riots reaches its full maturity when riots break out of monographic case studies to be incorporated into full histories. Roger Wells includes riot as one dimension of his rich attempt to comprehend the whole range of responses of British society to the famines of 1794-96 and 1799-1801. These famines dramatically revealed the fragile equilibrium underpinning national subsistence, and its propensity to collapse. Wells explains how and why the archaic

structure of state and society in Britain did just manage not to collapse.

John Belchem, *'Orator' Hunt, Henry Hunt and English Working Class Radicalism*

£14.00 • 248pp paperback • 191x235mm
ISBN 978-0-9564827-8-5

In the early 19th century, Henry Hunt became one of the most stirring orators of English Radicalism. His speech following the "Peterloo" massacre cost him three years in prison and gave him a reputation for inciting the rabble to violence. This book considers his place in the radical movement.

CPSIA information can be obtained
at www.ICGtesting.com
Printed in the USA
LVIW011911120812
2970LVUK00002B